Wild Rwanda

Wild Rwanda

Where to watch birds, primates, and other wildlife

By Ken Behrens, Christian Boix, and Keith Barnes

With contributions from Jason Anderson and Claver Ntoyinkima

/

MASTER FAMILY FUND

SUPPORTING SUSTAINABLE AVITOURISM
AND BIRD CONSERVATION WORLDWIDE

BirdLife South Africa is one of the leading bird conservation NGOs in Africa, and a partner of BirdLife International. It is very involved in assisting other African bird conservation organizations achieve their conservation and training objectives.

Keith Barnes is donating all his proceeds and royalties from this book to Bird-Life South Africa. To find out more about the mission and goals of BirdLife South Africa or to help support the organization, please visit www.birdlife.org.za.

Cover photographs: Nyungwe's misty forests ©Keith Barnes; Yellow-billed Oxpecker on a plains (*common*) zebra ©Ken Behrens; Gorilla ©Ken Behrens; Blue-headed Sunbird ©John Caddick.

First Edition: March 2015

© Lynx Edicions – Montseny, 8, 08193 Bellaterra, Barcelona, www.lynxeds.com
© texts: Ken Behrens, Christian Boix, Keith Barnes
© photographs: credited photographers

Design and layout: Elena Fonts
Printed by: Ingoprint, S.A.
Legal Deposit: B-7083-2015
ISBN: 978-84-96553-96-5

Contents

List of Side Boxes

Introduction

IMPRESSIONS AND ILLUSIONS OF RWANDA

The small country of Rwanda lies in the mountainous heart of Africa and has long been known for its biological riches, in particular its mountain gorillas, made famous by the work of Dian Fossey and the movie *Gorillas in the Mist* based on her life. Unfortunately, this country still suffers a considerable hangover as a result of the genocide that took place in 1994. International public perception cannot ignore these events and they are usually the first thing that anyone thinks of when the country's name is mentioned. However, on arriving in Kigali and meeting the vibrant, energetic, and friendly Rwandan people, the last thing that you can imagine is that they would turn on each other in a vicious ethnic conflict. Fortunately, the many social ills and deep divisions caused by the colonial segregations of Rwandans into two pseudo-ethnic classes, the Hutu and the Tutsi, seem to have been addressed by the government and indeed by the collective will of the people. There is definitely a strong desire among Rwandans to live together peacefully. All who experienced that darkest hour of Rwandan history are eager to move on and forgive, even if they can never forget what happened. There is hope that most Rwandan children will be unaffected by the divides that tore apart their parents' generation.

The Rwanda of today is a small, beautiful, friendly, happy country of agriculturally productive and well-cultivated rolling hills. The burgeoning human population of over 300 people per km^2 makes it the most densely populated country in Africa, and the effects of human activity are everywhere to be seen. Despite the genocide, the return of many refugees means that the country is now more crowded than ever. In all, 95% of Rwanda's economy is based on agriculture and 87% of the over one million hectares that are cultivated is devoted to subsistence crops. Outside of the national parks the majority of the country resembles a massive garden. Natural habitats are transformed and the vistas across the countryside encompass humble rural communities growing crops such as tea, coffee, cotton, manioc, and bananas, while more organized cooperatives and companies growing tea and coffee also occasionally punctuate the subsistence farmlands. The verdant rolling hills have a serene beauty, even if none of the habitat is natural. Alongside the large swathes of altered habitat exist a handful of well-protected areas that have managed to maintain their integrity. Chief amongst those are the Nyungwe, Volcanoes, and Akagera national parks, located in the southwest, northwest, and east of Rwanda, respectively. Kigali is the only real city in Rwanda. Small towns, most

Rwanda is sometimes called "land of a thousand hills". ©Ken Behrens

with the typical character and ambiance of small colonially influenced African towns, are scattered across the countryside. Germany took control of Rwanda in 1885 but in 1916 Belgium invaded and was officially handed control at the end of the First World War. Belgium administered Rwanda until 1962 and many of the country's trials and tribulations in the twentieth century can be traced back to the colonial promotion of one people over another.

A visit to Rwanda to witness the country's recovery from its past sufferings is a worthwhile experience in itself. But this country is also a treasure trove of exquisite and excellent natural history experiences. Despite the great overall population density, it usually feels as if you have the whole of the immense Nyungwe forest to yourself, shared only with chimpanzees shrieking somewhere off in the endless misty expanses of forest. And of course, there are Volcanoes' mountain gorillas, one of the most incredible wild creatures of them all. These are but highlights of the many rewards that await a naturalist making a trip to this little-visited country.

RWANDA AS A NATURAL HISTORY DESTINATION

Many African countries with abundant megafauna including lions and elephants are thought of as more obvious wildlife watching destinations than Rwanda. Although this country cannot rival nations like Kenya, Uganda, or South Africa in terms of large mammals or overall diversity, Rwanda can provide a high quality experience that is very different from that on offer in other African countries. And despite being compact and easy-to-access, Rwanda still offers a good range of different habitats and features.

Rwanda is very small and landlocked. Its surface area of 26,328 km^2

Seeing gorillas is one of the world's most incredible natural history experiences. ©Ken Behrens

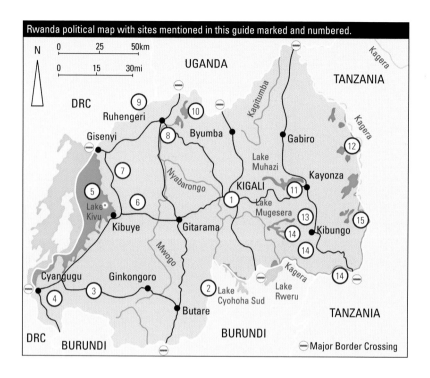

N

0   25   50km
0   15   30mi

UGANDA

TANZANIA

Kagera

DRC

Ruhengeri

Gisenyi

Byumba

Gabiro

Lake Muhazi

Kayonza

Kagera

Nyabarongo

KIGALI

Lake Kivu

Kibuye

Gitarama

Lake Mugesera

Kibungo

Mwogo

Cyangugu

Ginkongoro

Lake Cyohoha Sud

Lake Rweru

Kagera

Butare

TANZANIA

DRC

BURUNDI

BURUNDI

Major Border Crossing

(10,169 sq. miles) makes it slightly larger than Wales and about the size of the US state of Maryland. Most of the country is rugged and mountainous, and lies more than 1500 m above sea level. In the west the rugged mountains of the Albertine Rift (1600–4500 m) run along the border with the Democratic Republic of the Congo (DRC). These mountains mark the watershed between Africa's two greatest river systems, the Nile and the Congo. The northern part of the Rwandan Rift is volcanic and is home to several huge mountains including Karisimbi (4507 m), Africa's seventh highest peak. In this western region lie Rwanda's most significant wildlife areas and national parks, blanketed in montane forest and bounded to the west by the huge Lake Kivu. This region is also the lair of Rwanda's great-

est natural riches, chief of which are the great apes. Mountain gorillas are Rwanda's most obvious drawcard and very little can compare with the experience of spending an hour with a group of the most poignant and soulful creatures on the planet. The antics of chimpanzees (often called "chimps") are almost as alluring; as well, Rwanda has an array of smaller cercopithecine monkeys, including the localized L'Hoest's, Dent's (mona), Virungas golden (gentle), and owl-faced monkeys, along with troops of up to 400 Angolan (pied) colobus, making it a primate-lover's delight.

Despite being small and land-locked, Rwanda supports almost 700 species of birds, of which about 475 are resident and 200 are migrants or vagrants. However, these numbers alone do not tell the whole story. De-

Dusky Crimson-wing is just one of 25 Albertine Rift endemic birds found in Rwanda. ©Josh Engel/Field Museum

spite not supporting any "political" endemic bird species, Rwanda shares 25 Albertine Rift endemics that are only found in a small portion of Africa that includes parts of Uganda, Burundi, Tanzania, and the Democratic Republic of the Congo (DRC). The Albertine Rift is the richest Endemic Bird Area (as defined by BirdLife International) in Africa and given that the DRC is currently unsafe Rwanda supports the most accessible Albertine Rift forests on Earth. In particular, Nyungwe NP in the southwest of the country is a treasure chest of Afro-montane forest species. Nyungwe is second only to the DRC's Itombwe Mountains as a key locality for Albertine Rift endemics. A key specialty in Nyungwe is the Red-collared Mountain-Babbler, a handsome but strange bird that forms boisterous parties and can be found

clinging to the branches of moss-clad cloud-forest trees. The only close relatives of this mountain-babbler live in the mountains of DRC, Cameroon, and Nigeria. Other targets in Nyungwe include the spectacular Ruwenzori Turaco, the rare Buff-throated (*Kungwe*) Apalis, and the gorgeous Regal and Purple-breasted sunbirds. Not all endemics are easily seen and inevitably one has to invest time in finding species such as the scarce Albertine Owlet. It is also possible that some of the very least known birds in Africa are hiding somewhere in the vast forests of Nyungwe, including Rockefeller's Sunbird, Schouteden's Swift, and the enigmatic Congo Bay-Owl. The birding in Nyungwe tends to be better than in more frequently visited Albertine Rift sites in adjacent Uganda. The much more visited Bwindi

NP in Uganda has fewer endemics and the only Albertine Rift endemic (ARE) found in Bwindi but unknown in Rwanda is the enigmatic Grauer's (*African Green*) Broadbill. However, with a little more searching, this easily overlooked species may yet be found to occur in Rwanda. Endemics aside, Rwanda's Albertine Rift forests support an incredible variety of forest birds, including an ensemble of 74 montane forest species, more than in any other

The papyrus swamps of Akagera in eastern Rwanda hold the one-of-a-kind Shoebill. ©Ken Behrens

Afro-montane region. An additional 23 lowland Guinea-Congo forest species are also found here; nevertheless, Rwanda is not an ideal country for focusing on this latter group of birds as virtually all are more easily found in other countries, including adjacent Uganda or Cameroon on the other side of the Congo Basin.

The eastern portion of Rwanda is lower in elevation (1300–1500 m) and forms part of the Lake Victoria basin. Here the vegetation morphs into an open woodland and savannah matrix. Akagera NP is the prime site in this part of the country. Although its size has been reduced by some 60%, this is still the largest park in the country. It is also the richest for birds and mammals, supporting over 50 species of mammals including such marquee species as leopard, "Masai" giraffe, hippopotamus, African savanna elephant, and plains (*common*) zebra. Along with these, there is a strong supporting cast of species such as sable, roan, Uganda topi, common impala, Sudan oribi, common eland, spotted hyena, and many others. There are also exciting plans to re-introduce black rhinos and lions in the near future. Akagera's lakes also boast high concentrations of prehistoric-looking Nile crocodiles. Akagera is certainly one of Africa's best parks for birding. Before huge portions of the park were degazetted in 1997, it was a contender for the park with the longest bird list in Africa (527 species confirmed) and despite its reduced size it still marshals an impressive array of approximately 480 birds. Here several birds reach the northern limit of their range. These include Purple-crested Turaco, the recently split Ruaha (*White-headed Black*) Chat, Souza's Shrike, and Miombo Wren-Warbler.

The Ruwenzori three-horned chameleon is endemic to the Albertine Rift. ©Christian Boix

Green-headed Sunbird, just one of a dazzling array of sunbirds in Rwanda. ©Keith Barnes

The park is one of the best places in Africa to find the localized Red-faced Barbet. Also worthy of special mention are Akagera's wetland species, the most significant of which is the Shoebill, which occurs on its papyrus-fringed lakes.

Rwanda's impressive wetlands support the characteristic avifauna of East Africa's papyrus-dominated marshes, which includes Papyrus Gonolek, Papyrus Yellow-Warbler, White-winged Swamp-Warbler, Papyrus Canary, and White-collared Oliveback. Eleven of the twelve species restricted to the Lake Victoria Basin biome occur in Rwanda, the exception being the localized Fox's Weaver that is endemic to Uganda. Though Rwanda's best wetlands are found in and around Akagera, there are other significant wetlands scattered throughout the country. The main such sites are Akanyaru and Nyabarongo on the southern border with Burundi, Rugezi in the north near the Ugandan border, and Mugesera-Rugwero in the southeast. Unfor-

tunately, only the Rugezi Wetland is currently protected and most of these sites have already lost much of their diversity and original splendor.

It is obvious that despite its small size, Rwanda musters a surprising diversity of flora and fauna, which together offer a tantalizing set of must-see attractions for those interested in a shortish African journey. Although a trip of 10–12 days would be sufficient for a keen naturalist to cover the main sites in Rwanda, a longer trip would also be rewarding. A short trip could include gorilla and chimp tracking, encounters with several other primates, plus good general mammal viewing in Akagera NP. On the bird front, one could expect to record the vast majority of the Albertine Rift endemics, plus most of the East African papyrus specialists including a chance of seeing Shoebill. The total list should reach 250–350 species, almost half of Rwanda's birds and 15% of those in Africa. See "Suggested Rwanda Itinerary" on page 23 for more details.

PLANNING A TRIP

WHEN TO VISIT

The most popular time for tourists to visit Rwanda is during the European and North American vacation period of June to September. This is the dry season and trails are easy to walk. If planning a visit at this busy time, be sure to line up your gorilla-tracking permits well in advance to avoid disappointment as they are in high demand. Another shorter dry season during December and January also offers a good opportunity for birding and wildlife watching. Note that, although the west may still see rain during these months, the birding remains good.

In our experience one of the most productive periods for birding is between March and May during the main wet season, when many birds are responsive to calls and are very active. The good infrastructure and paved roads mean that wet-season travel is not that much different from that in the dry season. However, be aware that trails become more slippery and parts of Akagera may become inaccessible. During this time of year one may also lose a few afternoons to rain. If you are planning only a short birding trip during which the loss of a day would be crucial, then plan your visit for the dry season. But if you are on a more relaxed or longer itinerary and can afford to lose some time to inclement weather, a wet season trip during March–May will probably produce a better tally and overall be a more enjoyable birding experience. We do not

During the rainy season, birds like this Vieillot's (*Black*) Weaver become more vocal, active, and easier to see. ©Keith Barnes

recommend visiting during the second week of April, the genocide memorial week, which is a time of remembrance and private mourning for the people of Rwanda, and not the best time to be a tourist in Rwanda.

GETTING TO RWANDA

The capital, Kigali, receives flights from several international airlines and destinations. Belgian Airways flies directly from Brussels, while Kenyan and Ethiopian Airlines connect much of the world with Rwanda via their hubs in Nairobi and Addis Ababa. Rwandair Express (www.rwandair.com) is a local carrier that is well connected in East Africa and seems to be doing its best to open new routes and services to other parts of the country.

It is possible to cross the land border to or from Uganda, which fits in well with visiting Volcanoes NP and gorilla tracking since the Cyanika/Kisoro border crossing is just east of Volcanoes. Another option is the direct route between Kampala and Kigali, which buses and minibuses cover in 10–12 hours, and which costs less than $20. Something to consider when making a Rwanda trip is a flight up to Kampala to search for Shoebill in Mabamba Swamp and very good chances of a close encounter with this incredible bird. Flights between Kigali and Kampala are not very expensive (usually $200–300). Rwanda can also be accessed overland from Tanzania via Rusumo. There is a bus from Dar es Salaam, which takes about 24 hours. There are also border crossings from Burundi and DRC, but these are unlikely to be suitable ports of entry or exit for most visitors.

Eastern Rwanda's Akagera NP offers classic safari scenes like this one: a Yellow-billed Oxpecker on a Cape buffalo. ©Ken Behrens

At time of writing, citizens of the US, Canada, the UK, Germany, South Africa, and several other countries do not require a visa and can be granted an entry permit upon arrival. Nevertheless, beware that these policies can change at a moment's notice and so be sure to check visa regulations before you visit.

DESIGNING AN ITINERARY

Rwanda really only has a handful of essential sites. For the Albertine Rift endemics – in particular birds – Nyungwe NP is non-negotiable. Nyungwe is also the key site for chimps. To see mountain gorillas, Volcanoes NP is likewise non-negotiable. All other sites then add padding to these key localities. Akagera NP is a great place but, Red-faced Barbet and Shoebill aside, it is like many other savanna parks in Africa. The other sites covered in this book can fill in the gaps on an itinerary, but are not worth much time, except for explorers intent on making new discoveries or for those who eschew the well-trodden path.

Rwanda is easily combined with Uganda to make a more comprehensive but still fairly compact itinerary. Uganda offers a much better variety of Guinea-Congo-rainforest and Guinea-savanna bird species, more diverse savanna mammal viewing, and better chances at a close encounter with a Shoebill. For many birders, the best trip is ultimately a combination of these two countries. For those interested in a trip that includes Uganda, there is already a good if slightly dated site guide to the country by Jonathan Rossouw and Marco Sacchi, which is out-of-print and potentially difficult to acquire. East Africa is increasingly well

connected by fairly cheap commercial flights, meaning that Rwanda can easily be combined with Kenya, Tanzania, or even Ethiopia. Rwanda's endemics on top of Kenya's vast diversity would make for an incredible "mega-safari".

VEHICLE HIRE, ACCOMMODATION, AND TOUR OPERATORS

Rwanda is a reasonably easy destination to visit independently. Cars can

Suggested Rwanda Itinerary

Day 1: Arrival Kigali, drive to Akagera NP.

Days 2–3: Akagera NP.

Day 4: Akagera NP to Nyungwe NP (full day's drive). Stop in Kigali for lunch.

Days 5–8: Nyungwe NP, including chimp tracking at Cyamudongo.

Day 9: Nyungwe NP to Volcanoes NP. The easiest route runs through Kigali but you can also drive via Lake Kivu and stop in Gishwati Forest. Nevertheless, this long winding unpaved route is not recommended during the wet season.

Day 10: Morning gorilla tracking in Volcanoes NP. Afternoon Buhanga Forest.

Day 11: Additional day in Volcanoes NP. Virungas golden (*gentle*) monkey tracking; hike to Mount Bisoke, visit to Dian Fossey memorial, and/or forest birding.

Day 12: Return to Kigali for departure (with possible stop at Rugezi Wetland) OR cross into Uganda to continue an itinerary that combines the two countries.

Great Blue Turaco, a cartoon character of a bird. ©Keith Barnes

be rented in Kigali, either as self-drive or with a driver. Most of the roads to access the sites in this book are paved and you could easily get the best out of Rwanda in a small sedan or any non-4x4 hire vehicle. See "Driving and Roads" below for more information.

There is a range of accommodation, from camping to luxury lodges, available at most of Rwanda's major wildlife sites. For some of the less-visited and more remote sites, the only option will be to stay in a basic hotel some distance away in the nearest major town or to camp at the site itself. Lodging in Africa is generally more expensive than in Asia or South America and in Rwanda is expensive even by African standards. It is to be hoped that as Rwanda gains greater popularity as an ecotourism destination, more accommodation options – including cheaper ones – will become more widely available. Some accommodation in Rwanda is easy to book via e-mail, some can be tricky without the assistance of a tour company.

Several international natural history tour companies offer trips to Rwanda (see contacts on page 41). If money is not a major concern this is by far the easiest way to visit Rwanda and ensures encounters with the majority of the bird specialties, plus hassle-free arrangement of accommodation, local guides, and primate-tracking permits.

There are a large and growing number of tour operators within Rwanda (see contacts). Most of these operators are well prepared for arranging a primate safari but have little experience with other kinds of trips such as birding tours.

PUBLIC TRANSPORT

It would be possible to travel across Rwanda using buses and minibuses and see an excellent variety of mammals and birds, including some of its endemics. Unfortunately, most of the sites covered in this book are difficult to visit without your own vehicle, particularly Nyungwe and Akagera NPs. In Nyungwe, you could travel to Uwinka or Gisakura and then walk or hitchhike to access different forest sites, but you would lose much time in transit. Akagera is almost impossible to visit without your own vehicle. Some backpackers do manage to do gorilla tracking by taking public transport to Ruhengeri and then arranging a 4x4 for their day of gorilla tracking. However, the savings this implies will pale in comparison with the $750 cost of a gorilla-tracking permit in the eyes of most people. Trying to organize a focused wildlife-watching trip on public transport would probably be frustrating but would certainly give one a taste of this gem of a country. Rwanda is generally a safe, clean, and well-organized country, and backpacking here is easy compared to many other African countries. A good travel book such as the Rwanda Bradt guide is essential for this kind of travel.

CLIMATE

Although Rwanda is located close to the equator in the tropics, its moderate-to-high elevations provide it with a mostly temperate feel; indeed, the highlands can be positively cool, with temperatures from 12–25°C (53–77°F) but also with extremes of 0–30°C (32–86°F). The lower areas around Akagera are warm and humid. The annual rainfall varies from 1600–2200 mm (63–87 inches) at Nyungwe to 600 mm (24 inches) at Akagera. The main rainy season lasts from February to May, while June to September is the driest time of year; October to January is an intermediate period.

TRAVEL SPECIFICS

DRIVING AND ROADS

Apart from the fact that there are few road signs, driving is not too difficult in Rwanda. Roads are good and since there are relatively few it is hard to get lost for too long! If you are driving yourself, be careful as the police are everywhere and watch carefully for vehicles that appear to be speeding. Stick to the speed limit both to avoid fines and for the sake of Rwanda's many pedestrians and domestic animals. Tracks4africa.com is an excellent resource for GPS maps for those interested in driving themselves around Rwanda.

LANGUAGE

All Rwandans speak to each other in Kinyarwanda, a Bantu language, with a tiny minority of Twa language speakers in isolated communities. French was the official second language until 2010, when it was replaced by English, meaning that many older Rwandans speak good French, while the younger people often speak English. Swahili is also widely spoken.

MONEY MATTERS

Rwanda's currency is the Rwandan Franc (RWF). The main expenses on a Rwandan trip are vehicle rental (normally including the services of a driver), fuel, accommodation, food, park entry and guiding fees, primate-tracking permits (if you opt for those activities), and flights to and from the country. Exchanging money can be more complicated than might be expected. US Dollars and Euros (preferable) are the main choices for exchange, even at the international airport. If you bring any other currency you can expect poor exchange rates. ATMs are becoming common in Kigali and other major towns and function with most major credit/debit cards; nevertheless, relying on ATMs for all of your cash is inadvisable. Visa is the most widely accepted card.

ACCOMMODATION AND FOOD

In most sites in Rwanda there is a variety of accommodation. It seems that the return of tourists to Rwanda after the genocide has encouraged a recovery of high-end lodges. Thus, places such as Nyungwe, Volcanoes, and Akagera all have luxurious lodges if necessary and often mid-range and budget options too. Camping is possible at Nyungwe, Akagera, and elsewhere.

Food in restaurants is good-to-excellent and often not that expensive. Perhaps as a result of the Belgian influence, restaurant standards are higher than in most East African countries. Western-style menus are common, along with Rwandan dishes such as goat kebabs and tilapia (a white and tasty freshwater fish), with ugali, plantain, or chapati. The incredibly rich and fertile farmlands mean that stopping anywhere at a roadside market will yield a luscious selection of fruit and vegetables (e.g. avocados, bananas, potatoes, papaya, mangos, and pineapples) for those who like to self-cater. Remember to plan your meals carefully when you are on the road as outside of the main urban centers there are few restaurants, although many roadside cafes will offer a wholesome buffet known as *mélange* (from the French). Rwanda is globally famous for its incredible coffee and tea and frequent cups of stellar brew can add considerable pleasure to a trip through this country.

REFERENCES AND RESOURCES

The Kingdon Field Guide to African Mammals by Jonathan Kingdon is the best guide to the mammals occurring in Rwanda. It is published in both slim pocket-size and in a larger and more complete version. The latter is recommended for those wanting in-depth information about the country's primates.

The Behavior Guide to African Mammals by Richard Estes contains excellent information about gorillas and chimpanzees, some of Rwanda's other primates, and most of Akagera's savannah mammal species.

Birds of East Africa by Stevenson and Fanshawe covers Rwanda. This is an excellent book and by far the best field-guide for the country's birds. It is now available as an App for tablets touch devices and includes an excellent set of recordings by Brian Finch (see below).

The Princeton Illustrated Checklist *Birds of Eastern Africa* by Ber van Perlo is a compact reference that covers Rwanda's birds but leaves a few things to be desired.

Birds of Africa South of the Sahara by Sinclair and Ryan is the only other book that currently covers all of the species in Rwanda but the small size and broad scope of most of the range maps make the distribution information for Rwanda almost useless.

The excellent *East African Bird Sounds* by Brian Finch covers Rwanda. This set of recordings can be accessed by buying and downloading the App version of the Stevenson and Fanshawe *Birds of East Africa*. The free website Xeno-canto also offers recordings of a growing number of Rwanda's birds (http://www.xeno-canto.org).

A Field Guide to the Reptiles of East Africa by Stephen Spawls, Kim Howell, Robert Drewes, and James Ashe gives excellent coverage of all of Rwanda's reptile species. The only problem with this guide – at least from the perspective of a travelling naturalist – is its large size. The Princeton pocket guide to Reptiles and Amphibians of East Africa by the same authors is largely taken from the larger volume. It is not exhaustive but is portable and covers the most commonly encountered species.

If you can find it, there is an excellent guide to Nyungwe NP. Look or

The tree hyrax is one of the loudest of Rwanda's mammals. Its deafening calls split the night in forested places like Nyungwe NP. ©Lee Hunter

Sneezed to extinction?

Poaching and habitat loss have driven the mountain gorilla to the brink of extinction. Today, a mere 880 individuals survive in their last stronghold, the Virunga Mountains. Like high-altitude "castaways", these surviving groups have nowhere to retreat and are surrounded by a sea of humanity that continues to chop and till the fringes of their forests into oblivion. With nowhere to turn, they find themselves confined to protected areas. Given that they are also visited on a daily basis by tourists, mountain gorillas have ended up sharing their entire lives with humans and this shared life leaves them vulnerable to a suite of human-borne infectious germs.

While gorilla tracking helps conserve gorillas by providing the funding needed to protect and manage the national parks, the hordes of people visiting from all over the world expose gorillas to one of the largest samples of human-borne infectious diseases that anybody – let alone a wild animal – is ever likely to face. Gorillas share 98.5% of their genes with humans and so most diseases are communicable. It is no exaggeration to say that humans' rapidly evolving arsenal of resistant strains of airborne diseases should now be considered as the greatest threat to these gorillas' continued existence. Infectious disease has become the second leading cause of death in mountain gorillas, exceeded only by deaths by trauma such as infanticide, accidents, and fights between silverbacks. Disease deaths are currently speculated to account for more than 20% of mortalities. Common respiratory infections ranging from mild colds to severe pneumonia are the most lethal to gorillas. Not only do they affect individuals but they can also spread like wildfire through whole groups.

A large amount of money and effort is spent every year on medical teams who closely monitor gorilla troops for any individuals that show symptoms of respiratory diseases. These medical checks also extend to the 400+ rangers, trackers, porters, and aides working in the gorilla-tracking industry in an attempt to ensure that those that come into the closest contact with these gentle giants do so with the cleanest possible bills of health. Disease prevention is also the reason why tourists are limited to one hour with the gorillas. Perhaps even more importantly, visitors are supposed to remain at a safe distance from the gorillas, which is determined by the distance that airborne spray particles are known to travel in a human sneeze, not by what is deemed necessary for human safety.

So consider all of this when you head for the hills to see your first gorilla. Just as you might load up on immune boosters before getting onto a transcontinental flight to Rwanda, also dig into your baggage and find a bandana to cover your nose and mouth while you enjoy your gorilla encounter. Also consider leaving your tracking until the end of your trip in the hope that any airborne illness you might have picked up on the plane will no longer be ▶

infectious. If you know you are coming down with something, do the right thing and stay behind. There is no better way to pay your respect to these incredible creatures.

ask for it at the RDB offices in Kigali or Nyungwe if you cannot get hold of a copy in advance. It provides an in-depth look at the national park and will heighten your appreciation of the area.

The Bradt Travel Guide to Rwanda by Briggs and Booth is highly valuable. It includes discussions of history, religion, culture, the genocide, and many details of travel practicalities, and will definitely enhance your understanding of this country. There is also good coverage of birds and other wildlife in Rwanda. The details regarding accommodation, restaurants, and getting around the country are very accurate.

The website www.tracks4Africa. co.za contains good GPS maps of Rwanda that will be very useful for those who are driving themselves and will also be of interest to those with a hired driver.

HEALTH AND SAFETY

HEALTH
Proof of yellow fever immunization is technically required to enter the country and in general being immunized is a good idea. Immunizations against tetanus, diphtheria, typhoid, and polio are also recommended. Malaria exists in Rwanda and it would be wise to take prophylaxis for this debilitating and occasionally deadly disease, especially if visiting the lower elevation eastern parts of the country such as Akagera NP. Although malaria is rare at higher altitudes (1800–3000 m), it does still occur. Prophylaxis is essential if you visit during the rainy season as this is when most cases occur. The best bet is to avoid being bitten and it is wise to speak to your travel clinic for advice on avoiding the carrier *Anopheles* mosquito. Ticks, tse-tse flies, blackflies, and putsi-flies are the other biting insects that carry a variety of diseases, none of which is quite as serious as malaria. Swamps and other fresh water areas carry the risk of bilharzia (*Schistosomiasis*) and so avoid swimming close to villages or reeds, although swimming at the major resorts on Lake Kivu is safe. As in most less-developed countries, you should only drink bottled, filtered, or boiled water to avoid digestive upsets.

SAFETY AND ETIQUETTE
It may sound strange for a country that suffered the world's most recent and horrific genocide, but it would be harder to find a safer African country to travel in! Rwanda is remarkably safe. Petty crime is mainly confined to Kigali and violent crime is almost unheard of. Do be alert for pickpockets, particularly in Kigali. Elsewhere in the country your driver or guide should warn you about any appropriate etiquette when interacting with local people. Rural Rwandans are

Hippos are not to be trifled with. ©Keith Barnes

exceptionally engaging and friendly: if you want to walk across land that is privately owned, try to get permission if possible, and be careful not to trample crops for what seems like a minor misstep for you may be a significant loss of precious food for a local family. A good rule of thumb is never to photograph anyone without first asking permission. Also be sensitive when discussing the genocide. There is virtually no one who was not affected in a very personal way by this horror and appropriate compassion is urged when discussing its details. If in doubt, don't ask. If you'd like to find out more, pay a visit to the thoughtfully presented and moving Genocide Memorial in Kigali.

DANGEROUS ANIMALS
Rwanda has very few of the potentially dangerous large mammals found elsewhere in East Africa. You can walk into the countryside almost anywhere

without worrying much about lions, leopards, buffalo, or elephants. The exception to this is Akagera NP, where you need to be careful, as buffalo, elephant, and hippopotamus are common, and leopard also occurs. Volcanoes NP has buffalo but access to this park is not allowed without an armed escort.

Proper etiquette around the mountain gorillas is an important subject that your park guide will address before you hike to see these incredible animals. Silverback male gorillas, which can weigh over 200 kg, have been known to mock charge tourists, although this is rare. The best advice is to listen very carefully to what your guide tells you before your hike – it could save you from a somewhat worrying experience. All the larger lakes except Lake Kivu have hippos and crocodiles and so be careful if you take a swim or bird any lakeshore. Like most of Africa, poisonous snakes are possible anywhere, but rarely encountered. Count yourself lucky if you see a beauty like a mamba!

ANNOYANCES

In this densely populated country, don't be surprised if inquisitive local children accompany you on birding trips outside the parks (they are not present in the parks). They are usually just curious. Say *inyonyi* (birds) and point, and they'll laugh. They may ask for money or pens in areas where tourists are common, but just say "no". They will usually get the message quickly. If you have an urge to donate pens or other small gifts, stop at a local school and give them to the headmaster directly to avoid encouraging begging among Rwanda's children. Help them to be proud. Most

adults who approach you are merely curious or are eager to practice their English.

BIOGEOGRAPHY

VOLCANOES, ICE AGES, AND THE GREAT RIFT

Discovery and National Geographic regularly showcase the megafauna of Africa's savannas. But most of Africa's prime biodiversity hotspots are actually montane forests that differ dramatically from the surrounding savannas and lowland forests. For the last 30 million years the Great Rift Valley, which stretches from Ethiopia to Zimbabwe, has been buckling Africa in two. As the Earth's crust has diverged at its plate boundaries, lava has exploded from beneath and created a se-

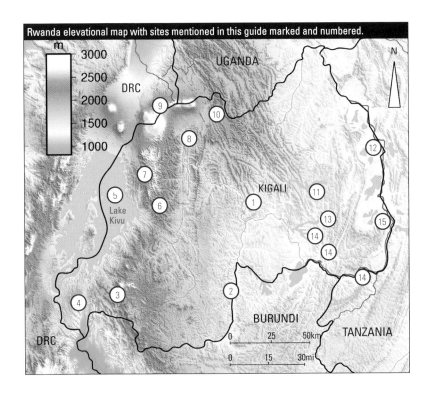
Rwanda elevational map with sites mentioned in this guide marked and numbered.

ries of volcanoes that litter the central spine of the continent. This process has produced an ever-evolving series of mountains, several of which were once higher than Kilimanjaro, Africa's highest peak today. The interchange of plants and animals between these mountains has influenced the patterns of biodiversity that we currently see across Africa.

The patterns found on Africa's mountains mimic island chains such as the Galapagos, where over time old islands erode away as new ones form, which are then gradually colonized by plants and animals. However, unlike true archipelagos where land is separated by uninhabitable ocean, species in montane forests are able to shift between adjacent montane forest blocks by moving through lowland forests or other corridors of suitable habitat, thereby creating complex pat-terns of isolation and endemism. After 30 million years of continuous volca-nic activity, modern-day Africa retains seven main montane forest blocks: the 1) Cameroon-Nigerian mountains, 2) Ethiopian highlands, 3) Kenyan-Tanzanian mountains, 4) Eastern Arc (mostly in Tanzania), 5) Malawi-Zim-babwe chain, 6) South African moun-tains and, one of the main subjects of this book, 7) Albertine Rift mountains. Within each of these complexes, the levels of diversity and endemism are driven by three major factors: i) the height of the mountains, which deter-mines the range of habitats and eco-types they can support; ii) their age, which determines how long they have had to accumulate species; and iii) their position relative to other mon-tane systems, which influences coloni-zation and the exchange of species. Of all of Africa's forest blocks, the Alber-

Rwanda's Afro-montane forests are the richest in Africa. This is the Albertine Rift endemic Black-faced (*Mountain Masked*) Apalis. ©Keith Barnes

Yellow-crowned Canary is found in most of Africa's montane forest blocks. ©Keith Barnes

tine Rift has the greatest levels of both biodiversity and endemism, which, if you examine its history and geography, is somewhat less than surprising.

Of all the present-day mountain ranges in Africa, the Albertine Rift is one of the oldest, most geologically active, and highest, and both the Virunga and Ruwenzori ranges reach over 4000 meters. The mountains of the Albertine Rift are ancient and the continuous geological activity they have experienced throughout their existence has driven further speciation. The highest-altitude environments, which the Albertine Rift possesses in abundance, are thought to be the most important generators of new endemic species and forms. Additionally, the range of habitats, from lowland forest to moorland and alpine habitats at the highest altitudes, has enabled these mountains to maintain high levels of

biodiversity. Finally, the Albertine Rift mountains are the most centrally located of the major forest blocks and are flanked by three others, the Eastern Arc, Kenyan-Tanzanian mountains, and Malawi-Zimbabwe chain. These other ranges have all acted as sources of colonization and biotic exchange for the Albertine Rift – today, these mountains are a true epicenter for all of Africa's montane forests, a feature reflected in the levels of biodiversity and endemism they harbor. A further factor in the Albertine Rift's biological richness affecting the lowlands as much as the mountains is the way in which the upheavals during the ice ages drove speciation across the Congo Basin, on whose eastern side these mountains lie.

The Congo Basin, whose vast lowland rainforests abut the Albertine Rift's western margin, may have act-

33

In Nyungwe one finds Angolan (pied) Colobus, one of several members of the pied colobus complex in East Africa's mountains. ©Keith Barnes

ed as a giant corridor fueling biotic exchange between the Rift and the Cameroon-Nigerian highlands to the west and the Angolan highlands to the southwest. During the coldest periods of the ice ages – as recently as 10,000 years ago – much of central Africa's lowland forest dried out and became savanna. At these times the moist mountainous western edge of the Albertine Rift acted as a refuge for a vital part of the Afrotropical forest flora and fauna that would subsequently recolonize the lowlands once the ice ages had finished. During wetter periods, forests would spread through the savanna, creating a continuum of forest linking the western Rift to the Cameroon-Nigerian and Angolan highlands, thereby permitting species interchange. The net result of all these phenomena is that the Albertine Rift is arguably the most biologically complex mountain chain in Africa. It is also one of the most important mountain areas from a conservation perspective due to its 1) current biodiversity, 2) role as an *in-situ* creator of new endemic species, and 3) historical and potential future role as a refuge for lowland forest biota during periods of climate change.

BIOGEOGRAPHY IN BIRDS AND MAMMALS

A number of fascinating patterns begin to emerge if you examine the avifauna of African mountains and, in particular, that of the Albertine Rift. Several genera of Albertine Rift endemics share stronger affinities with extant or extinct Asian genera than they do with any other African species, a fact that emphasizes the age and antiquity of these forests. The Congo Bay-Owl, Neumann's (*Short-tailed*) Warbler, Grauer's (*African Green*) Broadbill, and Grauer's Cuckooshrike are all possible examples of taxa that are isolated relicts of Asian stock, once more widespread across the Old World, that has subsequently been replaced by more modern African derivatives. The bay-owls have a healthy fossil record dating back some 25 million years and it is thought that these primitive barn-owls were probably quite widespread and successful until modern *Tyto* barn-owls evolved and replaced them, leaving only a couple of bay-owl species in geologically ancient refugia. Genetic studies of Neumann's (*Short-tailed*) Warbler have found that taxonomically it is nested within the Asian family Cettidae, seemingly having diverged from its nearest Asian relative some 17 million years ago. The broadbills are primarily Asian in distribution: Grauer's (*African Green*) Broadbill, thought to be the most ancient of all African broadbills, occurs only in small isolated refugia and is on the brink of natural extinction. The fact that the broadbills have close relatives in Madagascar, the asities, suggests that this is indeed an ancient group of birds. Another excellent example of these ancient and vanishing lineages is the *Micropotamogale* genus of ottershrews, which is only found in the Albertine Rift and Mount Nimba in West Africa. Away from western and central Africa, representatives of this relict family survive only in Madagascar in the form of the strange tenrecs. This lineage dates back some 50 million years and provides important clues as to the history of these mountains.

Some species are derived from more recent events. Genetic analyses suggest that the complex of forest robins in the Albertine Rift evolved in the late Pliocene between 3.2 and 2.2 million years ago. Other groups such as Stuhlmann's (*Rwenzori Double-collared*) and Regal sunbirds are similarly more recent derivatives. The evolution of the mountain gorillas, the Rift's celebrities, is a very interesting case. Although gorilla and human lineages parted about 9 million years ago, western lowland gorillas separated from the eastern populations only about 2 million years ago; furthermore, the Albertine Rift endemic subspecies *beringei* only diverged from the gorillas that inhabit the lowland forests to the west of the Virungas (*graueri*) about 400,000 years ago. Thus, the origins of the diversity and endemism of animals in the Albertine Rift are both ancient and relatively recent. It is important to realize that the species assemblages we see today have a history but that the processes driving speciation are ongoing.

HABITATS

Historically, the rugged and higher western half of Rwanda was covered by moist, lush montane forest and grassland associated with the Albertine Rift. The lower and less rugged eastern half of Rwanda was more open, boasting grassland and woodland that support classic African trees such as *Acacieae* (the tribe which contains the African members of the recently split *Acacia* genus), *Combretum*, and *Commiphora*. Although the general habitat boundaries remain the same, over 80% of the country has been transformed into subsistence agriculture, some of

Rwanda's vast papyrus marshes hold a set of special birds. ©Grant Atkinson

which is so ancient that it is difficult to know exactly what the habitat was like before the first plough broke the land and the first crop was grown. Today, most of Rwanda resembles an intricate chessboard of agricultural smallholdings, tea, coffee, and exotic tree plantations, small villages, and the occasional remnants of the indigenous scrub or wetlands. Very few mammals and a severely reduced subset of birds survive in these human-modified habitats.

Another key habitat are the wetlands, where important species such as *Typha* and papyrus and other *Cyperus* thrive. The best remaining wetlands are along the eastern border with Tanzania and the southeastern border with Burundi, although historically there were once large wetlands scattered throughout the country. Many of these have been heavily altered by human use. More information on specific habitats is included in the site accounts below.

the era of profound human impact on the natural landscape that continues up to the present day. As long as 1000 years ago, the middle-elevation areas between the Nyungwe and Volcanoes forest blocks may already have been largely deforested. More recently, the rinderpest epidemic of the 1880s forced pastoralists into the remaining forests and many fires and loss of habitat resulted. The discovery of gold in the 1930s had a further severe impact on the forests and the intensity of land use in the forest led to the local extinction of Cape buffalo and African savanna elephant in Nyungwe in the 1970s and 1990s, respectively.

Today, Rwanda is the most densely populated country in Africa. Between 1934 and 1991 the population grew from 1.6 to 7.2 million and it currently supports over 8.5 million people. Perhaps even more alarming is the fact that the country's population is still growing at a rate of around 2.3% per year. Most of these people dwell in rural areas and their impact on the landscape is profound. The majority of the country bears the marks of severe human impact. Increasingly intensive agriculture and higher population densities have seen vast portions of natural Rwanda disappear under cultivation in the last century. Nowadays only a few islands of natural vegetation hold their ground.

Africa's first national park, Volcanoes, was declared in northwest Rwanda in 1925 to protect the mountain gorillas. Despite some early successes, however, the conservation history of Rwanda is bleak. The Volcanoes-Gishwati-Mukura Forests covered around 830 km^2 in 1934 but by 1955 this forest block had become severely

CONSERVATION

Ancestors of the Batwa people first arrived in Rwanda some 500,000 years ago. Their traditional hunter-gatherer lifestyles had little impact on the natural environment. Things changed with the arrival of the Bantu people some 2000 years ago. They brought with them more advanced techniques of cultivation and animal domestication, which permitted much greater population densities and instigated

fragmented; by 1998 only 18% of its original surface area remained. Similarly, Nyungwe NP has lost 35% of its area, above all in the Cyamudongo tract of the park where some 70% has been lost. In 1997, about 15% of the country was included in national parks and reserves but widespread degazetting of parks occurred after the tragic genocide of 1994, one of whose causes could have been land pressure. Rwanda's largest national park, Akagera, was reduced to 40% of its original size. Today, only 8% of Rwanda's land area is preserved for wildlife. The fact that huge portions of national parks and reserves have been degazetted in the past 15 years to create space for people emphasizes the frailty of the country's current network of protected areas. The

apparent local extinction of species including Leaf-love, Blue-shouldered Robin-Chat, Olive-green Camaroptera, Forest Robin, Cassin's Flycatcher, and Kenya (*Eastern*) Violet-backed Sunbird also suggests that natural habitat in the country is disappearing fast.

Nevertheless, more recently there have been certain positive conservation developments. The Wildlife Conservation Society has been heavily involved in surveying Nyungwe and the Virunga Mountains, the parts of Rwanda with the highest conservation priority. Nyungwe was proclaimed a National Park by the government in 2004, an excellent development that gives more protection to this vital site for the conservation of Afro-montane environments. Volcanoes NP has been

Tea estates extend right up to many of the borders of Nyungwe NP. All of Rwanda's protected areas are hemmed in by people. ©Keith Barnes

Bronze Sunbird has disjunct populations in eastern and southern Africa, as well as Angola. Some of these populations must have been isolated for a long time. ©Keith Barnes

designated as a Biosphere Reserve under UNESCO's Man and Biosphere Program. Elsewhere, programs have been launched to shore up the remnants of the Mukura and Gishwati Forest Reserves. Rwanda has ratified a number of treaties including international UNESCO agreements on 1) biodiversity, 2) trade in endangered species (CITES), 3) climate change, and 4) desertification. However, unless the scourge of poverty and the predominance of subsistence agricultural are challenged – above all, by bringing the population growth rate under control – Rwanda's environmental problems will persist. There are no easy solutions but if the population can be stabilized, the economy developed, and the protected areas managed to create significant income, the parks are much more likely to survive.

Most Rwandans engage in subsistence agriculture and depend on firewood for cooking. Even though this may be unsustainable in the long term, it does mean that income from tourism can be very influential in the short term. Foreign visitors are already making a big impact, with tourism second only to agriculture as a source of national income. In 1989, tourism income from the gorilla-tracking mecca of Volcanoes NP earned the country $4–6 million, and in Nyungwe NP $0.5–1 million. Since then, the numbers of tourists have doubled and the country's full potential is still to be developed, particularly as a more diverse range of activities such as tracking other primates, mountain climbing, and birding is now on offer. The enlightened national parks administration is attempting to share revenue with neighboring communities, which seems the only likely strategy for preventing future degazetting. When comparing Rwandan park administration with that of an emerging superpower such as India (which is struggling to conserve its flagship mammal, the tiger), the job being done by the Rwanda Development Board (formerly ORTPN) to protect what remains of Rwanda's natural resources appears nothing short of phenomenal. Rwanda needs tourism badly and the world needs Rwanda's resources – above all in the Albertine Rift – to be protected. So please consider visiting this marvelous little country

NOMENCLATURE AND TAXONOMY

Mammal taxonomy and nomenclature follow the *Handbook of the Mammals of the World* (HMW) published by Lynx Edicions (2009–2013) for the families already covered by this work and *The Kingdon Field Guide to African Mammals* (1997) for species not yet covered. Because the former reference work follows more liberal phylogenetic taxonomic principles, there are many species that are split by HMW that are not split by Kingdon. When names differ between the two works, we default to the HMW name and sometimes give the Kingdon name in parentheses. In the species lists, we use the Kingdon order, as that of the HMW is not yet complete.

Bird taxonomy follows the sixth edition of *The Clements Checklist of Birds of the World* published by Cornell University Press, including updates through to 2013. There are some generally accepted "splits" that Clements does not recognize, several

of which are recognized in the Stevenson and Fanshawe *Birds of East Africa*. Throughout the text, when the Stevenson and Fanshawe name differs from the names in Clements, the Stevenson and Fanshawe name is included in parentheses and italics. In some cases, other alternate bird names (usually potential splits) are included in parentheses, but these are not italicized. The specialty birds section in the back of the book discusses some of the cases where Stevenson and Fanshawe's taxonomy differs from that of Clements.

Regardless of which populations are currently considered as distinct species, the Albertine Rift is a rich center of endemism. With the increasing popularity and prevalence of the Phylogenetic Species Concept, which recognizes more species than previous species concepts, there are many potential splits that would create endemic or near-endemic species that are not currently recognized by any major authority. It seems in particular that bird species that have disjoint populations in the Cameroon-Nigerian and/or Angola Mountains and again in East Africa, and which are separated by the entire Congo Basin (e.g. Mountain Sooty (*Black*) Boubou), may actually be significantly different and could be separate species. Occasionally, the same subspecies (e.g. *atriceps* African Hill Babbler) is considered to occur in the Cameroon-Nigerian mountains and then again along the Albertine Rift. This is highly unlikely given the evolutionary history of this region and future phylogenetic analyses are bound to reveal many cryptic species and subspecies. Another interesting pattern lies within the Albertine Rift itself.

Copper Sunbird, a species mainly found in eastern Rwanda. ©Kevin Bartlett

The mountains of southwest Uganda and northwest Rwanda, including the Virungas, occasionally support different taxa from Nyungwe NP and there may well be cryptic species lurking within these discrete nodes. The "Specialty Species" section at the back of the book addresses the most distinctive endemic or near-endemic subspecies and also highlights other taxonomic enigmas. Knowledge of such taxa when visiting a country is useful as it allows list-keeping naturalists to "bank" these species in case of a future split.

CONTACTS

RDB (the Rwanda Development Board), formerly known as ORTPN (Office Rwandaise du Tourisme et des Parcs Nationaux) is perhaps the most important contact in Rwanda. The RDB can advise on gorilla, chimp, and other primate-tracking permits, facilitate bookings for RDB-run accommodation such as Nyungwe's Gisakura guesthouse, and provide advice on most other aspects of a Rwanda natural-history trip. Web: www.rwandatourism.com; e-mail: info@rwandatourism.com, reservations@rwandatourism.com; telephone: +250 (0)252502350/573396.

Tropical Birding arranges birding, natural history, and specialist photography trips throughout Africa including Rwanda. Web: www.tropicalbirding.com; e-mail: info@tropicalbirding.com; telephone: 1-800-348-5941.

41

Lesser Striped-Swallow is found throughout the country. ©Ken Behrens

There is a large and growing number of tour operators within Rwanda. Many of the best are members of the Rwanda Tours and Travel Association. Web: http://www.rttarwanda.org/members.php **Access Rwanda Safaris** is a very good Rwandan tour operator. Web: http://www.access-rwanda-safaris.com; e-mail: info@access-rwanda-safaris.com Most tour operators in Rwanda are well prepared to arrange a primate safari, but less experienced with other kinds of trips such as birding tours.

HOW TO USE THIS BOOK

OVERALL ORGANIZATION

Each site account starts with a brief introduction that highlights the appeal of the site and provides some basic information about it.

Next comes a list of "Key species" and "Other species of interest". Key species are those that are difficult to find worldwide (due to their small range or general scarcity) and are found in very few sites anywhere in the world. Thus, the Albertine Rift endemic species are always considered as key species. "Other species of interest" have a broader range and/or are more abundant. Such evaluations are necessarily subjective but aim to give the reader a good idea of the main species to focus on at each site. There may be many other interesting species at a given locality, but this valuation will depend on whether the reader is mainly a Palearctic, Afrotropical, or Nearctic naturalist. In the text and "Other species of interest", we discuss species that may be of interest to one or another of these groups; nevertheless, the key species are restricted to those that will be priorities for almost any keen naturalist visiting Rwanda. A couple of sites have no true key species and so only "Species of interest" are listed.

The "Habitat" section briefly describes the wildlife habitat at the site. The "Mammaling/Birding" section gives specific information about how to maximize your wildlife watching success and enjoyment at a particular site, including exact locations to try for specific species.

Under "Directions," there are instructions on how to reach the site. Sometimes this type of information is also included under "Mammaling/Birding", depending on the best strategy for wildlife watching in the area. The directions section also includes information on entrance fees, guides, and food and lodging in the area.

Some sites include sidebars with more detailed information on a particularly interesting aspect of the site.

SPECIALTIES SECTION

At the back of this book, you will find a section on the most interesting mammals and birds of Rwanda and a discussion of the best sites at which to find them. This section covers all of the Albertine Rift endemics, most endemic subspecies, all scarce and local African specialties such as most of the Lake Victoria bird endemics, and globally endangered or scarce species such as the Shoebill. If you want to check that your itinerary includes good chances for all of your target species, read this section to make sure you visit the right localities.

MAPS AND GPS

All of the accounts include GPS coordinates for specific spots. These can

Little Bittern is a shy denizen of Rwanda's extensive wetlands. ©Ken Behrens

be extremely useful for navigation. The datum used for all of these points is WGS84, in a degrees, minutes, and fractions of minutes format. An excel spreadsheet of all the waypoints mentioned in this book is available at the following site: <http://www.tropical-birding.com/wild-rwanda/>. This site also includes online applications that allow the easy conversion of an Excel spreadsheet into a format that is transferrable to a GPS unit.

Google Earth is an incredible tool for exploring and understanding wildlife-watching sites. Readers are encouraged to plug the GPS coordinates from this book into Google Earth, which will allow them to virtually explore the sites prior to visiting. If no map is included for a given site and/or the directions seem confusing, viewing the associated coordinates on Google Earth is likely to clear things up.

KILOMETER READINGS

Distances in kilometers are used extensively in the maps and the text. While these can be extremely useful, take them with a pinch of salt. Odometers vary considerably, particularly in Africa where vehicles take a lot of hard use. If you have a GPS, it will be very useful in navigating precisely to places that kilometer readings will get you close to. Some maps are annotated with marker points and kilometer readings, where we label the distance between each major marker point (as if you had reset your odometer at every marker point).

Acknowledgements

Many thanks to our sponsors: the Master Family Fund, Columbus Zoo, Tropical Birding, Africa Geographic, Africa Geographic Travel, and Access Rwanda Safaris. Without them, the creation of this guide would have been impossible. Claver Ntoyinkima provided a tremendous amount of information about Nyungwe National Park and lots of additional information about other parts of Rwanda. His humble passion and incredible self-taught knowledge were instrumental to our love and understanding of Rwanda and in making it a place that we can recommend to others. Jason Anderson wrote part of the Kigali site account and all of the southeastern papyrus, Makera Forest, and Mashoza Parike site accounts. He also provided invaluable input on the manuscript as a whole. Marcell Claassen, Brian Finch, Norbert Gatera, Sarah Hall, Kavuna Muhire, Claudien Nsabagasani, Madeleine Nyiratuza, Faansie Peacock, and Emmanuel Werabe provided various types of information and insight. The Rwanda Development Board provided guidance and access to national parks during the research phase of the book. Africa Geographic created the maps for this guide and we are particularly grateful to Cindy Armstrong and Sarah Borchert. Trip reports from Marcell Claassen, Ross Goode, Nigel Moorhouse, Dave Sargeant, Rainer Summers, and Keith Valentine were useful. Janet Behrens and Lucy Witts generously donated their time by proofreading the manuscript and spotted errors that would otherwise have escaped our attention. Josh Engel of the Chicago Field Museum of Natural History commented on the biogeography section. Thanks also to the Tropical Birding clients who shared Rwanda trips with us and allowed additional research for the book, especially to Bernie Master who was so impressed by his birding experience in Rwanda that he envisaged the need for and conceptualized the birth of this guide. Many thanks to our publisher Lynx Edicions, particularly to Yolanda Aguayo, Josep del Hoyo, and Susanna Silva.

Ken wishes to thank Rojo Johnarson for her patience during the long hours of work required by this project, and her all-around support.

Christian would like to thank Simon Espley for his support and understanding throughout the many hours that it took to produce the book. To his wife Lucy, and children Kayla and Oliver, he wishes to dedicate this book, and pledges to bring them to Rwanda one day.

Keith would like to thank his parents for instilling a passion for birds and wildlife in a young man, and his wife Yi-fang and son Joshua for putting up with it in an old one.

Site Accounts

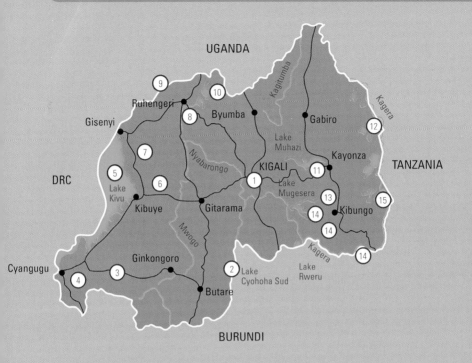

1. Kigali and surrounds
2. Akanyaru Wetland
3. Nyungwe National Park
4. Cyamudongo Forest
5. Lake Kivu
6. Mukura Forest
7. Gishwati Forest
8. Buhanga Forest
9. Volcanoes National Park
10. Rugezi Marsh
11. Route from Kigali to Akagera NP
12. Akagera National Park
13. Mashoza Parike Woodland and Abudada Dam
14. Papyrus Swamps of Southeastern Rwanda
15. Makera Forest

Kigali and surrounds

Kigali is not remarkably "birdy" but there is some decent birding to be had in and around the city, in particular in the Nyarutarama Lake area on the northern side of the city and at the wetlands along the Nyabarongo River, accessible either from the south or the west of the city. The lake and surrounding areas are good for a variety of birds that subsist in humanized habitats, while the wetlands hold a good set of marsh birds including some papyrus specialists such as White-winged Swamp-Warbler and Papyrus Gonolek.

KEY SPECIES

Birds: White-winged and Greater Swamp-warblers, Papyrus Gonolek.

OTHER SPECIES OF INTEREST

Birds: Fulvous Whistling-Duck, Hottentot Teal, Scaly Francolin, Great White and Pink-backed pelicans, Little Bittern, Goliath Heron, Bat Hawk (rare), Palm-nut Vulture, African Marsh-Harrier, African Goshawk, Little Sparrowhawk, Long-crested Eagle, African Rail, African Crake, Lesser Jacana, Long-toed Lapwing, African Snipe, Greater Painted-Snipe, Blue-headed Coucal, African Hobby, Spot-flanked Barbet, Brown-throated Wattle-eye, Black-headed Gonolek, Red-backed Shrike (boreal winter), African, Great, and Eurasian reed-warblers (latter two in boreal winter), Chubb's and Trilling cis-

Some widespread but great-looking waterbirds like Long-toed Lapwing can be found right in Kigali.
©Keith Barnes

ticolas, Gray-capped Warbler, Black-lored Babbler, Swamp Flycatcher, Purple-banded, Green-headed, and Red-chested sunbirds, Thick-billed Seedeater, Northern Brown-throated, Grosbeak, and Red-headed weavers, White-collared Oliveback, Crimson-rumped Waxbill, African Firefinch.

HABITAT

Much of Nyarutarama Lake is surrounded by marsh vegetation, a mixture of *Typha*, *Miscanthidium*, and papyrus and other *Cyperus*. The area immediately around the lake is covered by a mixture of exotic grasses and scrub (mostly dominated by *Lantana*) that form dense thickets. A small grove of large silver oaks and *Eucalyptus* surrounds a derelict settlement on the lake's northeastern shores. The slopes on the southern edge of the lake and upstream (southeast) have largely been transformed into cultivated fields, with some isolated indigenous trees and shrubs. A sizeable patch of *Acacieae* woodland persists about 250 m upstream along the rivulet that feeds the lake, on the slopes below Nyarutarama Avenue.

The western bridge over the Nyabarongo River crosses a swath of marsh habitat, mainly papyrus. Unfortunately, it suffers much human disturbance but some birds remain. The marsh habitat along the Nyabarongo to the south of the city is more extensive and in better condition.

BIRDING

Urban Kigali holds a few birds. Certain species such as Hooded Vulture, Black Kite, White-rumped Swift, and African Palm-Swift can float overhead anywhere, even downtown. Some very decent birding can be had on the outskirts of the city, as detailed below.

Nyarutarama Lake: "Lovers Lake", as it is often referred to by locals, is found in Kigali's affluent suburb of Nyarutarama, adjacent to the Nyarutarama Golf Course. The lake is surrounded by a walking track and the surrounding habitat is crisscrossed by many footpaths, allowing easy exploration of both wet and dry habitats. While far from being an essential birding spot, you can easily rack up 80+ species in a couple of hours of birding here and as such it is a good place to bird if you have a few extra hours in Kigali.

One of the best places to bird is along the 300 m-long gravel track that runs along the north side of the lake, parallel to Nyarutarama Avenue (⊞ of mid-point on gravel track: S1° 56.237 E30° 5.796). This track cuts through a grove of large *Eucalyptus* and silver oak trees that are mostly above the track. On the track's eastern side lies a set of derelict buildings (⊞ S1° 56.288 E30° 5.882). Focus on the vegetation south of the track towards the lake's shores. Walking along here slowly will allow thorough exploration of the lake's banks and bring you into contact with a number of habitats such as scrub, reeds, muddy patches, floating rafts of vegetation, and open water, viewable through a few good breaks in the reeds. Several small trails run between the gravel track and the edge of the lake.

The lake's shores and open waters can be scanned from the main parking area (described under "Directions" below) or from the road along the dam. A telescope will come in handy. White-faced Whistling-Ducks are always present and can be expected in large numbers (50–100). Scan carefully through the whistling-duck flocks as the odd Fulvous Whistling-Duck often hides in their midst. Hottentot Teal and Red-billed Duck (*Teal*) occur in smaller numbers, with Yellow-billed and Comb (*Knob-billed*) ducks seen regularly, and Spur-winged Geese occasionally. Residents include Little Grebe, Red-knobbed Coot, Eurasian (*Common*) Moorhen, and African Jacana. Carefully scan any rafts of floating vegetation (*Potamogeton* or waterlily), as these are favored foraging grounds for Lesser Jacana, which occasionally shows up. The lake's shallows lure African Spoonbill, African Openbill, Yellow-billed and Marabou storks, and Hamerkop. Occasionally, Goliath Heron and Great White and Pink-backed pelicans are recorded at the lake, and there is a recent unconfirmed report of Shoebill.

Moderate "pishing" along the lake's edge should easily yield a few Winding Cisticolas and quite likely elicit a response from the always-alert Trilling Cisticola or groups of Gray-backed Fiscals, normally from the drier scrub. Stay focused on the reeds and you may pick up Tropical Boubou, African Reed-Warbler, Tawny-flanked Prinia, Common Waxbill, and during the boreal winter Palearctic migrants such as Great and Eurasian reed-warblers and Sedge Warbler. Weaver traffic in the reeds is hard to miss, especially when they are nesting. Village, Baglafecht, Grosbeak, and Northern Brown-throated weavers, and Holub's Golden-Weaver can all be seen. Black Crakes are loud and ubiquitous in the marsh, while the shier African Rails can be teased out into view with playback. African Crake has even oc-

casionally been spotted. Both African Snipe and the smart-looking Greater Painted-Snipe have been flushed by a lucky few. Pied and Malachite Kingfishers are often seen perched or hovering above the lake. Swamp Flycatcher and Little Bee-eater sally out in pursuit of their winged prey.

The grassy areas around the lake often hold Water Thick-knee, Yellow-throated Longclaw, African (*Grassland*) Pipit, and the regal (*African*) Wattled Lapwing. Cattle, Squacco, and Great White egrets, and Black-headed and Gray herons are often spotted resting on the taller lakeshore vegetation or occasionally in the large silver oaks and *Eucalyptus*. The denser *Typha* beds hide the odd Black-crowned Night-Heron and a good ear might be able to pick out the vocalizations of Little Bittern.

As elsewhere in central Africa, the skies are bound to fill with raptors as thermals generate the necessary lift by mid-morning. You can expect good numbers of Yellow-billed Kites and Hooded Vultures, as well as the odd African Fish-Eagle, African Harrier Hawk, and Palm-nut Vulture, plus no shortage of Pied Crows. Although flocks of swallows and swifts will often pose an identification challenge given their height and the hazy visibility, such flocks commonly hold Lesser Striped-Swallow, Barn and Angola swallows, Plain Martin, and Little and White-rumped swifts. Occasionally, Wire-tailed, Red-rumped, and Mosque swallows, Common Swift, and Black Sawwing are also spotted.

Dry and thick *Lantana* scrub covers the area to the east of the lake, where the source stream meets and feeds the lake. Ugly as this habitat

Black-headed (*Yellow-backed*) Weaver is common throughout most of Rwanda. ©Ken Behrens

may be, it cannot be ignored as it provides protection, fruit, and nectar for a gamut of species such as Blue-headed and White-browed coucals, Black-headed Gonolek, Grey-capped Warbler, White-browed Robin-Chat, and several seed-eating species including Red-billed and African firefinches, Green-winged Pytilia, and Bronze Mannikin. You may also sometimes come across Village Indigobird or Pin-tailed Whydah, both brood parasites of the seed-eating birds. When the *Lantana* is in fruit, lookout for Brimstone and Black-throated canaries, and sometimes Western Citril.

The best access point for the mature *Acacieae* woodlands upstream (southeast) of the lake is described under "Directions". Drive over the dam, then turn east and continue for about 500 m, cross a small stream, and enter the woodland. Exploring this area can prove fairly productive, though depending on how new you are to Africa, it may require more time and effort than this sort of habitat is really worth. The best woodland patch extends from the parking area up the slope to the east and all the way to the paved road for about 200 m upstream and 100 m downstream. Birding these open woodlands might yield Emerald-spotted Wood-Dove, Spot-flanked Barbet, Lesser and Greater honeyguides, Cinnamon-chested Bee-eater, Brown-

Nyarutarama Lake can hold Yellow-billed Stork. ©Ken Behrens

throated Wattle-eye, Black Cuckoo-shrike, Chubb's and Trilling cisticolas, Yellow-breasted Apalis, Willow Warbler, Southern Black-Flycatcher, African Yellow White-eye, Thick-billed Seedeater, and Black-throated Canary. During the boreal winter, Palearctic migrants such as European Roller and European Bee-eater are possible. Always be on the lookout for fruiting or flowering mistletoes and *Lantana*, as well as any *Eucalyptus* or silver oaks in bloom, as these attract nectar-feeding species such as Scarlet-chested, Collared, Green-headed, Red-chested, Marico, Variable, and Bronzy sunbirds, and other opportunists such as Rueppell's (*Rüppell's*) Glossy-Starling and Red-headed Weaver. The woodland understory is good for African Paradise-Flycatcher, shy and retiring coveys of Scaly Francolin, the stealthy and darting African Pygmy-Kingfisher, the loquacious Red-chested Cuckoo, and Garden Warbler during the boreal winter. This wooded area holds some raptors including a few African and Gabar goshawks, Little Sparrowhawk, which likes the dense cover at the bottom of the valley, and Long-crested Eagle, which favors the woodland edge. At dusk keep an eye out for Bat Hawk and African Hobby, which are occasionally seen.

Birding is also good just north of the lake on the Nyarutarama Golf Course. You can walk around the golf course itself and through the small tracts of exotic woodland adjacent to the course but take care not to obstruct any golfers using the course. Investigate overgrown thickets for species such as Lesser Honeyguide, Brown-throated Wattle-eye, Green-backed (*Gray-backed*) Camaroptera, Collared Sunbird, and even Thick-billed Seedeater. Open parts of the golf course are home to African (*Common*) Stonechat and Red-backed Shrike (boreal winter). Migrant warblers found here include Garden and Willow warblers. There is a roost of Hooded Vultures in the tall trees north of the golf course.

Nyabarongo South Crossing: The Nyabarongo river (becoming the Akagera or Kagera river farther downstream) where it is crossed by the Kigali-Nyamata road is the most ac-cessible good-quality papyrus marsh near Kigali. You can park on the edge of Gahanga village just before the marsh (⬛ S2° 3.080 E30° 5.345). The northern shore of the papyrus beds is just east of the road here and makes a good dawn vantage point, with several pools visible from the fields within 300 m of the road. There are heartening numbers of large waterbirds at this site, including Spur-winged Geese, Great, Cattle, and Little egrets, Squacco, Gray, and Black-headed herons, African Openbill, and Yellow-billed Stork. The papyrus around Gahanga holds the reclusive White-winged and Greater swamp-warblers and other papyrus specialties. There are several tracks and roads going into the marsh. To find them either drive or walk on the main road south towards the bridge, exploring left and right as appropriate. A car-navigable track runs east from the main road into the marsh (from ⬛ S2° 3.381 E30° 5.257), entering ever-expanding sugar cane plantations, where some tracts of papyrus and pools still remain. To the west of the main road, the papyrus was still in good condition at writing and there is a small path that follows electricity pylons into a good area of papyrus. Throughout the wetland and adjacent scrub, watch for Goliath Heron, African Marsh-Harrier, Long-toed Lapwing, Little and Blue-breasted bee-eaters (the latter much less common), Blue-headed Coucal, Black-headed Gonolek, Sedge (boreal winter) and African reed-warblers, Winding Cisticola, Western Yellow Wagtail (boreal winter), and Crimson-rumped Waxbill.

Once across the bridge, there is a good patch of native trees on a farm on the left (📷 S2° 3.912 E30° 5.293) that often hold some interesting woodland birds such as Lesser Honeyguide, Black-headed Gonolek, Gray-backed Fiscal, Spotted Flycatcher (boreal winter), Willow Warbler, Black-lored Babbler, and the uncommon Purple-banded Sunbird. Wet scrub along the edge can hold species including Great Reed-Warbler during the boreal winter and even the scarce White-collared Oliveback. To the west of the main road, across from this small woodland, explore small footpaths that offer views over several pools (such as from near the main road at 📷 S2° 4.021 E30° 5.294) for marsh species and occasional waterfowl.

Nyabarongo West Crossing: Another place to access the Nyabarongo is the bridge west of Kigali on the road to Butare and the rest of southwestern Rwanda. The best papyrus birding here is along the causeway across the floodplain, west of the main river channel and bridge. If coming from Kigali, first cross the bridge (📷 S1° 57.700 E30° 00.193), then proceed about 500 m west to where there is a small pull-off close to the main swath of papyrus (📷 S1° 57.763 E29° 59.956). Search here and along the main road to the west for Swamp Flycatcher, Carruthers's Cisticola, White-winged Swamp-Warbler, and Papyrus Gonolek. The latter two are extremely shy species and this busy road is a difficult place to coax them into view. The main merit of this spot is that it lies along the road from Kigali to Nyungwe NP.

TIME

Nyarutarama Lake seems to gather birding momentum through the day and equal – if not better tallies – can be scored by birding the lake in the late morning as opposed to very early in the day. An hour or two will suffice for birding the lake and surrounds, although interesting finds may surprise anyone willing to invest more time. The western Nyabarongo site is only worth a stop if you are not visiting Akagera NP, which offers better papyrus birding. An hour or less is more than sufficient for this small site. The southern Nyabarongo site holds better papyrus and general bird habitat and is worth a couple of hours, although Akagera and other papyrus sites in the southeast are much better.

DIRECTIONS

Nyarutarama Lake: Since Nyarutarama Lake is located in the northern suburbs of Kigali, only a couple of kilometers from the city center, it can be reached by a variety of routes. To simplify matters, we provide here directions from the Rwanda Development Board (RDB) headquarters, which are just east of the Rwandan parliament. The RDB headquarters is a massive and monolithic building at the major intersection of the road to Kibungo (shown as "Vers Kibungo Road" on many maps) and the road that heads north to the Nyarutarama suburb (📷 of intersection: S1° 57.203 E30° 6.117). The Gishushu bus stop is at this intersection, which may be useful for those heading for the lake on public transport, and also makes a good reference point for taxi drivers. Turn north onto the Nyarutarama Road, proceed for 350 m, and then turn left onto the smaller Nyarutarama Avenue (📷 of intersection: S1° 57.045 E30°

6.198). Zero your odometer here. Nyarutarama Avenue winds gently downhill into the valley. After driving for about 2 km, you will see the lake to the west, along with the tall silver oaks and *Eucalyptus* that grow on its northern side. At 2.2 km, turn left onto a gravel track (▨ of turn: S1° 56.181 E30° 5.721) that runs over the lake's earthen dam. If you miss this turnoff, you will start to see the fairways and roughs of the Nyarutarama Golf Course on your left, in which case you should retrace your steps. Once on the gravel road, park depending on how you wish to bird this area. If lake and wetland species are your targets, park at the main parking area on the left, just 30 m down the gravel track. If you prefer to start by birding the best woodlands, drive on and along the dam wall for 300 m, then turn left onto a track leading along the lake's southern edge and beyond towards the woodlands. About 500 m along this track (800 m from the paved road) you will cross a stream, and 40 m further on you will have reached the core of the woodland described in the "Birding" section above (▨ S1° 56.491 E30° 5.932). A 4x4 may be required for this stretch, depending on rain and road conditions. Make sure you do not park your vehicle on this narrow track and avoid leaving any valuables in sight when you leave your car.

Nyabarongo South Crossing: Drive south from Kigali on the road to Nyatama. About 8 km after leaving the southern edge of Kigali, you arrive at the edge of the Nyabarongo floodplain. The directions above in "Birding" start from here. To the south, 1.3 km farther on, the road crosses the main river channel on a large bridge.

Nyabarongo West Crossing: To reach the river, drive west from central Kigali on the main highway. After about 3.5 km, you reach a major intersection where the road to Volcanoes NP heads north, while the road to Butare and Nyungwe NP continues west (▨ of intersection: S1° 56.952 E30° 1.330). Drive west on the Butare road for 3.4 km until you reach the large bridge over the Nyabarongo River. The main patch of papyrus is another 500 m west, beyond the bridge.

There are abundant options for accommodation and dining in Kigali. Staying near Nyarutarama Lake makes some sense, as this site is in the heart of an up-market residential suburb, surrounded by embassies, high commission residences, international schools, and 4-star hotels. Visitors can find good food, shopping, and accommodation nearby, all in a fairly secure environment. ◆

Akanyaru Wetland

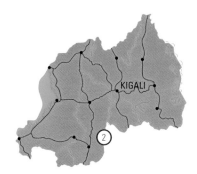

This huge wetland covers around 30,000 ha in south-central Rwanda on the border with Burundi. Historically, it was one of the most important wetlands in Rwanda and was home to some very interesting birds including Papyrus Yellow-Warbler, White-collared Oliveback, and Papyrus Canary, along with a good variety of more common marsh birds such as Papyrus Gonolek, White-winged Swamp-Warbler, Carruthers's Cisticola, Red-chested Sunbird, and Northern Brown-throated Weaver. Unfortunately, this marsh is not currently protected and as a result has been severely affected by human activities. Most of the marsh has been converted into cultivation and the patches of natural vegetation that remain are heavily utilized for thatch and fodder for animals. In its current state, this site is not worth a visit and most of the species that are certain to be seen are common birds of degraded habitat such as Black-headed Heron, African Pied Wagtail, Variable Sunbird, and Northern Gray-headed Sparrow. If the marsh is pro-

tected in the future and given a chance to regenerate, it may again become a good birding site.

DIRECTIONS

Reaching Akanyaru requires a long drive along bumpy dirt roads and is unlikely to be worthwhile for the vast majority of visitors. The directions here are included in case there are intrepid naturalists or scientists who want to reach the wetland. Take the main paved road from Kigali west and south towards Butare. About 13 km before Butare (**GPS** S2° 29.899 E29° 46.368), turn east off the main road onto a dirt track signed for Gikonko. From here, you follow a maze of dirt roads through a matrix of villages, agricultural fields, and exotic tree plantations. The center of the marsh is about 20 km due east of the turn off the main road, though the twists and turns of the access roads amount to about 30 km. The best way to navigate may be to ask local people along the way which road to take. Any intrepid potential visitors can also download a GPS track and waypoints from the following site: <http://www.tropicalbirding.com/wild-rwanda/>. ◆

The highly degraded Akanyaru Wetland is now mainly the domain of common and widespread birds like African Pied Wagtail. ©Keith Barnes

Nyungwe National Park

This huge forest (*c.* 1012 km²) is reputed to be the single largest block of montane forest in Africa. Without doubt, it is the most important birding site and most diverse site for primates in Rwanda. It ranges in altitude from around 1600 m at its lowest point on its western boundary to 2950 m at its highest peak, Bigugu. Rains hit Nyungwe mostly between September and May, but it is dry from June to August. Located in far southwestern Rwanda near the borders with Burundi and DRC, it lies just south of massive Lake Kivu and adjoins Burundi's Kibira NP.

Nyungwe has a total bird list of 278 species that includes 71 of the 74 Afromontane forest species occurring in Rwanda. At least in terms of birds, it may be the richest montane forest in the whole of Africa. It harbors 25 Albertine Rift endemics, including three that currently cannot be seen safely anywhere else in the world, as well as several others that are common here but difficult to see in neighboring Uganda (Bwindi). The Itombwe Mountains in neighboring DRC are, arguably, the only site in the world that is more important for Albertine Rift birds.

There are also some impressive primates to be seen, including habituated chimpanzees, the endemic L'Hoest's monkey, and a large troop of Angolan (*pied*) colobus. There are even owl-faced monkeys in the park's remote southern reaches, but they are essentially inaccessible to visitors. To all this, add the birds, more mammals, some absolutely stunning scenery, and a lovely climate, and you have one of the finest natural hideaways in the whole of Africa.

Although seemingly pristine, Nyungwe was damaged in the previous century and, for example, the destruction of forest at lower altitudes between 1958 and 1979 led to the local extirpation of several low-elevation species. The Buffalo and African savanna elephant that used to flourish in the park are now extinct, the last elephant being killed in Kamiranzovu in 2000. Mammals such as duikers and bush pigs are extremely shy and rare, probably as a result of extensive poaching.

KEY SPECIES

Mammals: Chimpanzee, Angolan (*pied*) colobus, Johnston's (gray-cheeked) mangabey, L'Hoest's, Dent's (*mona*), owl-faced (rare and access difficult), and silver (*gentle*) monkeys, Carruther's mountain, Boehm's, and Ruwenzori sun squirrels, Lestrade's (*Peter's*) duiker.

Birds: Handsome Francolin, Ruwenzori Turaco, Albertine Owlet, Dwarf Honeyguide, Stripe-breasted Tit, Red-collared Mountain-Babbler, Neumann's (*Short-tailed*) Warbler, Yellow-eyed Black-Flycatcher, Kivu Ground-Thrush, Red-throated Alethe, Archer's Robin-Chat, Blue-headed, Stuhlmann's (*Ruwenzori Double-collared*), Regal, and Purple-breasted

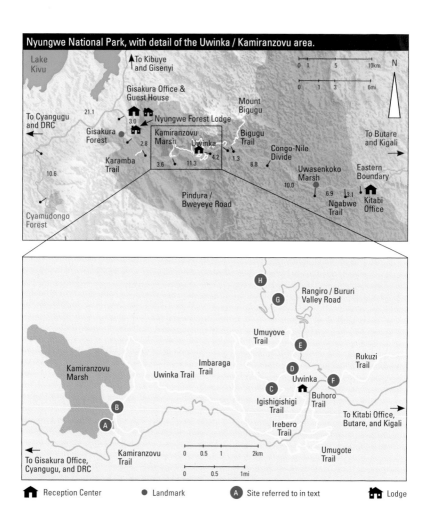

Nyungwe National Park, with detail of the Uwinka / Kamiranzovu area.

Lake Kivu

To Kibuye and Gisenyi

Gisakura Office & Guest House

Mount Bigugu

0 1 5 10km
0 1 3 6mi

N

To Cyangugu and DRC

21.1

3.0

Nyungwe Forest Lodge

Gisakura Forest

2.8

Kamiranzovu Marsh

Uwinka

Bigugu Trail

1.3

Congo-Nile Divide

8.8

To Butare and Kigali

Karamba Trail

3.6

11.3

4.2

10.6

Cyamudongo Forest

Pindura / Bweyeye Road

Uwasenkoko Marsh

10.0

6.9

3.1

Ngabwe Trail

Eastern Boundary

Kitabi Office

H

Rangiro / Bururi Valley Road

G

Umuyove Trail

E

Rukuzi Trail

Kamiranzovu Marsh

Uwinka Trail

Imbaraga Trail

D

Uwinka

F

Igishigishigi Trail

C

Buhoro Trail

To Kitabi Office, Butare, and Kigali

B

Irebero Trail

A

Umugote Trail

To Gisakura Office, Cyangugu, and DRC

Kamiranzovu Trail

0 0.5 1 2km
0 0.5 1mi

🏠 Reception Center   ● Landmark   Ⓐ Site referred to in text   🏠 Lodge

sunbirds, Doherty's Bushshrike, Willard's Sooty Boubou (rare), Ruwenzori (*Collared*), Black-faced (*Mountain Masked*), and Buff-throated (*Kungwe*) apalises, Grauer's Swamp-Warbler, Grauer's Warbler, Red-faced Woodland-Warbler, Ruwenzori Batis, Dusky and Shelley's (very rare) crimson-wings, Strange Weaver, Dusky Twinspot (rare), Kandt's (*Black-headed*) Waxbill.

OTHER SPECIES OF INTEREST

Mammals: olive baboon, red-tailed (uncommon) and vervet monkeys, African potto (unconfirmed), thick-tailed greater galago, African giant squirrel, Lord Derby's anomalure, brush-tailed porcupine (uncommon), side-striped jackal, African clawless (*swamp*) otter, marsh, Egyptian (*ichneumon*), and common slender (*slender*) mongooses, rusty-spotted (*blotched*) and servaline genets, African civet, African palm civet, wild cat, serval, African golden cat (rare), leopard (rare), southern tree hyrax, bush-pig (rare), (*giant*) forest hog (rare), black-fronted and eastern yellow-backed (rare) duikers.

Birds: Mountain Buzzard, Cassin's and Ayres's hawk-eagles, Dusky Turtle-Dove, Great Blue and Black-billed turacos, Barred Long-tailed Cuckoo, Fraser's Eagle-Owl, Red-chested Owl-et, Montane (*Rwenzori*) Nightjar, Scarce Swift,

Bar-tailed and Narina trogons, Cinnamon-chested Bee-eater, Black-and-white-casqued Hornbill, Western (*Green*) Tinkerbird, Tullberg's and Elliott's woodpeckers, Mountain Sooty (*Black*) Boubou, Many-colored and Lagden's bushshrikes, Gray Cuckooshrike, Black-tailed (*Montane*) Oriole, White-bellied Crested-Flycatcher, White-tailed Blue-Flycatcher, Dusky Tit, Shelley's (Kakamega) Greenbul, Eastern (Olive-breasted) Mountain-Greenbul, White-browed Crombec, Brown Woodland-Warbler, Mountain Yellow-Warbler, Cinnamon Bracken-Warbler, Evergreen-forest Warbler, Chestnut-throated and Black-throated apalises, Chubb's Cisticola, African (Ruwenzori) Hill Babbler, Mountain and Gray-chested illadopsis, Violet-backed Hyliota, White-eyed Slaty-Flycatcher (subsp. *toruensis*), White-bellied and Gray-winged robin-chats, White-starred Robin, Equatorial Akalat, Ruaha (*White-headed Black*) Chat, Waller's, Stuhlmann's, Slender-billed, and Sharpe's (rare) starlings, Northern Double-collared and Bronze sunbirds, Oriole Finch (rare), Western (*African*) Citril, Streaky and Thick-billed seedeaters, Baglafecht, Black-billed, and Brown-capped (rare) weavers, Yellow-bellied and Black-crowned waxbills, Red-faced and Abyssinian crimsonwings (both rare).

HABITAT

Nyungwe is covered by a mosaic of diverse vegetation, from tall closed-canopy forest to open flower-filled marshes. For the most part the highest altitudes between 2500–2950 m are covered with stunted sub-alpine forest and heath. Lower down between 2000–2500 m diverse montane forest communities predominate, while at the park's lowest altitudinal limits elements of lowland forest begin to infiltrate. Tall, complex forest covers the fertile moist valleys, while shorter and thicker forest is more typical of the drier ridge lines. Flooded forests, marshes, streams, open heaths, and herbaceous slopes are interspersed throughout.

The eastern and western halves of the park differ significantly. Nyungwe is divided by a north-south-running range of mountains that reach 2600–2900 m in altitude and the edaphic characteristics of the park differ greatly on the eastern and western sides of this range. The schists in the west support dense forest between 1700–2000 m, with dominant tree genera that

Black-billed Turaco is just one of an amazing four turaco species in Nyungwe. ©Ken Behrens

include *Newtonia, Symphonia, Podocarpus, Chrysophyllum, Syzygium, Carapa,* and *Ocotea.* Spectacular *Impatiens* cover much of the forest floor. Watch for distinctive giant *Lobelia* along the roadsides as this species can attract sunbirds when flowering. The east is granitic and higher (2200–2500 m) and the vegetation comprises trees such as *Macaranga* and *Polyscias* that are more characteristic of secondary forest. Higher up there are heaths and open areas dominated by *Philippa* and *Erica kingaensis.* The forest edges here also frequently support the fire-resistant *Hagenia.* One of the most distinctive (but also most difficult-to-access) habitats in Nyungwe is the massive and virtually monospecific stand (about 30 km²) of *Arundinaria alpina* bamboo that occurs in the southeast.

Nyungwe is the easiest place in the world to see the ARE Handsome Francolin. ©Ken Behrens

MAMMALING/BIRDING

Access to Nyungwe is straightforward. The excellent paved road from Butare to Cyangugu on the DRC border runs through the heart of the forest, providing far easier access to high altitude habitats than in the more popular Bwindi Impenetrable Forest in Uganda.

This park is huge and to get the most out of it you ideally need your

THE NYUNGWE KIDS BIRDWATCHING CLUB

The Nyungwe Kids Birdwatching Club was created and is sustained by the efforts of birding guides Narcisse Ndayambaje and Claver Ntoyinkima. It aims to inspire local children to view the forest as both a fascinating and wonderful place, and as an important resource for the future. As well as learning to value their forest, the children gain valuable skills that they might use as the next generation of birding guides. Narcisse and Claver are always looking for extra binoculars and field guides to support their program and so if you feel like donating and are planning a visit to Nyungwe, bring them to Rwanda with you. If you're lucky, you might even be able to pit your identification skills against those of the kids... and will probably lose! Find out about the club's latest activities on its Facebook page: https://www.facebook.com/nyungwekbw.club

own transport for your entire stay. Otherwise, a few happy days' birding may be had by camping at Uwinka, where the many trails will keep you busy. Though there is not a great deal of traffic, you may even be able to catch rides within the forest to access areas farther afield. A further benefit of having your own transport is being able to stay in one of the guesthouses or hotels in the Gisakura area.

If you only plan a short 1–2 day stay, the premier trails that are not to be missed are Bigugu and Kamiran-zovu. It would also be good to spend some time on the lower stretches of the Rangiro road. If you have more time, add the Karamba and Rukuzi trails, the Isumo (Waterfall) Trail near Gisakura, and spend extra time in the Uwinka area; then add whatever else you need to try for the remainder of the species that you are pursuing. Cyamudongo Forest (described in the next site account) is a key site for chimp tracking and an interesting but far-from-essential birding location.

Ruwenzori Batis is a sharp little Albertine Rift endemic. ©Ken Behrens

MAMMAL OVERVIEW

At least thirteen species of primates (11 diurnal) occur in Nyungwe, including a healthy population of the amazing chimpanzee, which can sometimes even be encountered by chance outside an official tracking expedition. If you find a *Syzygium*, *Olea* (olive), or *Ficus* (fig) tree with ripe fruit, scan it carefully, as these are preferred fruit trees for chimps. It may be worth returning to a good fruiting tree on several occasions. Remember to approach stealthily because although there are two habituated troops, the remainder of the population is still wisely wary of humans. If you have your heart

set on seeing chimps, the best way is to arrange through the RDB chimp-tracking permits and a skilled tracking guide prior to arrival. Unlike gorillas, success on a single chimp-tracking excursion is never guaranteed and so the safest strategy is to book two days of tracking. Extra time spent with these amazing animals should be relished if you happen to succeed in finding them on both days. Chimp permits are much cheaper and less likely to sell out than gorilla permits in Volcanoes NP, but can still become unavailable, especially on busy dry-season weekends when many foreigners living in Kigali tend to visit. The normal site for chimp tracking is Cyamudongo, which lies over an hour's drive away from Gisakura. This site is covered in the next account, which also includes further information on chimp tracking.

There are several other habituated primate species in Nyungwe: Angolan (*pied*) colobus, Johnston's (*gray-cheeked*) mangabey, and silver (*gentle*) monkey. Tracking them can be arranged through the national park staff at the reception centers and costs an extra fee on top of the daily park entrance and guiding fee. Owl-faced monkeys exist in the park's southeastern bamboo zone, but although a habituation program has been considered in the past, they are currently inaccessible to visitors. The southeastern section of the park is also the stronghold of (*giant*) forest hog.

The local *ruwenzorii* race of the Angolan (*pied*) colobus is considered to be globally vulnerable. This is hard to believe when you come across Nyungwe's famous Uwinka-area troop of around 400 individuals, almost 10 times the size of the next largest colobus troops in Africa! The colobus is one of the most common monkeys in Nyungwe and can be encountered almost anywhere in the park. They even occur in the tiny forest patch on the Gisakura Tea Estate. This leaf-eating monkey has a stomach that can process highly fibrous foods, thereby allowing large troops to live in closer proximity to each other and making them a very social species. The increased safety that comes with the large number of watchful eyes in a colobus troops is inviting to other monkeys, which often forage alongside colobus and so you should keep your eyes peeled for other species.

Johnston's (*gray-cheeked*) mangabey (*Lophocebus johnstoni*) can be found in the vicinity of Uwinka, especially below Uwinka along the Bururi

road. It is also present on the western side of the park on, for example, the Isumo (Waterfall) Trail. This omnivore mostly eats fruits, nuts, seeds, and leaves. It prefers lower forest, below 2300 m. Among their preferred foods are the seedpods of *Entandrophragma*, *Newtonia*, and *Albizia* and so you should concentrate your search on these trees.

The gentle monkey group (*Cercopithecus mitis*) may be represented in Nyungwe by two separate taxa variously considered as good species (HMW) or subspecies (Kingdon). There is speculation that the rare Albertine Rift endemic Virungas golden (*gentle*) monkey (*Cercopithecus kandti*) occurs in the bamboo zone in the southeast of the park. The literature is confusing, but if it does occur here it is very rare. Virungas golden (*gentle*) monkeys are better searched for in Volcanoes NP, where there are two habituated troops that are relatively easily seen. If you are going to track mountain gorillas at Volcanoes, then it also makes sense to try for this monkey there. Much more commonly seen (and similar in appearance to the Virungas golden (*gentle*) monkey) is the silver (gentle) monkey (*Cercopithecus dogetti*), which is found in the higher reaches of the park. The Bigugu Trail and the upper reaches of the Bururi road are good areas to look for this species. To add further confusion and complexity, species in the gentle monkey group (e.g. silver) have been known to hybridize with species as different as red-tailed monkeys!

Although it is one of the most localized monkeys in terms of its global distribution, the good-looking L'Hoest's monkey is common throughout the main part of the park and is easily seen along the roadside. This long-legged monkey is the most terrestrial of Nyungwe's guenons (members of the genus *Cercopithecus*) and unlike other forest monkeys they flee from danger on the ground rather than through the trees. Troops generally number 6–8, but up to 40 have been seen together. Although common in Nyungwe, this ARE monkey is considered "vulnerable" by the IUCN.

Cyamudongo is the best area to look for both Dent's (*mona*) and redtailed monkeys, as these prefer lowerlying terrain and this is one of the last forests in Rwanda supporting these two species. Red-tailed appears to be on the verge of extirpation and sightings are becoming rare.

The rare owl-faced monkey (*Cercopithecus hamylni*) was only discovered in Nyungwe in 1989. Although more or less a bamboo specialist, it can sometimes be found away from this habitat. It is restricted to the remote southeastern portion of the park where there are massive stands of bamboo. Unfortunately, access to this area is currently difficult.

Olive baboon is found throughout the park but prefers more open and lower areas on the edge of the forest. Vervet monkey is also more of a savanna species but is found in the lowerlying and more open areas of Nyungwe, often emerging from the forest edges to raid cultivated fields.

The prosimians are a group of primates whose most famous representa-

Equatorial Akalat is more frequently recorded once you learn its quiet, African Scops-Owl–like call. ©Ken Behrens

Nyungwe is one of the best places in the world for the stunning Doherty's Bushshrike. ©Mike Gaudaur

tives globally are Madagascar's lemurs. Elsewhere in the Old World, monkeys have essentially forced this group of ancient primates into niches that restrict them to nocturnal activity. In Africa, the best-known representatives are the galagos (or bushbabies). Often the only clue to their presence are their loud nocturnal wails. Galagos are almost exclusively arboreal and can leap great distances. Their diet consists mostly of tree sap and insects. Nyungwe definitely supports thick-tailed greater galago, while Demidoff's and Thomas's dwarf galagos, spectacled lesser galago, and east African potto are also suspected to occur. Nocturnal spotlighting expeditions offer the best chance of seeing prosimians.

Nyungwe supports six squirrel species, which are among the most visible members of the mammalian fauna of the park. The most spectacular of these is the immense African giant squirrel. It can reach 40 cm in length and 1 kg in weight, and has a long striped tail. The Ruwenzori sun squirrel is medium-sized and has a reddish head and feet. Boehm's Squirrel is a small chipmunk-like member of the group. Carruther's mountain squirrel is plain in appearance but is an interesting link between two major groups of squirrels, and is endemic to the Albertine Rift. Red-legged sun squirrel and fire-footed rope squirrel both have bright rufous-red legs and are found in Nyungwe's lower-elevation forest. Anomalures or flying squirrels form a separate family that is closely related to the typical squirrels. This family is represented in Nyungwe by Lord Derby's anomalure, a good-looking gray, white, and black species that is nocturnal and rarely seen. As with the galagos, nocturnal spotlighting expeditions give the best chance of seeing an anomalure.

The song of Black-faced Rufous-Warbler sounds like the beep of a large truck backing up. ©Lee Hunter

Ruwenzori *(Collared)* Apalis, a feisty little endemic. ©Josh Engel/Field Museum

A Rufous-chested *(Rufous-breasted)* Sparrowhawk about to feast on an Abyssinian *(Olive)* Thrush. ©Trevor Hardaker

Other mammals such as common slender *(slender)*, marsh, and Egyptian *(ichneumon)* mongooses, African civet, African palm civet, servaline and rusty-spotted *(blotched)* genets, leopard, African golden cat, bushpig, *(giant)* forest hog, and black-fronted and eastern yellow-backed duikers, are all present, but much less numerous and difficult to observe. African clawless *(swamp)* otter is found in Kamiranzovu Marsh. Past poaching has decimated the populations of most of these animals, particularly the palatable

Nyungwe's misty forests seem endless, timeless, and pristine. ©Keith Barnes

The subspecies of Baglafecht Weaver in western Rwanda is an Albertine Rift endemic. ©Keith Barnes

ones such as pigs and duikers. Much of this poaching occurred in conjunction with illegal activities such as gold mining during Rwanda's political and social problems of past decades. Their populations can be expected to rebound if the high current level of protection is maintained. Hopefully in a decade or less, mammal sightings will be a much more prominent part of a visit to Nyungwe.

A highly obvious but seldom-seen mammal is the noisy nocturnal southern tree hyrax. Its shrill phantom-like cry is characteristic of the nocturnal soundscape. Those unfamiliar with its voice expect something much larger and more imposing than a stubby little hyrax!

There are 12 shrew species in Nyungwe, of which seven are AREs. The Rift also boasts a scarce cave-dwelling bat (*Rousettus lanosus*) and an endemic chameleon (Ruwenzori Three-horned Chameleon *Chameleo johnstoni*), both of which are found in Nyungwe. There is also a Rwandan endemic caecilian (*Boulengerula fisheri*), and two endemic butterflies: *Bebearia dowsetti* and *Acraea turlini*, while *Papilio leucotaenia* is nearly endemic but is also found in a few other parts of the Rift. The park supports over 1050 plant species, including more than 240 tree species. This is one of the world's best sites for orchids; there are over 150 species, including some Rwandan endemics. For an easy introduction to the local orchids, visit the orchid garden at the Uwinka reception center.

BIRD OVERVIEW

Nyungwe's most obvious drawcard is its birds as this is one of the world's

(Giant) forest hog lives in Nyungwe but is very hard to see. ©Keith Barnes

Gray-headed Nigrita (*Negrofinch*) is usually detected by its loud and distinctive song. ©Lee Hunter

premier sites for Afro-montane and Albertine Rift species. Most of the Nyungwe site account below is focused on birds, both because they are the most obvious vertebrates in the park and because birding is a major

The Great Blue Turaco is one of Africa's most amazing birds. It's wonderfully common in Nyungwe.
©John Wilkinson

pursuit for most of the park's visitors.

Many bird species are common and found throughout much of the national park. We deal first with these species before delving into the specifics of individual sites and how to find the less common birds, including the localized Albertine Rift endemics.

Several endemics are widespread and commonly seen almost anywhere in the park, both along the main road and on the trails. These include Ruwenzori Batis, Ruwenzori (*Collared*), and Black-faced (*Mountain Masked*) apalises, Red-faced Woodland-Warbler, Archer's Robin-Chat, and Regal Sunbird. Obviously, even these species have microhabitat preferences; nevertheless, at least 70% of the sites detailed in this account will provide good opportunities for finding them and you can easily bump into them elsewhere. Other birds that are common throughout the park and often form mixed flocks include Yellow-

rumped Tinkerbird, Chinspot Batis, Northern Puffback, Black-tailed (*Montane*) Oriole, Yellow-whiskered Greenbul, Eastern (Olive-breasted) Mountain-Greenbul, Chestnut-throated and Black-throated apalises, African (Ruwenzori) Hill Babbler, African Yellow White-eye, Collared Sunbird, and Forest (*Dark-backed*) Weaver.

Both the odd hoots of Great Blue Turaco and the guttural calls of Black-billed Turaco can be heard wherever there is forest at moderate altitudes. Fruiting trees attract Rameron (*Olive*) and African Green-Pigeons, as well as Waller's Starling. Also check any fruiting trees for scarcer species such as Sharpe's and Stuhlmann's starlings. Snags in the canopy and along the forest edges commonly produce Cinnamon-chested Bee-eater, Dusky-brown (*African Dusky*) Flycatcher, and White-eyed Slaty-Flycatcher. The understory can hold Lemon Dove traipsing quietly along the ground, while the calls of Tambourine Dove suggest that this bird is more common than sight records alone would seem to suggest. Walking forest trails slowly and watchfully is the best way to see both of these doves. White-starred Robin is another common understory and thicket resident. Mountain Sooty (*Black*) Boubou can be easily heard and reluctantly coaxed into view almost anywhere in the park above 1900 m, especially in dense thicket habitats. At night, African Wood-Owl can be found almost anywhere, while the much-less common Verreaux's Eagle-Owl is also widely distributed.

Any open habitat, particularly disturbed edges, should yield Yellow-bellied Waxbill and the abundant Chubb's Cisticola, and in moister habitats Black-crowned Waxbill. At lower altitude and on the forest edges, particularly in garden-like habitats, one can find Shikra, Red-eyed Dove, Blue-spotted Wood-Dove, Speckled Mousebird, Cardinal Woodpecker, African Paradise-Flycatcher, Common Bulbul, White-browed Robin-Chat, African (*Common*) Stonechat, Abyssinian (*Olive*) Thrush, Scarlet-chested Sunbird, African Pied Wagtail, Bronze Mannikin, Western (*African*) Citril, and Streaky Seedeater. The Cinnamon Bracken-Warbler is commonly heard but hard to see wherever there is some thicket. Wherever there are flowers along the forest edge, watch for the omnipresent Bronze, Northern Double-collared, and Variable sunbirds. Any open area regularly produces Black Sawwing, Angola, Red-rumped, and Wire-tailed swallows, and Rock

From Nyungwe you can often see the mysterious eastern edge of DRC, realm of endemics like Schouteden's Swift and the enigmatic Congo Bay-Owl. ©Ken Behrens

Tullberg's Woodpecker is low-density and inconspicuous within Nyungwe. ©Ken Behrens

The widespread Variable Sunbird has a beautiful Albertine Rift endemic race *igneiventris*. ©Ken Behrens

Martin, and somewhat less frequently raptors such as Mountain and Augur buzzards, African Harrier-Hawk, and Crowned Hawk-Eagle (*African Crowned Eagle*). The light and incessant "chit" call of the African Goshawk is commonly heard and is the easiest way to pick up this mid-sized accipiter. African Cuckoo-Hawk and Ayres's and Cassin's hawk-eagles are much rarer and require a lot more searching. Some more typical savanna raptors will overfly the park, perhaps breeding in the degraded habitat outside of Nyungwe or in the park's more open eastern side. These include Tawny and Wahlberg's eagles and Lanner. Long-crested Eagle can sometimes be found along the forest edges or in the buffer zones. As everywhere in Africa, degraded forest quickly loses forest species and begins to attract species more typical of savannahs and mixed habitats and so the fringes of Nyungwe hold species such as African Scops-

Owl, Tropical Boubou, Black Cuckoo-shrike, and Holub's Golden-Weaver.

Other species are less common but similarly widespread, and one needs a bit of luck to bump into them. Among these we include Green-backed (*Gray-backed*) Camaroptera, which is uncommon at this site but should not be a priority bird given its abundance elsewhere in Africa. The giant Black-and-white-casqued Hornbill can be found in a lot of places and its heavy wing beats often give it away. The trilling crescendo of Scaly-throated Honeyguide reveals this species as it sits still in the dense canopy: but beware the incredibly similar-sounding Grauer's Warbler, whose call will much more likely emanate from the understory. Greater and Lesser honeyguides are fairly common, often in secondary and forest edge habitats, or even in the exotic trees of the park's buffer zones. Several cuckoo species are low-density but widespread in Nyungwe, including African Emerald, Dideric, and the highly sought-after but aggravatingly difficult-to-see Barred Long-tailed Cuckoo, whose call is heard incessantly. Other cuckoos occur seasonally, although their movements are poorly understood. These include Levaillant's, Common, and African Cuckoos. Creeping through the tangles, keep an eye out for Yellowbill. Scarce and African (*Black*) Swifts are uncommon, but can turn up almost anywhere. Crowned Hornbill, Gray-winged Robin-Chat, Violet-backed Hyliota, Thick-billed Seedeater, Black-and-white Mannikin, and Kandt's (*Black-headed*) Waxbill are uncommon-to-rare, but have all been found at a variety of sites. Sharpe's Starling is rare and its occurrence is poorly understood and probably seasonal, but likewise it has been recorded widely in the forest.

Although not exactly a migrant trap, several migrants, particularly raptors, use the mountains as a flyway. Fairly common boreal migrants in Nyungwe include European Honey-Buzzard, Common (Steppe) Buzzard, Tree Pipit, Barn Swallow, Willow Warbler and large flocks of European Bee-eaters. Less common are Lesser Spotted Eagle, rare falcons including Lesser Kestrel, Amur, and Sooty falcons, and Eurasian Hobby, as well as European Nightjar. Wet spots here and there can attract a few migrant shorebirds, including Common Snipe and Marsh, Green, and Wood sandpipers. There are a handful of scarce species present along Nyungwe's montane streams, including Mountain Wagtail and African Black Duck.

In terms of possibilities and extreme rarities, the one species never to have been recorded at Nyungwe

White-bellied Robin-Chat is extremely shy, and much harder to see than the very similar Equatorial Akalat. ©Lee Hunter

is Grauer's (*African Green*) Broadbill. This is surprising because plenty of habitat seems to exist for this species, especially around Kamiranzovu Marsh, although this area is higher in elevation than the places inhabited by this broadbill in Uganda. Rockefeller's Sunbird and Chapin's Flycatcher have both been claimed from Nyungwe and there are also reports of Schouteden's Swift. However, no photographic or any other type of documentary evidence exists for any of these birds and their occurrence still needs to be definitively proven. There are also suggestions that the incredibly scarce Congo Bay-Owl and Itombwe Nightjar may occur.

EASTERN NYUNGWE

It is best to explore the sites in the east of the park as you enter from Butare. These sites are less interesting than those in the west and are only worth a couple of hours for most visitors. The vast majority of visitors will access the prime western sites while based at Gisakura or Uwinka and so we have separated the descriptions of the eastern and western sites. The eastern sites will be dealt with as if you were birding them on your way into the park from Kigali and Butare, while the western sites are treated in order from Gisakura.

About 20 km before entering Nyungwe on the approach road from Butare, watch out for Ruaha (*White-headed Black*) Chat and Trilling Cisticola. The chat is found in villages such as Gisaka (GPS S2° 29.097 E29° 31.822), where it likes to perch on the houses. Angola Swallow is another species that breeds in these small villages. Be respectful when using binoculars as many Rwandans equate binoculars with cameras and do not like having their pictures taken without permission. It is especially worthwhile trying for the chat if you do not visit Akagera as this latter area provides your best chance of seeing this newly split species. The cisticola occurs in the degraded woodlands, seemingly preferring *Lantana*.

After you pass through the small settlement of Kitabi (GPS S2° 31.153 E29° 25.927), you will reach the official park boundary after 800 m (GPS of boundary: S2° 31.573 E29° 24.965). Even though the forest does not start for a while, zero your odometer here. There is a large reception center at the Kitabi entrance where visitors arriving from the east should check in, and where park information is available. There are good views from here over the tea plantations to the edge of the forest. Trails are being developed in the Kitabi area, although they are unlikely to prove as interesting as those in the Uwinka and Gisakura areas.

Continuing into the park on the main road you will see a peak to the south of the road after 3 km. This is Mount Ngabwe, which at 2763 m is the second-highest peak in Nyungwe. This area can be good for Scarce, Alpine, and White-rumped swifts. The eastern side of Nyungwe is also particularly good for Mountain Buzzard, although beware of the Common (Steppe) Buzzards that also occur during the boreal winter.

The key measurements along the main road through the eastern part of the national park are given below. Kilometer readings are only approximations and so should be used with due discretion. Note that the Nyungwe NP map included in this guide shows the distances *between* each landmark, rather than the "running" distances given here. If you zero your odometer at the national park entrance 800 m west of Kitabi and drive west, the following kilometer readings apply:

0.0   Eastern boundary of Nyungwe NP
      (📷 S2° 31.573 E29° 24.965)
3.1   Ngabwe Trail trailhead
10.0 Uwasenkoko Marsh
      (📷 S2° 31.736 E29° 21.190)
20.0 Congo-Nile Divide
      (📷 S2° 29.590 E29° 17.567)

Ngabwe Trail

This moderately difficult trail is about 4-km long. It is one of the highest trails in altitude in the park and the habitat here is mostly *Hagenia* and *Macaranga* forest and moorland. The granitic rock substrate permits the growth of fewer tree species here than in western Nyungwe and the forest has a secondary feel. This part of the park has also historically been subject to fires and other forms of disturbance, which may contribute to the nature of the habitat. This is one of the best places in the park to search for Stuhlmann's (*Ruwenzori Double-collared*) Sunbird; Cinnamon Bracken-Warbler is very common here.

Grauer's Swamp-Warbler is an endangered endemic that can be found at Uwasenkoko and Kamiranzovu Marshes in Nyungwe. ©Ken Behrens

Uwasenkoko Marsh
GPS S2° 31.736 E29° 21.190

This small marsh lies approximately 10 km from the eastern edge of Nyungwe NP. Although it straddles the main road, it is easily missed as it looks more like a sedgy riverbed than a marsh. The soils in this region are black and bog-like. The adjacent vegetation comprises *Hagenia* and a heather-like mix of *Erica* and *Phillipia* species. In certain seasons, striking red-hot pokers (*Kniphofia*) decorate the marsh. If you are not going to walk the trail to the Kamiranzovu Marsh, this is the crucial site for Grauer's Swamp-Warbler. The sedge beds here support a couple of pairs that are easily seen if they respond to recordings, but very difficult if they don't! Though always difficult to see, Red-chested Flufftail can be heard calling here. The surrounding habitat is scrubby, and Cinnamon Bracken-Warbler is particularly common. This is one of the only areas in the park where the uncommon Kandt's (*Black-headed*) Waxbill has been regularly recorded. The wetland and edges also support Common Waxbill and seedeaters such as Streaky Seedeater, Western (*African*) Citril, and the locally scarce Yellow-crowned Canary. Brown Woodland-Warbler (generally very scarce in the park) and Stuhlmann's (*Ruwenzori Double-collared*) Sunbird have been found in the thicker scrub adjacent to the marsh. Watch overhead for aerial hunters such as Scarce Swift, Angola and Red-rumped swallows, and Plain Martin.

Congo-Nile Divide
GPS S2° 29.590 E29° 17.567

The divide lies approximately 20 km from the eastern edge of Nyungwe NP. This site is mainly of geographical interest. The ridgeline running north to south here (including Mount Bigugu) separates the catchments of Africa's two greatest river systems: to the east the waters flow into the Nile basin, while to the west they flow into the Congo. The topography and nature of the forest also changes along this watershed. The forests to the west are steeper, denser, and wetter, with a greater diversity of plant species and birds. This is one end of the recently developed Congo/Nile Trail, a 10-day trek between Nyungwe and Volcanoes NPs. Although the trail runs mostly through cultivated areas, including coffee and tea plantations, the section within Nyungwe NP could prove an interesting place for exploration.

WESTERN NYUNGWE

The directions for the western side of the park (west of the Congo-Nile divide) are given starting from the Gisakura reception center near the park's western boundary because most visitors stay at one of the lodges in the Gisakura area and access the park from the west. If you are arriving in Nyungwe from the east and want to make some stops along the way, reverse the following kilometer readings or refer to the map in this site account, which simply gives the distance between each landmark rather than the "running" distances below.

If driving east from Gisakura, zero your odometer at the Gisakura guesthouse and park reception center and the following apply:

0.0   Gisakura Guesthouse/RDB office and reception center (GPS S2° 26.483 E29° 05.533)

1.2   Turn-off to Gisakura Tea Estate ( S2° 27.079 E29° 05.464)

3.0   Western boundary of Nyungwe NP ( S2° 27.752 E29° 06.007)

5.8   Karamba Trail trailhead ( S2° 28.703 E29° 06.690)

9.4   Kamiranzovu Trail western trailhead ( S2° 29.461 E29° 09.317)

10.1 Kamiranzovu Trail eastern trailhead ( S2° 29.349 E29° 9.601)

20.7 Turn-off to Uwinka Reception Center and Museum, starting point for the Umugote (Blue), Irebero (Yellow), Uwinka, Buhoro (Gray), Igishigishigi (Green), Imbaraga (Red), and Umuyove (Pink) Trails ( S2° 28.729 E29° 12.032)

21.7 Start of Rangiro/Bururi Valley road, running north ( S2° 28.607 E29° 12.362)

24.9 Start of Pindura/Bweyeye Road, running south ( S2° 28.478 E29° 13.721)

25.0 Rukuzi Trail, eastern trailhead ( S2° 28.445 E29° 13.765)

26.2 Bigugu Trail, trailhead ( S2° 28.412 E29° 14.381)

35.0 Congo-Nile Divide, covered in "Eastern Nyungwe" ( S2° 29.590 E29° 17.567).

Gisakura

The most popular accommodation option in Nyungwe is the RDB-administered Gisakura Guesthouse ( S2° 26.483 E29° 05.533), which is adjacent to the Gisakura office and reception center. The scrubby surrounding

The gardens at Gisakura are a sunbird paradise. Northern Double-collared Sunbird is one of the most common species here. ©Ken Behrens

forest is worth birding and is productive in the middle of the day, especially when the cultivated gardens are in flower. The flowers in the gardens are a magnet for sunbirds in mid-morning and afternoon once the sun heats them up; of the sunbirds, Northern Double-collared and Variable (of the attractive local subspecies *igneiventris*) are abundant, Collared, Bronze, and Green-headed are less common, and Blue-headed and Stuhlmann's (*Ruwenzori Double-collared*) are only very occasional. Be careful when identifying double-collared sunbirds – Northerns are abundant but Stuhlmann's (*Ruwenzori Double-collared*) only occasionally make visits to the guesthouse. Although the plumages of these birds are almost identical, Stuhlmann's (*Ruwenzori Double-collared*) is significantly larger and has a proportionately much longer tail. Streaky Seedeater abounds and White-eyed Slaty-Flycatcher occurs in the garden. Occasionally scarcer species such as Thick-billed Seedeater are also encountered. Bird parties move through the scrubby forest remnants bordering on the garden and species of interest recorded here include Least Honeyguide, White-tailed Blue-Flycatcher, Black-faced (*Mountain Masked*) Apalis, and Gray-headed Nigrita (*Negrofinch*). In particular this appears to be a reliable locality for Brown-throated Wattle-eye and Black-billed Weaver, which can both be difficult to catch up with elsewhere in Nyungwe. Remember to zero your odometer as you leave Gisakura to maximize the usefulness of the directions given here. As you drive through the tea plantations and open areas before the park entrance, remember to watch out for Mackinnon's Shrike (*Fiscal*), as it is unlikely to be seen once you enter the forest. A nocturnal excursion from Gisakura is well worthwhile: a 6-km drive to the head of the Karamba trail should reveal several Montane (*Rwenzori*) Nightjars in flight, sitting on the road, or vocalizing. The national park gates are always open, as the road receives some through traffic.

Gisakura Forest

This is a small and isolated forest patch located on the Gisakura Tea Estate. To reach it, drive along the main road 1.2 km south of the Gisakura Guesthouse/RDB office and then turn west into the Gisakura Tea Estate (GPS of turn: S2° 27.079 E29° 05.464). Pass through a gate and then drive west about 200 m to where you can park and access the tiny forest patch to the north. A trail runs around the perimeter of this forest. Although there is nothing really outstanding in this forest, it is an ideal place for getting good views of birds as is often the case in degraded forest. There are also some characteristic species of scrubby and degraded areas that can be hard to find in Nyungwe's generally pristine forests. Species here include Ross's Turaco, Yellowbill, Luehder's (*Lühder's*) Bushshrike, Red-rumped and Angola swallows, White-tailed Blue-Flycatcher, Dusky Tit, White-browed Crombec, Black-throated Apalis, White-chinned Prinia, Gray-capped Warbler, White-eyed Slaty-Flycatcher, White-browed and Snowy-crowned robin-chats, Equatorial Akalat, Green-headed, Olive-bellied, and Western Olive sunbirds, Golden-breasted Bunting, and Black-billed Weaver. Seedeaters seem to thrive along the edges of this small forest and common species include

The tiny Gisakura Tea Estate Forest offers abundant edge habitat, and birds like White-chinned Prinia.
©Ken Behrens

Bronze Mannikin and Western (*African*) Citril. More rare are Red-faced and Dusky crimson-wings and this is also one of few places in Nyungwe where the rare Dusky Twinspot has been recorded. A small and fairly tame troop of Angolan (*pied*) colobus spends most of its time in this Forest, often providing excellent views.

Isumo (Waterfall) Trail

This easy trail takes a hiker into some magical forest and ends at the impressive 40-m high Kamiranzovu Falls. The trail is about 10.6 km long and takes a couple of hours to walk. It starts 400 m from the Gisakura reception center. This is a good hike for primates, including Dent's (*mona*) and L'Hoest's monkeys, Johnston's (*gray-cheeked*) mangabey, and Angolan (*pied*) colobus. Despite the excellent birding, this trail does not rank as one of the park's unmissable sites. Look for Ruwenzori and Great Blue turacos, Ruwenzori and Chinspot batises, Red-faced Woodland-Warbler, Gray Apalis, shy White-bellied Robin-Chat, Equatorial Akalat, Yellow-eyed Black-Flycatcher, and Regal, Purple-breasted, Northern Double-collared, and Blue-headed sunbirds. Scarce species that can be found here include Black-faced Rufous-Warbler, Mountain Illadopsis, Mountain Wagtail, and the rare White-tailed Ant-Thrush. This area also supports Willard's Sooty Boubou (this species is not included in *Birds of East Africa*; see "Specialty Species" for more information). Once you are near the falls, the trail splits into an easier trail that goes to the top of the falls, and a more difficult one that descends to the base of the falls. Near the falls look for Slender-billed Starling. In the more open country along the way (above all, the tea plantations) look for Mountain Buzzard, European Bee-eaters (mainly on migration), Brown-crowned Tchagra, Mackinnon's Shrike (*Fiscal*), Siffling Cisticola, Fawn-breasted and Common waxbills, and Streaky Seedeater.

Main road
Between the park entrance ([GPS] S2° 27.752 E29° 06.007) and the trailhead for the Karamba Trail, there is excellent and easily accessible road-side forest. Most of the common endemics have been recorded here and it also supports White-bellied Crested-Flycatcher, Yellow-eyed Black-Flycatcher, and the scarce Violet-backed Hyliota. Check the tall *Symphonia* trees for Purple-breasted and Blue-headed sunbirds, and watch the roadside tangles for Stripe-breasted Tit, Strange Weaver, and Dusky Crimsonwing. Willard's Sooty Boubou was first confirmed in Rwanda along this stretch of road, near the Karamba trailhead. If driving here at dawn or dusk, watch for the rare Bat Hawk and much commoner Handsome Francolin. Nocturnal birding for species such as Montane (*Rwenzori*) Nightjar, African Wood-Owl, and Red-chested Owlet can also be productive.

Karamba Trail
If driving into the park from Gisakura, you will come across the trailhead for the Karamba Trail ([GPS] S2° 28.703 E29° 06.690) on the southern side of the main road after 5.8 km. The

NYUNGWE'S ANTBIRDS

The highlands of Africa have a characteristic set of driver ants (*siafu* in Swahili) that are amongst the forest's most important predators. The biomass that these micro-carnivores consume is far greater than that consumed by all the mammalian predators combined. A select band of birds have learned to take advantage of the chaos created by the marching columns of ants and feed above all on the invertebrates flushed out by the approaching ants. In Nyungwe, the endemic Red-throated Alethe seems to be the most dominant species; White-starred Robin and Equatorial Akalat will also attend and any morsel that tries to flee the ants is instantly snapped up by one of these opportunists. Although not documented for the Red-throated Alethe, elsewhere in Africa the Fire-crested Alethe will only breed if its territory supports a colony of driver ants, so reliant are the Antbirds on their ant partners.

The open areas at the start of the Karamba trail often hold Black-crowned Waxbill. ©Ken Behrens

gold miners' settlement that formerly existed at this site was removed after Nyungwe became a national park. There is now an army campground, which is sometimes used during military exercises. If the camp is occupied by soldiers, take care when using binoculars and cameras on the first stretch of the trail to avoid suspicion. The open areas around the trailhead and along the first 200 m of the trail are worth checking as this is one of the few areas in the park where one can expect Golden-breasted Bunting, the occasional Cape Wagtail, and pipits that may belong to the recently split Jackson's Pipit group, restricted to a small part of East Africa. The thickets here are also a good place to find African Broadbill, African Green-Pigeon is often obvious in flight around the trailhead, and Black-crowned Waxbills flock in the rank grasses.

After a few hundred meters you come to an area where there is a steep drop-off on the left. Barred Long-tailed Cuckoo, Oriole Finch, and Thick-billed Seedeater have been seen here. Yellow-eyed Black-Flycatchers are usually easy to see in this area.

After about another 100 meters, the vegetation becomes thicker and this is one of the best sites in Nyungwe for White-bellied Robin-Chat. Also watch and listen for Equatorial Akalat, which is similar but lacks the robin-chat's small white supercilium and bicolored tail. In this area you might also find Handsome Francolin, Doherty's and Many-colored bushshrikes, Mountain Sooty (*Black*) Boubou, Gray Cuckoo-shrike, and Red-throated Alethe. In the canopy search for Waller's and Stuhlmann's starlings (the former fairly dependable here), Dusky Tit, the locally scarce Brown-capped Weaver, and Gray-headed Nigrita (*Negrofinch*). This lower-lying forest is good for greenbuls including the omnipresent Eastern (Olive-breasted) Mountain-Greenbul, plus Yellow-whiskered and the scarcer Slender-billed greenbul. The latter half of the trail is one of the best places in Nyungwe for the stunning Bar-tailed Trogon. Be aware that this species' call can still seem to come from far off even when the bird is only 15 or 20 m away! Other Albertine Rift endemics that occur at Karamba include Ruwenzori Turaco, Red-throated Alethe, Archer's Robin-Chat, and Grauer's Warbler. Although a little rarer, Scarce Swift, Tullberg's Woodpecker, African (*Blue-mantled*) Crested-Flycatcher, Evergreen-forest Warbler, Plain (*Cameroon Sombre*) Greenbul, and Purple-breasted Sunbird have been seen here as well. The rare Dwarf Honeyguide has occasionally been recorded at Karamba, as has Dent's (*mona*) monkey, which is scarce at higher altitudes. Chimp troops frequent this area as well and though shy it is sometimes possible to get good views of them before they take flight.

After hiking for about 1.5 km listen carefully for the staccato, scratchy, and repetitive calls of Buff-throated (*Kungwe*) Apalis, as this is one of the easiest places to see this species on Earth. The trail becomes narrow and indistinct after about 1.7 km (📍 S2° 29.159 E29° 06.230) in an area with very thick undergrowth. Before turning back, stop and listen for the distinctive calls of skulking Neumann's (*Short-tailed*) Warbler and Gray-chested Illadopsis.

Hiking this trail in the late afternoon can work well as you can wait for dark and do a bit of night birding.

The area around the trailhead is excellent for Montane (*Rwenzori*) Nightjar and African Wood-Owl. The nightjar likes to perch on the small rocky cliff across the road from the trailhead and to feed over the fields of the military camp. Noisy coveys of Handsome Francolin fly up into trees to spend the night and can sometimes be located with a spotlight.

Kamiranzovu Marsh Trail

Kamiranzovu Marsh is a huge (13 km²) wetland that was created tens of thousands of years ago by block faulting that essentially created a huge dammed basin. Kamiranzovu is a poetic name meaning "the place that swallows elephants," although the elephants have unfortunately been extirpated from the park. To access the marsh, there is an excellent loop trail that drops down from the main road before winding its way back up. This is one of the most important birding sites in Nyungwe, not to mention one of its most scenically beautiful and unique spots. Walking this trail also gives you chances of seeing some unusual mammals such as serval and African clawless (*swamp*) otter. This trail is about 4-km long and is moderately difficult due to the 130-m (430-ft) height difference between the trailheads and the marsh below. It takes three hours to walk down into the wetland and back, but at least five hours are needed to bird the trail properly, thereby making this an excellent full morning or afternoon activity. This is definitely one of the better birding trails and is highly recommended. Your strategy should depend on the birds that you are pursuing. If Grauer's Swamp-Warbler is a priority, it makes sense to take the

The Kamiranzovu Trail is the best place in Nyungwe to search for Neumann's (*Short-tailed*) Warbler. ©Ken Behrens

Moist edge habitats around Kamiranzovu Marsh are very good for the endemic Yellow-eyed Black-Flycatcher. ©Christian Boix

steeper western trail down as it allows for the quickest access to the marsh. From here, you can continue around to the eastern trailhead. On the other hand, if your priority is to search for species such as Willard's Sooty Boubou, Neumann's (*Short-tailed*) Warbler, Kivu Ground-Thrush, and Gray-chested Illadopsis in the moist forest adjacent to the marsh, it is best to use the eastern trailhead, which will take you into the correct habitat more quickly. Once you reach the bottom, you can either return by the same (eastern) trail or continue along the main trail and climb back up to the western trailhead. One consideration is whether your driver will meet you at your desired return point, although the two trailheads are only about 500 m apart on the park's main paved road.

These directions will begin from the western trailhead (📷 S2° 29.461 E29° 09.317). The interesting birding begins quickly. About 150 m down the trail you will reach an excellent spot for the shy and scarce

Doherty's Bushshrike (📷 S2° 29.391 E29° 09.268). Other interesting species in the vicinity include Bar-tailed Trogon, Many-colored Bushshrike, Buff-throated (*Kungwe*) Apalis, Violet-backed Hyliota, and Sharpe's Starling. The forest here is very open, allowing sweeping views of the marsh and the sky above, and is a good place to scan for Mountain Buzzard, Cassin's and Crowned hawk-eagles, and probably the most reliable place in Nyungwe for the well-named Scarce Swift. Continue down the trail, following a big switchback that drops you into a moist and open valley (📷 S2° 29.363 E29° 09.291) that is a reliable spot for Yellow-eyed Black-Flycatcher.

Continue walking for just over 500 m until you reach the transition zone between the forest and the marsh vegetation at the bottom of the fault. This swampy forest and scrub ecotone is good for Evergreen-forest Warbler, a scarce bird across most of its range, even in Nyungwe. Coaxing this skulker out of the undergrowth requires some serious dedication and a fair amount of luck. For the next couple of hundred meters, the trail becomes a boardwalk that crosses the southeastern corner of the vast Kamiranzovu Marsh (see map on page 58). This whole stretch is excellent for Grauer's Swamp-Warbler (GPS of one spot along the trail for this warbler: S2° 29.169 E29° 09.157). Listen for its strange display flight that involves much wing snapping. Other birds that live in the marsh include Red-chested Flufftail, Blue-headed Coucal, and Chubb's Cisticola. On the mammal front, the marsh supports serval, bush pig, marsh mongoose, and African clawless (*swamp*) otter. Arriving very early or staying late is the best way of seeing one or more of these mammals but does require a long walk in the dark. The plant communities are different in the marshy areas and the vegetation is rich in epiphytes, particularly orchids. There are some endemic woody plants in this marsh that have not yet been described by science.

An extensive exploration of the marsh would require some bushwhacking or wading, as the main trail soon leaves the marsh and re-enters the forest. The next stretch of the trail traverses some thick, swampy, lower-elevation forest that is among the best birding areas in the national park. Near the forest edge, soon after leaving the marsh, is one of the park's best sites for Pink-footed Puffback (GPS S2° 29.126 E29° 09.174). Other species in this area include Ruwenzori Batis, White-bellied Crested-Flycatcher, Buff-throated (*Kungwe*) Apalis, and Yellow-eyed Black-Flycatcher. About 200 m after entering the forest, you reach the junction with the very

Kamiranzovu Marsh is one of Nyungwe's most outstanding features. ©Ken Behrens

long Uwinka trail (icon of junction: S2° 29.010 E29° 09.192) that winds north and east and eventually all the way to the Uwinka park office area. It is worthwhile to walk down the Uwinka trail for at least 700 m as the birding along this first stretch is excellent. Soon after the this trail junction, there is a three-way junction signed for the Orchid Trail, a short side trail giving access to yet another area for the tireless to explore. To stay on the main Uwinka trail, take the right-hand of the three trails. The next 150 m of the Uwinka trail **B** may be the best site in Nyungwe for Neumann's (*Short-tailed*) Warbler (icon of good spot: S2° 28.930 E29° 09.266) and Gray-chested Illadopsis (icon S2° 28.890 E29° 09.273). This area is also very good for the incredibly shy and scarce endemic Kivu Ground-Thrush. The best spot for this species lies another 500 m beyond the main Neumann's (*Short-tailed*) Warbler site (icon of Kivu spot: S2° 28.715 E29° 09.454). You have to be lucky to find this species and the only available recordings are largely ineffective at attracting this bird. The best approach is to walk the trail very slowly and quietly, watching for any movement on the trail or in the undergrowth. If you hear the ground-thrush singing, expect it to be perched motionless, very well camouflaged, and fairly high (but usually below the canopy). The best way of seeing this almost crepuscular species is probably to arrive at dawn or even earlier, but this would require a long hike in the dark that could even be turned into an owling expedition for the hardiest of birders!

The thick dense forest at the Kamiranzovu/Uwinka Trail junction area also supports Buff-spotted Flufftail (rare), Many-colored Bushshrike, African (*Blue-mantled*) Crested-Flycatcher, Dusky Tit, White-bellied and Gray-winged robin-chats, Equatorial Akalat, and Waller's and Stuhlmann's starlings. Rare birds that have been recorded near the swamp include Yellow-billed Barbet, Willard's Sooty Boubou, Violet-backed Hyliota, White-tailed Ant-thrush, Oriole Finch, and White-breasted Nigrita (*Negrofinch*). As well, if you fancy an extended owling session, this trail is an excellent place to try for Fraser's Eagle-Owl, the endemic Albertine Owlet, and other owls. Fraser's Eagle-Owl can sometimes even be spotted or flushed from its day-roost site along the trail down from the eastern trailhead. Red-chested Owlet also occurs in the forest along this trail and Marsh Owl can be found in the marsh itself. So, if you can find a way to either start early or stay up late, this would be the best trail on which to do so. Other interesting species that can be encountered along the Kamiranzovu Trail and the western end of the Uwinka Trail include Black-billed and Ruwenzori turacos, Dusky Turtle-Dove (generally scarce in Nyungwe), Tullberg's Woodpecker, Slender-billed Greenbul, Red-throated Alethe, Banded Prinia, Mountain Illadopsis, Strange and Black-billed weavers, Gray-headed Nigrita (*Negrofinch*), Dusky Crimson-wing, and Kandt's (*Black-headed*) Waxbill.

From the moist forest mentioned in the previous paragraph, hearty hikers can continue along the Uwinka trail. Nevertheless, most will prefer to turn around and go back to the Kamiranzovu Trail for a shorter loop and then back to the eastern trailhead. The slopes along the way up to the eastern trailhead provide excellent visibility into the mid-story and canopy and provide access to many understory skulkers. Neumann's (*Short-tailed*) Warbler can occur all along this stretch, although it is not so easily seen as in the dense forest at the bottom. Other good species along the eastern trail include African Broadbill, White-bellied Crested-Flycatcher, Grauer's Warbler, Yellow-eyed Black-Flycatcher, and both Lagden's and Doherty's bushshrikes, both of which can be difficult to find in Nyungwe. This whole area is particularly good for Brown-capped Weaver and Blue-headed Sunbird. Listen carefully for the distinctive up-and-down song of this sunbird, which can otherwise be rather inconspicuous, especially when there are not many plants in flower.

A lush drainage line (⊞GPS S2° 29.122 E29° 09.915) crosses the main road about 500 m east of the eastern Kamiranzovu trailhead and is a good spot for both White-bellied Robin-Chat and Brown-capped Weaver.

Uwinka area

The Uwinka reception center, park office, and campsite (⊞GPS S2° 28.699 E29° 11.995) lie at about 2450 m, towards the higher end of the park's heavily forested mountains. The views of Lake Kivu and the misty mountains of the DRC from here are spectacular. Thanks to a handsome project by US-AID, much new infrastructure, including an interpretive visitor center, orchid nursery, and a canopy walkway, have recently been constructed at Uwinka, and its educational value alone makes this a worthwhile stop. From here you have the opportunity

The area around Uwinka is good for Western (*Green*) Tinkerbird. ©John Wilkinson

to hike, picnic, camp, and take a variety of guided tours to see primates.

Do not ignore the open forest around the visitor center and along the road between Uwinka and Bururi, as it will often provide more birds than any of the networked trails. Fairly common birds include Black-billed and Ruwenzori turacos, Ruwenzori Batis, Stripe-breasted Tit, Red-faced Woodland-Warbler, Regal and Western Olive sunbirds, and many more. The open skies around Uwinka are particularly good for Crowned (*African Crowned Eagle*) and Cassin's hawk-eagles, so keep your eyes peeled. Crowned Hawk-Eagles sometimes even nest near the center. This area is one of the few in the park that supports Western (*Green*) Tinkerbird, but it would appear to be seasonal, vanishing in the dry season. Right around Uwinka watch for White-naped Raven, which is bold and tame here. The Uwinka area is frequented by an enormous troop of 400-some Angolan (*pied*) colobus, certainly one of the more remarkable natural spectacles on offer in Rwanda. Those keen to see this troop should inquire about their whereabouts from national park staff, who may be able to offer a guided tracking experience for an extra fee.

The main road around Uwinka – and in particular the 1-km stretch between the turn-off to Uwinka and the turn-off along the Bururi road – is very good for Handsome Francolin. Try to be the first vehicle along here in the early morning for an excellent chance of seeing this bird. Albertine Owlet is occasionally heard in the forest just west of Uwinka but seems more frequent on the Kamiranzovu Trail. Backtracking towards Gisakura from Uwinka by 5 km there is a good stretch of roadside forest that has revealed both Violet-backed Hyliota and Gray-winged Robin-Chat, two very scarce birds in Nyungwe. Commoner here are species such as Stripe-breasted Tit and Grosbeak Weaver. Angolan (*pied*) colobusis are often seen from the main road in the western part of Nyungwe, both around Uwinka and elsewhere.

The Uwinka area is the starting point for an impressive system of trails. The trails have recently undergone a name change and so in this guide we provide both sets of names for each of the trails. Note that most of the trails form loops that coincide with other trails or roads for part of their course. This can cause confusion and so you should consult the national park maps or the Uwinka trail map in this guide carefully. For example, when you head north on the main trail from Uwinka you are simultaneously walking the Umuyove (Pink), Imbaraga (Red), Igishigishi (Green), and Buhoro (Gray) trails! The Umuyove (Pink), Buhoro (Gray), Igishigishi (Green), and Imbaraga (Red) trails all start at Uwinka. The Uwinka, Irebero (Yellow), and Umugote (Blue) trails start from the main road about 400 m back towards Gisakura (west) from the Uwinka reception center. You can

Nyungwe's handsome new visitor center. ©John Wilkinson

also connect with these trails via the Buhoro (Gray)/Imbaraga (Red) trail. For each trail, we will give a general idea of the length of the walk, its difficulty, its features, and the mammals and birds that can be expected. The rare Lagden's Bushshrike and Sharpe's Starling can occur on any of the trails in the Uwinka area.

Umugote (Blue) Trail

This is the only trail in the Uwinka area that lies south of the main road. It is about 3.5-km long, takes about 2–3 hours to walk or 4–5 hours to bird, and is moderately difficult. There are a couple of different loop options and so it is wise to ask your park guide which is best in terms of your interests and energy levels. This is regarded as one of the better general birding trails at Uwinka. It is short enough to not require a whole day and is also good for primates since silver (*gentle*) monkeys and chimpanzees occur in this area. There are fine vistas south towards Burundi. The very rare Yellow-bellied Wattle-eye has been recorded on this trail, although the likelihood of encountering it is low.

Irebero (Yellow) Trail

This trail is about 3.2-km long and takes about 3–4 hours to walk or 5–6 hours to bird. It is a moderately difficult walk. There are good views down into the Bururi Valley from this trail.

Uwinka Trail

This is a long and tough trail of about 10.5 km that takes most of the day to walk. As such, it will only be attractive to the most hardy of visitors. It runs all the way to the Kamiranzovu Marsh area, where it connects with the Kamiranzovu Trail. The far western end of the Uwinka Trail offers some of the best birding in the park, but is best accessed via the Kamiranzovu Trail (see page 82).

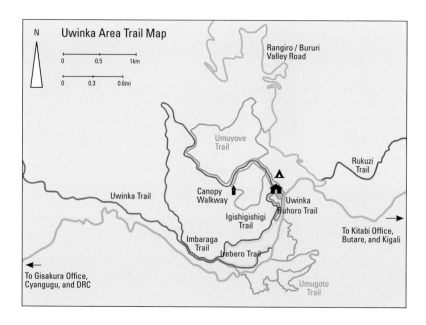

Buhoro (Gray) Trail

This is a short and easy 1–2-km trail that is suitable for those who find walking on forest trails difficult. The first 100 m of the trail (just north of Uwinka) are very good for Red-throated Alethe, which can often be seen hopping along the trail itself. Look especially around Campsite III. Note that the Buhoro (Gray) Trail shares this first stretch of trail with the Umuyove (Pink), Imbaraga (Red), and Igishigishigi (Green) trails and so watch for the alethe along this stretch whichever loop you have in mind. Handsome Francolin and Ruwenzori Turaco are both regularly seen along the Buhoro (Gray) trail. This is also a reliable place for Tullberg's Woodpecker, Luehder's (*Lühder's*) Bushshrike,

Gray Cuckooshrike, Stripe-breasted Tit, and White-browed Crombec. One particularly good spot is about halfway down the western leg of this loop trail (▢ S2° 28.660 E29° 11.959) on a steep slope where there are good views of a number of big trees reaching up from below. This is also a good place for Blue-headed and sometimes Purple-breasted sunbirds. For the second half of this trail loop, you walk on the main road and then the short access road to the Uwinka visitor center.

Igishigishigi (Green) Trail

This is a fairly short 1.7-km trail that starts at Uwinka and takes you to the newly constructed canopy walkway ⑥. It is suitable for those who find walking on forest trails difficult. It

Watch for Red-throated Alethe on the trails just north of Uwinka. ©Keith Barnes

The canopy tower is good for soaring raptors like Crowned Hawk-Eagle (*African Crowned Eagle*), which often nests nearby. ©Ken Behrens

takes about 1.5 hours to walk and 3 hours to bird this trail. The 90-m walkway offers beautiful views over the forest and is a convenient place to spot canopy-dwelling birds such as African Green-Pigeon, Rameron (*Olive*) Pigeon, a variety of sunbirds and apalises, and soaring raptors like Crowned (*African Crowned Eagle*) and Cassin's hawk-eagles, European Honey-Buzzard, Mountain Buzzard, and Eurasian (boreal winter) and African hobbies. If considering a visit, inquire at Uwinka about other visitors on the walkway since noisy groups (i.e. school fieldtrips) can greatly detract from a walkway experience. Note that a canopy walkway visit currently costs an extra $20 in addition to the normal entrance and guiding fees. Other bird species that can be seen along the Igishigishigi Trail include Neumann's (*Short-tailed*) Warbler, Archer's Robin-Chat, African (Ruwenzori) Hill Babbler, and Blue-headed Sunbird.

Imbaraga (Red) Trail

This is a long 9–10-km trail whose descent of over 500 m in altitude makes it one of the more difficult trails in Nyungwe. It takes at least 4–6 hours to walk and if you were birding it could take you all day – so bring a packed lunch! There are several beautiful waterfalls along this trail that are good for Slender-billed Starling, while Neumann's (*Short-tailed*) Warbler is common in the dank undergrowth. This trail offers a good chance of bumping into a wild and unhabituated chimpanzee troop.

Umuyove (Pink) Trail

This 3.8-km-long trail is moderately difficult due to the significant elevation change. Of all the trails in the Uwinka area, this is the best for birding. It offers good chances of seeing forest residents such as Black-and-white-casqued Hornbill, White-headed Woodhoopoe, Mountain Sooty (*Black*) Boubou, Black-tailed (*Montane*) Oriole, Yellow-streaked Greenbul, Red-throated Alethe, Grauer's Warbler, and African (Ruwenzori) Hill Babbler. The bench near the junction where the Umuyove (Pink) Trail splits from the Imbaraga (Red) and Igishigishigi (Green) Trails **D** (S2°28.434 E29° 11.859) is a good open spot that often provides excellent birding. Red-collared Mountain-Babbler has been seen here and elsewhere on the Uwinka trails, although it is more reliable on the Bigugu Trail. Continuing past the junction for about 70 m you reach a spot that has often produced Dwarf Honeyguide (S2°

Grauer's Warbler can be seen on the Umuyove (Pink) trail. ©Ken Behrens

28.374 E29° 11.831). The Umuyove (Pink) Trail continues to drop as it heads north, eventually losing about 200 m in elevation. At the northeastern corner of the trail, you can choose to go west and continue on the Umuyove (Pink) Trail or go east on a cut-off trail **E** that will bring you in around 200 m to the Rangiro/Bururi Valley Road. This cut-off can be good for Crowned Hornbill, Black-faced Rufous-Warbler, Mountain Illadopsis, and Strange Weaver. Search for the latter two in the thicket about halfway down the cut-off (S2° 28.146 E29° 11.916). The point where cut-off meets the Rangiro/Bururi road is an excellent place for both Narina and Bar-tailed trogons (of intersection: S2° 28.118 E29° 11.951). If you follow the road to return to the Uwinka area, take note of the information given below on birding this stretch and, in particular, watch for Dusky Crimson-wing.

Rangiro/Bururi Valley road
of intersection with main road: S2° 28.607 E29° 12.362

From the main road 1.1 km east of Uwinka, a broad and obvious road goes down into the Bururi Valley on the north side of the main road **F**. This road leads north to the village of Rangiro outside of the national park and local people often walk up and wait at this intersection for a passing bus. For convenience's sake, here we usually refer to this road as the "Bururi road" rather than by its more complete set of monikers. This road is one of the best birding areas in the park as it is wide and offers easy walking and visibility, and because it drops down steeply and has both higher- and lower-elevation forest types. Perhaps

COLOBUS MONKEYS

Within Africa's monkeys, colobus represent a completely different radiation from the "pouch-cheeked" monkeys that make up the majority of the continent's primates. Pouch-cheeked monkeys comprise groups such as the baboons, mangabeys, and the huge and diverse genus *Cercopithecus*. Within colobids, there are three groups: the monotypic olive colobus, the red colobus, and the most common and diverse group, the pied colobus, whose representative in Rwanda is Angolan (*pied*) colobus.

In most respects, the structure of colobus is unremarkable and they are not markedly different from pouch-cheeked monkeys. Colobus have large bodies, long limbs, and a small head. Their most obvious morphological trait is the near-absence of a thumb, which is reduced to a small stub. Their nearly thumbless hands form perfect hanging hooks for their arboreal lifestyle. They also mean that colobus prefer to feed directly with their mouths rather than pick up food with their hands as other monkeys do.

However, it is their innards that really make colobus special. They have a digestive system similar to that of a ruminant, with a multi-pouched stomach that uses bacterial fermentation to break down cellulose and other difficult-to-digest compounds. This special digestive system allows colobus to have a very different diet from other monkeys. Essentially, they are specialists in hard-to-digest parts of plants, which are also the most readily available plant materials in the forest. Hard seedpods, unripe fruits, old or even dry leaves, and other parts of plants that are toxic or unpalatable to other monkeys can all be eaten by colobus. Legumes are an important example, as they dominate African forests, but are largely inedible for other monkeys.

The alternate diet of colobus translates into a different social structure from that of pouch-cheeked monkeys. Since they are less dependent on seasonal flushes of resources such as ripe fruit, they have small rigid territories. The general abundance of their food (i.e. leguminous trees) also allows colobus to exist at higher densities (and in larger troop sizes) than other monkeys. A good example is the mega-troop of around 400 Angolan (*pied*) colobus that lives near Uwinka in Nyungwe NP, and the general abundance of this species, which is by far the park's commonest monkey.

Colobus are less active and aggressive than most pouch-cheeked monkeys, a fact that is again related to their diet. They spend less time searching for food and more time lounging around and digesting their easy-to-find food. Their striking black-and-white coloration is used in combination with loud vocalizations to broadcast clearly their possession of a certain territory and thereby avoid conflict with their neighbors. Territorial displays staged by a whole troop of boldly colored colobus giving their deafening Harley Davidson-like vocalizations usually occur at dawn and dusk. Visitors to Nyungwe NP have a good chance of experiencing this unforgettable spectacle.

The lower stretches of the Bururi road are very good for African Broadbill. ©Ken Behrens

most alluring of all, the area where the road leaves the forest is where Shelley's Crimson-wing is most frequently recorded in Nyungwe, although sightings remain very rare. Driving to the lower stretches of this track is advisable only in the dry season as in the wet season it may become impassable even with a 4x4. The problem is not that the road is in poor condition but rather its clay-like composition, which means that even a small amount of rain makes it extremely slippery. If you decide to venture down to the lower elevations, consider that it takes at least an hour of driving to get there and you can easily spend 5–7 hours birding below. Therefore, make sure you allow at least a half-day for this activity. Also bear in mind the condition of the road if you find yourself

on the lower stretches and it begins to rain.

Near its top the road is broad and easy to bird. Archer's Robin-Chat occurs here, close to the junction with the main road. The short stretch between the main road and the entrance to the Rukizi Trail is particularly good for the little ruby Dusky Crimson-wing (S2° 28.341 E29° 12.079). This area is also a good locality locality for Dwarf Honeyguide. Look for large *Symphonia* trees, which when in bloom attract many sunbirds including Purple-breasted.

Past the junction with the Rukuzi Trail watch for Handsome Francolin: it is easy to flush but not see well and so it is important to watch the road carefully. Strange Weaver, Black-tailed (*Montane*) Oriole, some of the other common endemics, and Banded Prinia are also found here. Red-collared Mountain-Babbler is occasionally seen along this road, but the densities here are not as high as on the Bigugu Trail.

About 1 km down the road is another excellent spot for Dusky Crimson-wing (S2° 28.341 E29° 12.079). In about another 500 m (1.5 km from the paved road), you start to skirt the pines of the park's buffer zone. This area is good for both Bar-tailed and Narina trogons, sometimes even in the pines (of trogon area: S2° 28.118 E29° 11.951). As the road continues to drop down, it completely exits the forest and enters a pine plantation about 2 km from the paved road. Continue for another 5–6 km, passing through plantation and cultivated fields and reaching an intersection where you turn left to continue down to the lower-lying forest (of intersection: S2° 27.150 E29° 11.715).

Silver (*gentle*) monkey is fairly common in Nyungwe, especially at higher elevations. ©John Wilkinson

At 7.3 km from the intersection with the main road, you will come to some lower-lying forest at around 1900 m in altitude **G**. This is one of the best birding areas in Nyungwe. These lower forests support a different mix of species and there are generally a lot of birds. The next 3 km of the road switchback and loop their way down into the forested valley and offer excellent birding, as well as a chance to observe some of the most beautiful forest in all of Nyungwe, with some huge mahogany, *Newtonia*, and *Symphonia* trees. These lower-elevation forests support African Emerald Cuckoo, Yellowbill, Elliot's Woodpecker, African Broadbill, Lagden's and Luehder's (*Lühder's*) bushshrikes, Pink-footed Puffback, White-bellied Crested-Flycatcher, Dusky Tit, Yellow-whiskered, Slender-billed, Plain (*Cameroon Sombre*), and Shelley's (Kakamega) greenbuls, Buff-throated (*Kungwe*) and all the rest of Nyungwe's apalis species, White-chinned Prinia, Equatorial Akalat, White-bellied Robin-Chat, Waller's Starling, Oriole Finch, Thick-billed Seedeater, Vieillot's (*Black*) Weaver, and Gray-headed Nigrita (*Negrofinch*). Moist and densely vegetated gullies in this area are excellent for the skulking but loud Black-faced Rufous-Warbler. Scarce species recorded at these elevations include African Pitta (rare and erratic), Cabanis's Greenbul, Yellow-bellied Hyliota, White-breasted Nigrita (*Negrofinch*), Dusky Twinspot, Red-faced Crimsonwing, and Red-headed Bluebill. The recently split Willard's Sooty Boubou has recently been found down here. These lower forests are also good for primates, namely chimpanzee, silver (*gentle*) monkey, and Johnston's (*gray-cheeked*) mangabey. There is a habituated mangabey troop that resides in this valley that has been studied by primatologists. Your best chance to see mangabeys is to arrange a primate-tracking visit with RDB officials, who keep tabs on the current whereabouts of these monkeys.

After 10.3 km (from the paved road), the Bururi road leaves the thick forest, although there is still some forest to the west of the road (of forest exit: S2° 27.253 E29° 11.452). The open areas along the next 700 m ⓗ are the best place in Nyungwe for Shelley's Crimson-wing, although one still has to be extremely lucky to see this extremely rare finch. This area is also good for Dusky Crimson-wing. In particular, watch for crimson-wings along the road 250 m after the track exits the forest (S2° 27.151 E29° 11.412). Crimson-wings tend to feed on seeding grasses along the road and can remain extremely inconspicuous until they are flushed. Otherwise, birding here is not too interesting, although there are some open country species such as Black-crowned Tchagra and Cape Wagtail.

Rukuzi Trail

The western end of the Rukuzi Trail starts on the Bururi road, which you should take down about 150 m and then look for the trailhead on your right. This junction (S2° 28.547 E29° 12.454) is a favored spot for Red-throated Alethe, which often holds territory here. Walking about 100 m down the Rukuzi Trail will bring you to some scrubby understory that is favored by Doherty's Bushshrike and a group of Mountain Illadopsis (S2° 28.537 E29° 12.514). This area can also be good for Banded Prinia and Archer's Robin-Chat. The haunting

Even in non-breeding plumage, Purple-breasted Sunbird is distinctive. ©Lee Hunter

call of Lagden's Bushshrike, which is a rare bird in Nyungwe, can sometimes be heard on the first kilometer of the Rukuzi Trail. This seems to be one of the best areas for this species in Rwanda. After you have birded the first kilometer or two of this trail it may pay to turn around and drive to its eastern section, which is very close to the junction with the Pindura/Bweyeye road (see below). On the north side of the main road about halfway between the two ends of the Rukuzi Trail is a *Symphonia* tree that is excellent for Purple-breasted and other sunbirds when in bloom (GPS S2° 28.698 E29° 13.147). Walking the eastern end of this trail for about 1 km can produce Ruwenzori Turaco, Lagden's Bushshrike (GPS of good spot: S2° 28.201 E29° 13.939), Grauer's Warbler, and Strange Weaver. The full Rukuzi trail is 7.8-km long.

Pindura/Bweyeye road
GPS of intersection with main road: S2° 28.478 E29° 13.721
This is a large road that leads south of the main road to the village of Bweyeye. This intersection was formerly the site of Pindura, one of the two trading posts removed by governmental decree. Travelling the 28 km south to Bweyeye takes about 2.5 hours and requires a 4x4 vehicle. Some birders have recorded Kivu Ground-Thrush and Shelley's Crimson-wing about 5–7 km down this road. In order to try for these species, the best bet may be a pre-dawn drive down the road in the hope of encountering one on the track at first light. The upper portion of the road is also good for Rufous-chested (*Rufous-breasted*) Sparrowhawk, Cassin's Hawk-Eagle, Barred Long-tailed Cuck-

oo, Tullberg's Woodpecker, Many-colored Bushshrike, Stripe-breasted Tit, Shelley's (Kakamega) Greenbul, Gray Apalis, Grauer's Warbler, Slender-billed Starling, Purple-breasted and Stuhlmann's (*Ruwenzori Double-collared*) sunbirds, and Thick-billed Seedeater.

Bigugu Trail
GPS of trailhead: S2 28.412 E29 14.381
This is a tough 7-km-long (14 km round trip) trail with about 600 m of elevation gain that takes you to the highest peak in Nyungwe, Mount Bigugu (2950 m). Fortunately, it is not necessary to walk more than 3 km up the trail (6 km round trip) for the best birding. Although the initial climb is tough, the walking is quite easy for the next couple of kilometers on what turns out to be a fabulous birding trail. This is the best trail in Nyungwe for Red-collared Mountain-Babbler and the first 3 km of the track supports at least three groups of this enigmatic and handsome flagship species. Although groups of mountain-babblers are often big (8–15 birds) and noisy, they may forage quietly and are surprisingly elusive. Focus your attention on the canopy of the biggest trees with moss- and lichen-clad trunks; these birds often probe and forage in these epiphyte-laden trees, which seem to be a key component of their favored habitat. While babblers occasionally join other species in mixed flocks, they are equally comfortable in mono-specific groups. When babblers flock with other species, they favor other fairly large and sluggish birds such as Black-tailed (*Montane*) Oriole and Gray Cuckooshrike. So, if you find a flock containing these species, watch carefully for babblers.

Red-collared Mountain-Babbler is Nyungwe's "flagship" bird. ©Ken Behrens

This trail starts as a series of steep switchbacks and then after about 500 m starts to level out. On the switchbacks watch for Lagden's Bushshrike, Yellow-streaked Greenbul, Chestnut-throated Apalis, and Mountain Illadopsis. After about 750 m the track flattens out and is easy to walk and bird and you may encounter the babbler anywhere from here onwards. There are a few vistas with excellent open views; remember to check for soaring raptors. This part of the trail is also excellent for Ruwenzori Turaco, both Narina and Bar tailed trogons, White-headed Woodhoopoe, Tullberg's and the locally scarce Olive woodpeckers, Gray Cuckooshrike, and White-browed Crombec. Handsome Francolin is common along here and it is heard everywhere but is difficult to see well on the narrow trail. Watch the canopy flocks for Stripe-breasted Tit. This area is one of the few in the park that support Western (*Green*) Tinkerbird that, as elsewhere

in Nyungwe, seems to be seasonal, disappearing in the dry season. The understory along this trail is particularly good for Archer's Robin-Chat, along with other skulkers such as Mountain Sooty (*Black*) Boubou, Cinnamon Bracken-Warbler, Equatorial Akalat, White-starred Robin, Red-throated Alethe, and Mountain Illadopsis. The scrubby edges and heaths hold several groups of Mountain Yellow-Warbler, which, despite their shyness, usually respond well to recorded calls. Shelley's Crimson-wing has been recorded from this trail, but is as rare here as it is elsewhere. The whole trail is good for silver (*gentle*) monkey, which thrives in this slightly higher-elevation forest. If you fail to find mountain-babbler quickly, remember that the biggest group's territory lies the farthest down the trail, 2–2.5 km from the trailhead. A few hours spent carefully birding the Bigugu Trail will give you at least a 75% chance of seeing this handsome species.

TIME

Three days is enough time to find most of the Albertine Rift endemic birds and a couple of species of primates. However, this is an incredibly beautiful place and it would be easy and pleasurable to spend a week or more in Nyungwe. More time will certainly be useful if you are hoping to find Albertine Owlet or Shelley's Crimson-wing, or to go searching for some of the rare species that have not yet been definitively recorded. Also remember that if you are going to make a dedicated chimpanzee tracking expedition, this will take at least one full morning – and because looking for chimps is so focused, there is little opportunity to watch birds.

DIRECTIONS

It takes 3–3.5 hours to drive from Kigali to Butare in the Southern Province and another 1.5–2 hours to get from Butare to the eastern boundary of the park. Between Kigali and Butare, about 2 km south of the village of Ruhango, and 24 km south of the larger town of Gitarama, there is a large tree that hosts a breeding colony of African Spoonbills and other waterbirds (📍 S2°14.870 E29°47.648).

Getting around the park is amazingly quick, courtesy of the excellent paved road that bisects it. This is the main road that runs from Cyangugu near the DRC border to Butare, the main administrative town in Rwanda's Southern Province. This paved road makes birding Nyungwe and accessing the park a joy, despite the presence of the occasional pothole or cargo truck speeding its way towards the border. It also means that getting to any of the trailheads in the park is straightforward. It only takes 1.5 hours to drive the 55 km from one edge of the park to the other, a journey that would take many hours in some other African national parks. If you are planning to spend the night on the western side, for example at the Gisakura Guest House, make sure to budget enough time for the drive through the forest. The directions for navigating within the main part of the park are included in the "Birding" section above.

For campers without their own transport, Uwinka is the best place to stay. For those who prefer a hotel – and ideally have a vehicle at their disposal – the western border of the park holds some good options. The national park runs the basic but comfortable Gisakura Guest House. The bathrooms are shared, but they do have hot water. Bookings for Gisakura should be made with the guest house directly (website: www.gisakuraguesthouse.com; e-mail: ghnyungwe@yahoo.com; phone: +250 (0)788675051). Reservations are always recommended, especially on dry-season weekends, when the guesthouse is popular with foreigners working in Kigali. The Gisakura Tea Estate has a very basic guesthouse that is not currently open to visitors but which may re-open in the future. This guesthouse is adjacent to the Gisakura Forest covered under "Birding" above. The cheapest option for the moment is a new guesthouse called Café-Resto Keza Nyungwe located near the main road, 400 m west of the Gisakura office (e-mail: nyirijecla@yahoo.fr or nyirijecla@gmail.com; phone: +250 (0)783396666). The upmarket Nyungwe Forest Lodge is available for those with an ample budget (website:

ALBERTINE RIFT ENDEMIC BIRDS

The Albertine Rift spans the border regions of five countries (Rwanda, Uganda, Burundi, Tanzania, and the Democratic Republic of the Congo). This region supports 36 traditionally designated restricted-range bird species, more than any other endemic bird area (EBA) in Africa. But modern taxonomic approaches may see that number elevated since a new Rift endemic, Willard's Black Boubou, has recently been described. The Albertine Rift is spliced by some of Africa's great lakes, including Albert, Edward, Kivu, and Tanganyika, and its topography is complex, with many isolated massifs and forest blocks. The result is that no single massif or forest contains all the species endemic to the Rift. The Ruwenzoris rise to an incredible 5110 m, but these dizzying altitudes support mostly elfin and heath moorland and most forest lies below 3500 m.

The heart of the EBA are the Itombwe Mountains to the west of Lake Kivu in DRC, which support 31 of the EBA's 36 endemics. Rwanda's Nyungwe and Uganda's Bwindi National Parks, the two most accessible and frequently visited sites, support 25 and 24 endemic species, respectively, while more peripheral sites in Burundi and Tanzania support fewer species. The Albertine Rift supports four monotypic genera: the impressive Ruwenzori Turaco (*Ruwenzorornis*), Grauer's (*African Green*) Broadbill (*Pseudocalyptomena*), the strange Grauer's Warbler (*Graueria*), and the tesia-like Neumann's (*Short-tailed*) Warbler (*Hemitesia*). It also supports a host of near-mythical birds, including Congo Bay-Owl, Itombwe Nightjar, Schouteden's Swift, and Grauer's Cuckooshrike. The nightjar was only described in 1990 and all of these species are known from only a handful of specimens. The Albertine Rift remains one of the most fascinating areas in Africa for a birder to explore. The intrepid could easily discover something totally unexpected if they stray from the beaten path and new discoveries may await even in well-surveyed sites.

Nyungwe National Park supports an excellent selection of Rift endemics, most importantly the Red-collared Mountain-Babbler, Albertine Owlet, and Buff-throated (*Kungwe*) Apalis, all of which are only safely seen here. Other endemic species, such as Handsome Francolin, Ruwenzori Turaco, Montane (*Rwenzori*) Nightjar, Neumann's (*Short-tailed*) Warbler, Grauer's Swamp-Warbler, and Purple-breasted and Stuhlmann's (*Rwenzori Double-collared*) sunbirds, are much more easily seen here than in neighboring Uganda.

www.nyungweforestlodge.com; e-mail: reservations@newmarkhotels.com; phone: +27 (0)41 509 3000). It is also located on a tea estate near Gisakura. Finally, there is a new, mid-range (though still pricey) option, the Nyungwe Top

View Hill Hotel located just north of Gisakura, and signed off the main road (website: www.nyungwehotel.com; e-mail: reservations@nyungwehotel.com; phone: +250 (0)787 109 335/+250 (0)725 535 455). The view from here is excellent and the fireplaces in the rooms are welcome on cold clammy mountain nights. The access road to Top View is rough and may require a 4x4 vehicle when it is wet. Most of the accommodation options around Gisakura are rather expensive for what they offer, even by the expensive standards of African hotels. There are cheap hotels in Butare, which is within striking distance of the eastern side of the forest but a long way from the better western sites. Likewise, hotels in Cyangugu, about 40 minutes west of the park, would offer an alternative for a desperate visitor who finds the closer options already fully booked.

There is a somewhat complicated fee system in Nyungwe that is prone to change. Just as this guide went to press, we heard about another round of changes to the fee system and so the information below may already be out-of-date. For a foreigner, it currently costs $40 for a single day of hikes totaling less than 5 km but $50 for longer hikes. These prices include both park entry and a guide and cover as many hikes as you want to do in a day. The total cost for 2–3 days of treks is $60, while 4–7 days cost $90

in total, making a longer stay in the park fairly economical. It costs an extra $20 to visit the canopy walkway at Uwinka. Although past policies have been unclear on whether a guide is mandatory, this combined fee system makes it clear that RDB wants guests to be accompanied by park staff when exploring Nyungwe. Supporting this park – and in particular its extensive and well-maintained trail infrastructure and tireless conservation efforts – by paying entry fees and employing its local guides is strongly recommended. Chimpanzee tracking costs $90 per person. There are two habituated troops, one in Nyungwe proper and one in Cyamudongo (covered in the subsequent site account). Tracking other primates costs $70. This price might be worthwhile for scarcer species such as Johnston's (*gray-cheeked*) mangabey or owl-faced monkey (if tracking them ever becomes possible), but is probably not worthwhile for Angolan (*pied*) colobus, which is usually easy to see along the road or on the trails. The exception might be the visitor who is determined to see the enormous Uwinka troop of around 400 colobus. ◆

Cyamudongo Forest

This relict patch of forest was once connected to Nyungwe but has become isolated by extensive forest destruction. It is still managed as part of Nyungwe NP and plans have recently been mooted that will allow a forest corridor to regenerate, thereby connecting Cyamudongo with the main part of Nyungwe. At Cyamudongo the vegetation is denser and more like mid-elevation rainforest, a taste of what Rwanda's mid-elevation forests, now largely destroyed, must once have been like. The forest is about 300 ha (740 acres) in extent and covers rolling hills that range from 1700 to 2000 m in elevation.

Most of Nyungwe's visitors trying to see a habituated group of chimpanzees are likely to head to this forest. Watch also for red-tailed and Dent's (*mona*) monkeys, as this is the site where you are most likely to find these primates. For people who are strictly

birding, this patch will definitely add to your trip list, although if you are mainly targeting Albertine Rift endemics and on a tight itinerary, it is probably better to skip Cyamudongo. A few species such as Ross's Turaco, Gray-throated Barbet, and Luehder's (*Lühder's*) Bushshrike are more easily found here than in the main forest. Anyone birding here should also watch carefully for lower-elevation birds such as Yellow-billed Barbet that have become extremely rare in Rwanda due to the destruction of most forest at this elevation.

KEY SPECIES

Mammals: Chimpanzee and Dent's (*mona*) monkey.

Birds: Ruwenzori Batis, Willard's Sooty Boubou (probable), Buff-throated (*Kungwe*), Ruwenzori (*Collared*), and Black-faced (*Mountain Masked*) apalises, Red-faced Woodland-Warbler, Strange Weaver.

OTHER SPECIES OF INTEREST

Mammals: Red-tailed monkey.

Birds: Mountain Buzzard, Montane (*Rwenzori*) Nightjar, Scarce Swift, Great Blue and

Ross's Turacos are conspicuous and spectacular residents of Cyamudongo. ©Ken Behrens

Black-billed turacos, Narina and Bar-tailed trogons, Cinnamon-chested Bee-eater, Black-and-white-casqued Hornbill, Luehder's (*Lühder's*) Bushshrike, Gray Cuckooshrike, White-tailed Blue-Flycatcher, Yellow-whiskered Greenbul, Eastern (Olive-breasted) Mountain-Greenbul, White-browed Crombec, Chubb's Cisticola, Gray, Chestnut-throated, and Black-throated apalises, White-eyed Slaty-Flycatcher (subsp. *toruensis*), Waller's Starling, Northern Double-collared and Western Olive sunbirds, Streaky and Thick-billed seedeaters, Black-headed (*Yellow-backed*) and Forest (*Dark-backed*) weavers, Green-backed Twinspot (rare), Black-crowned Waxbill.

HABITAT

Cyamudongo is different from most of the forest in Nyungwe NP inasmuch as its vegetation is denser and there are fewer open areas. The composition of the vegetation is much more typical of a mid-elevation forest and boasts more figs (*Ficus*), *Croton*, *Newtonia*, and *Chrysophyllum* trees.

MAMMALING/BIRDING

If you have your heart set on trying to see the habituated chimps at Cyamudongo, it is best to arrange permits in advance directly with RDB or via a tour operator, and to make sure that you will be assigned a skilled tracking guide. After arriving in Nyungwe, speak to the rangers at one of the reception centers to reconfirm all arrangements. Once at Cyamudongo, you will be briefed and then the search for the chimp group will take anything from 30 minutes to 6 hours. Chimps are much less predictable than gorillas, their great ape cousins, and they too have the capacity to move long distances very rapidly over difficult terrain, leaving us, their more terrestrial cousins, lagging behind in both pace and fitness. This means that chimp sightings are never guaranteed. Indeed, only about 70% of treks are successful and so if seeing chimps is crucial to your time here, make sure you book for two or more mornings to avoid disappointment. It would seem that it is more difficult to find chimps in the dry seasons (particularly June to September) as there are fewer fruiting trees, which means that these animals range over greater distances during this period. After the chimps come down from their nests, they move rapidly and quickly through the forest in search of food. In the more fruit-laden rainy season (particularly February to May) the troops move less and can be easier to observe. In addition to the chimps, Cyamudongo is the best area to look for both Dent's (*mona*) and red-tailed monkeys, as these prefer lower-lying terrain and this is one of the last forests in Rwanda supporting these species.

After turning south at Shagasha it is about 10 km to the forest proper (see "Directions" below for details of the route). As you pass through the tea plantations and scrub on the way to Cyamudongo, watch out for more open-country species such as Scaly Francolin, African Palm-Swift, Siffling Cisticola, Arrow-marked Babbler, Cape and White-browed robin-chats, African Thrush, Brimstone Canary, Western (*African*) Citril, Yellow Bishop, Village Weaver, Red-billed Firefinch, and Pin-tailed Whydah. The open areas immediately around the forest support species including Long-crested Eagle, Northern (*Common*) Fiscal, Mackinnon's Shrike (*Fiscal*), and African (*Common*) Stonechat. The area where you first drive into the forest has produced

The forest in Cyamudongo has a lower-elevation feel than that of Nyungwe proper. ©Ken Behrens

Buff-throated (*Kungwe*) Apalis. There are two small parking areas, the northern Mwinjiro, and the more southern Muyange. Most visitors, including those tracking chimps, are likely to start from Mwinjiro, as there are more trails in the northern portion of the forest. From the parking area, you ei-

A family of the incredible chimpanzee, humans' nearest relatives. ©Julie Larsen Maher/USAID Africa Bureau

ther walk along the small network of trails or bushwhack, as is sometimes required when chimp tracking.

One bird species that seems to be absent from the main part of Nyungwe NP but which is fairly common in Cyamudongo is Gray-throated Barbet. Other species that are easier at Cyamudongo include Narina Trogon, Ross's Turaco, Black-and-white-casqued Hornbill, White-headed Woodhoopoe, Luehder's (*Lühder's*) Bushshrike, and Yellow-whiskered and Cabanis's greenbuls. The seven Albertine Rift endemics recorded in Cyamudongo are Ruwenzori Turaco, Ruwenzori Batis, Ruwenzori (*Collared*), Black-faced (*Mountain Masked*), and Buff-throated (*Kungwe*) apalises, Red-faced Woodland-Warbler, and Strange Weaver. However, none of these is particularly common and all are better searched for in Nyungwe proper. Other species to watch for when exploring Cyamudongo include Mountain Buzzard, Scarce Swift, Narina and Bar-tailed trogons, Rameron (*Olive*) Pigeon, Tambourine Dove, Red-chested and Black cuckoos, Yellow-rumped Tinkerbird, Lesser Honeyguide, Cinnamon-chested

The huge Black-and-white-casqued Hornbill is usually easy to see in Cyamudongo. ©Lee Hunter

SOCIAL BEHAVIOR OF THE CHIMPANZEE

Of all the great apes, the chimpanzee is the most closely related to humans and shares the vast majority of our DNA. As such, an experience with these creatures is particularly profound and thought-provoking. Much like humans, chimps have developed such complex and regionally variable behavior that it is hard to make generalizations regarding their habits and society. Nonetheless, certain tendencies hold true across different study sites in Africa.

These highly vocal apes live in a fission-fusion type of society. At times when food is abundant, up to 30 animals may loosely associate, but will rove in splintered bands of only a handful of animals at other times. However, the basic social unit of the female, her infant, and the older sibling remain together at all times. Competition between the males of adjacent groups is fierce and lone males may be killed by groups of neighboring males on patrol. This danger seems to be a unifying force among males of a given band, who might otherwise compete fiercely for food and females. Males have to cooperate to protect each other and perhaps as a result they freely mate with all the females of the group.

Facial expressions communicate feelings of agitation, frustration, and fear, and also reveal an individual's social standing. Knowing when to show dominance or subordination, when to groom, and how to maintain alliances within the group structure are crucial to the welfare of each individual. Although the chimpanzee is primarily a frugivore, it is known to hunt for meat, including young antelope, bushpigs, and other primates. There have even been documented cases of cannibalism. Fascinatingly, chimps' diets vary significantly across Africa and different groups seem to possess and transmit differing traditions about what and how they eat. In Nyungwe, chimps are particularly fond of the fruits of *Ficus*, *Olea*, *Syzygium*, and *Strombosia*.

Males are generally 25% larger than females and, despite weighing on average only 40 kg, they are three times stronger than a fit male human. Infants are only fully weaned at three years and spend much time learning from their parents until they reach adolescence. This period of learning is especially important for females, who have to learn how to care for infants by being aunts; otherwise they will be poor mothers. Chimps are tool-users and are highly intelligent, able to solve puzzles, and capable of self-recognition. Nyungwe NP supports between 400 and 1000 chimpanzees.

Bee-eater, Northern Puffback, Tropical Boubou, Black-tailed (*Montane*) Oriole, White-tailed Blue-Flycatcher, White-browed Crombec, Chubb's Cisticola, Chestnut-throated Apalis, African Yellow White-eye, White-eyed Slaty-Flycatcher, Waller's Starling, Northern Double-collared, Collared, Green-headed, and Bronze sunbirds, Streaky and Thick-billed seedeaters, Forest (*Dark-backed*) Weaver, and Gray-headed Nigrita (*Negrofinch*). At

Some open-country species like Mackinnon's Shrike (*Fiscal*) can be seen in the tea plantations along the way to Cyamudongo. ©Ken Behrens

least one pair of African Goshawks also nests here. Although there are as yet no confirmed records of Willard's Sooty Boubous, there are records of sooty boubous here that very likely refer to Willard's given Cyamudongo's altitude. Although few birders are likely to spend the night here, Montane (*Rwenzori*) Nightjar is present. Little Green Sunbird is very rare here and the only record of Red-thighed Sparrowhawk in Rwanda comes from Cyamudongo. Several lower Guinea-Congo forest birds are known only from a handful of records but these may no longer occur in or around Nyungwe. If they do, they are very rare and you should document your sighting well. They include White-spotted Flufftail, Afep Pigeon, Yellow-billed Barbet, Gray Parrot, Forest Woodhoopoe, Willcocks's Honeyguide, Buff-spotted Woodpecker, Forest Robin, and Blue-throated Brown Sunbird.

TIME

Chimp tracking usually takes up a full morning and will sometimes continue into the afternoon if the chimps are proving elusive. Those strictly interested in birds will find a full morning sufficient time here.

DIRECTIONS

Cyamudongo Forest is an isolated forest patch that is managed as part of Nyungwe NP. It lies west of the main Nyungwe Forest and so reaching this site will take several hours from Kigali. The drive to Cyamudongo from Gisakura on the western side of Nyungwe takes 1h 15 min. You could also stay slightly closer in the town of Cyangugu on the shores of Lake Kivu and then drive back towards Gisakura, branching south at the Shagasha tea estate, which will get you to Cyamudongo in only 45 minutes.

Reaching this forest requires a fairly long and complicated drive through small villages and tea estates, with few signs to guide the way. Most visitors will prefer to rely on their driver or local guide to navigate them to Cyamudongo, although directions are included below. A GPS track is also available for download at <http://www.tropicalbirding.com/wild-rwanda/>.

Red-tailed monkey is almost extirpated from Rwanda, but can still be seen in Cyamudongo Forest.
©Keith Barnes

From Nyungwe NP's Gisakura reception center, drive west 21.1 km on the paved road towards Cyangugu until reaching a sign pointing along a dirt road "12 Km to Cyamudongo Forest" (GPS of intersection: S2° 28.857 E28° 57.844). If approaching from Cyangugu, this turn is about 7.5 km after leaving the town. Turn south and drive 0.6 km to an intersection where you turn left (GPS S2° 29.165 E28° 57.783). Drive another 0.9 km to a T-junction, where you again turn left (GPS S2° 29.412 E28° 58.021). Continue south for 3 km to another intersection, where you once again go left (GPS S2° 30.511 E28° 58.324). In another 0.6 km, continue past a road to the left (GPS S2° 30.772 E28° 58.468). Drive for another 2.2 km to a big bend in the road where there is another intersection (GPS S2° 31.418 E28° 57.856). Turn left at this intersection, and drive to the south. In 1.6 km you pass a small village, and in 2.2 km a road to the left. Finally, after 3.3 total km from the bend intersection, you will arrive at the main intersection near the forest (GPS S2° 32.705 E28° 58.693). This intersection is signed for Mwinjiro car park to the left and Muyange car park to the right. Most birding and chimp-tracking expeditions begin at Mwinjiro, which is 0.8 km down the left-hand road. If you want to reach Muyange, go right, and drive for 3.2 km. The last 1.5 km of this drive takes you through interesting forest, which can be an excellent place for birds and monkeys, and sometimes even chimps. ◆

Lake Kivu

Lake Kivu lies between lakes Tanganyika and Edward in the great chain of lakes that stretch along the western branch of the Great Rift Valley and defines most of Rwanda's western border with DRC. One thousand or more years ago, Kivu must have been a wilderness paradise, where great forests full of chimps and gorillas ran right down to the shore. But for centuries, Kivu and its pleasant climate and rich soil have been attracting humans and today most of the shoreline of this great lake has been transformed by human use. Nonetheless, Kivu still retains some of its natural grandeur. Most of the mammals are gone but there are still many birds

on and around Kivu. This is far from an essential location for most visiting naturalists but could be visited on transit between other sites or as a more relaxing addition to an otherwise intense trip. Of general interest is the fact that Kivu contains vast

The vast Lake Kivu. ©Ken Behrens

The wetlands around Kivu hold species like Gray Crowned-Crane. ©Keith Barnes

reservoirs of carbon dioxide under its surface, which have the potential to create a massive limnic eruption. Indeed, a look at Kivu's geological history suggests that such eruptions have occurred in the past and massive die-offs seem to have occurred around the lake about every 1000 years.

SPECIES OF INTEREST

Mammals: Spotted-necked (*spot-necked*) otter.

Birds: White-backed Night-Heron (rare), Gray Crowned-Crane, Black Goshawk (*Great Sparrowhawk*), African Goshawk, Palm-nut Vulture, Gray Parrot (rare), African (*Black*) Swift, Mosque Swallow, Yellow-throated Greenbul, Gray-capped Warbler, Red-chested and Green-headed sunbirds, Grosbeak Weaver, (*Southern*) Red Bishop, Black-crowned Waxbill, African Firefinch.

HABITAT

Vast, wide, deep rift lake surrounded by villages, exotic tree plantations, and cultivation. There are some scattered patches of native scrub, as well as small marshes and mudflats.

MAMMALING/BIRDING

Cyangugu lies at the southern end of Kivu, Gisenyi at its northern end, and

Grosbeak Weaver favors moist, lakeside scrub. ©Keith Barnes

Kibuye on its central eastern shore. An unpaved road runs between these three towns. Although this road frequently provides distant views of Lake Kivu, it seldom approaches the lakeshore closely. The towns themselves give the best access to the shore and some good bird habitat. From a birding perspective, the small wetlands and native scrub along this main lake route are almost as interesting as the lakeshore and are more easily accessible. One such stretch of roadside habitat is where the road crosses the Kamiranzovu River just before it flows into Lake Kivu (📷 S2° 20.471 E29° 07.120). This spot lies about 16 km north of the junction with the paved Cyangugu to Kigali road. This is not an exceptional birding site but is worth a scan if you are driving this route. Here you may find typical scrub species such as Emerald-spotted Wood-Dove, Speckled Mousebird, Northern (*Common*) Fiscal, Common Bulbul, Tropical Boubou, Bronze Sunbird, Baglafecht Weaver, Holub's Golden-Weaver, and Common Waxbill, plus wetland species including Hamerkop, Lesser Swamp-Warbler, Red-faced Cisticola, Fan-tailed Widowbird, and Grosbeak Weaver. Another similar place is where the road crosses the Mugonero River just before it flows into Lake Kivu, 45 km farther north on the same road (GPS S2° 11.514 E29° 17.114). Gray Crowned-Crane often graces this more open wetland.

Scrub- and *Eucalyptus*-birding along the whole stretch of road between Cyangugu and Kibuye can be surprisingly productive. Common species include the ubiquitous Pied Crow, African Pied Wagtail, Bronze Sunbird, Northern Gray-headed Sparrow, and Bronze Mannikin. Slightly less common but still frequently encountered are Augur Buzzard, Red-eyed Dove, Little Swift, Speckled Mousebird, Northern (*Common*) Fiscal, Chubb's Cisticola, African (*Common*) Stonechat, Western (*African*) Citril, Streaky Seedeater, Village and Baglafecht weavers, and Yellow Bishop. It takes a little more effort to find Black-headed Heron, Mountain Buzzard, African Goshawk, Eurasian (*Common*) Kestrel, Red-chested Cuckoo, Cinnamon-chested Bee-eater, Scaly-throated Honeyguide, African Thrush, Red-rumped, Wire-tailed, and Angola swallows, Black and White-headed sawwings, Rock Martin, White-tailed Blue-Flycatcher, Mackinnon's Shrike (*Fiscal*), Ruaha (*White-headed Black*) Chat, Dusky-brown (*African Dusky*) Flycatcher, White-eyed Slaty-Flycatcher, White-browed Robin-Chat, Green-headed, Red-chested, and Variable sunbirds, Brimstone Canary, and Black-crowned Waxbill.

Someone travelling the lake route along the western side of Rwanda should consider stops at Mukura and/or Gishwati Forests for a taste of Afro-montane forest birds that include a good selection of Albertine Rift endemics. Mukura lies east of Kibuye (about an hour's drive), while Gishwati is right alongside the main lake road.

The northern town of Gisenyi enjoys a wide lakefront that runs right up to the DRC border. There are several pleasant hotels that sit on or near the shore. One of the best of these in terms of birding is Paradise Malahide (web: www.paradisemalahide.com; GPS of hotel: S1° 44.028 E29° 16.391), located on a peninsula a few kilometers south of the main part of Gisenyi. The species found here are quite similar to those found in many spots around Lake Kivu including Cyangugu and Kibuye. Along the lake look out for a variety of herons and egrets, Sacred and Hadada ibises, Hamerkop, Long-tailed and Great cormorants, White-winged (boreal winter) and Whiskered terns, Black Crake, Pied and Malachite kingfishers, and the occasional spotted-necked (*spotnecked*) otter. The hotel gardens can be rather productive and often yield Little Bee-eater, Brown-throated Wattle-eye, African Paradise-Flycatcher, Cape Wagtail, Tawny-flanked Prinia, Gray-capped Warbler, African Yellow White-eye, Red-chested, Scarlet-chested, Bronze, and Green-headed sunbirds, Yellow-fronted Canary, Western (*African*) Citril, Baglafecht Weaver, (*Southern*) Red Bishop, African and Red-billed firefinches, Common and Black-crowned waxbills, and Pin-tailed Whydah. Yellow-throated Greenbul seems to be something of a Malahide specialty – listen for its distinctive "yapping puppy" calls. Gray Parrot has even been recorded at sites along the Gisenyi lakefront! A handful of boreal migrants such as Willow and Sedge warblers filter through the area. A few shorebirds drop onto Kivu's rocky shores, with Common Sandpiper by far the

Spotted-necked (*spot-necked*) otter is occasionally seen along Lake Kivu. ©Ken Behrens

most common. Keep an eye out for vagrant waders like Black-bellied Plover. Kivu seems to attract a lot of aerialists, including African Palm-Swift, Little and African (*Black*) swifts, Red-rumped, Mosque, and Angola swallows, Lesser Striped-Swallow, and Black Sawwing. Watch for raptors such as the common Augur Buzzard and Black Kite, and scarcer Palm-nut Vulture, African Harrier-Hawk, Black Goshawk (*Great Sparrowhawk*), and Lanner Falcon. Evening boat trips from Gisenyi to the islands out in the lake have turned up White-backed Night-Heron. Such offshore trips can be arranged through Paradise Malahide and other hotels.

TIME

The Cyangugu-Kibuye-Gisenyi road is in fairly good condition but endless twists and turns make progress slow. It would take a full day to drive this route even if only a few stops were made. Parts of the route can become difficult when there is heavy rain. Stopping at a hotel in Kibuye or camping at Mukura Forest is recommended as a way of breaking up the drive.

DIRECTIONS

There are several excellent hotels in Gisenyi, including Paradise Malahide. Although options are more limited in Cyangugu and Kibuye, comfortable basic hotels can still be found. ◆

Mukura Forest

Mukura Forest lies at 2500 m in west/central Rwanda, about halfway between Volcanoes and Nyungwe NPs. As recently as 1934, Volcanoes NP and Mukura and Gishwati Forests (the latter lying to the north of Mukura) were connected and formed a contiguous area of 833 km². By 1955, these forests were still extensive but had been fragmented into three discrete parcels: Volcanoes, Mukura, and Gishwati. By 1998, only 18% of the original interconnected forest swath remained, mainly as a result of population pressure from refugees returning in the peace that followed the 1994 genocide. Most of the losses were sustained by the Mukura and Gishwati Forests, which were never as well protected as Volcanoes NP. In the past, Mukura supported a set of Afro-montane species including Albertine Rift endemic birds that matched or even exceeded that of Volcanoes NP. In fact, this forest may have been even richer still, given its position closer to Nyungwe and its lush habitat that closely resembles the rich western slopes of this latter park. Unfortunately, Mukura has been whittled down to a skinny fragment of its former self, totaling no more than a few square kilometers, and has lost much of its former diversity. However, the NGO ARECO has recently implemented a plan to protect and manage this forest and, if it succeeds, it will be just in time to prevent the complete conversion of the remaining natural habitat into cultivated fields and exotic tree plantations. At the time of writing, there

were still some interesting species to be seen, including the Albertine Rift endemics Ruwenzori Turaco, Stripe-breasted Tit, Grauer's Rush-Warbler, Blue-headed and Regal sunbirds, and Strange Weaver. Interestingly, despite its small size, Mukura still offers a better birding experience than Volcanoes! Nonetheless, this forest should not be an essential site for most visiting naturalists as there are no Afro-montane or Albertine Rift bird species that are best found in Mukura and very few mammals left at all.

KEY SPECIES

Birds: Ruwenzori Turaco, Ruwenzori Batis, Stripe-breasted Tit, Red-faced Woodland-Warbler, Grauer's Rush-Warbler, Ruwenzori (*Collared*) and Black-faced (*Mountain Masked*) apalises, Archer's Robin-Chat, Blue-headed, Stuhlmann's (*Ruwenzori Double-collared*), and Regal sunbirds, Strange Weaver, Kandt's (*Black-headed*) Waxbill.

OTHER SPECIES OF INTEREST

Birds: Barred Long-tailed Cuckoo, African Wood-Owl, Cardinal Woodpecker, Mountain Sooty (*Black*) Boubou, Black-tailed (*Montane*) Oriole, White-headed Sawwing, Yellow-whiskered Greenbul, Eastern (Olive-breasted)

The loud and bold Chubb's Cisticola can be seen throughout western Rwanda. ©Keith Barnes

Mountain-Greenbul, White-starred Robin, White-browed Crombec, Chubb's Cisticola, Chestnut-throated Apalis, African (Ruwenzori) Hill Babbler, White-eyed Slaty-Flycatcher.

HABITAT

Most of the habitats of Nyungwe are present here, albeit on a vastly reduced scale. The main habitat is lush Afro-montane forest similar to that of Nyungwe. Within the forest there are a couple of small marshes. There is abundant thicket habitat at the forest edges in the form of natural vegetation without taller trees that is the first step towards recovery after the destruction of the forest. The area surrounding the forest has been transformed by human needs, like most of Rwanda. There are small villages surrounded by extensive cultivated fields and exotic tree plantations. The mountains here are exceptionally rugged, and the views are among the most spectacular in Rwanda, even when they embrace nothing but farms.

BIRDING

Although it may appeal to an adventurous few, this is not a high-priority site for most visiting naturalists. Reaching Mukura from Kigali requires a two-hour drive on a paved road, followed by a 30- to 45-minute drive on a fairly good dirt road. The directions provided here will focus on the northern end of the forest, which is the most accessible due to its proximity to a major road. Detailed instructions on how to drive to the forest are included in "Directions" below.

After leaving the paved Kigali to Kibuye Road, drive about 15 km on a dirt road to reach the northern end of the forest. Although there are few birds along this stretch, do watch out for raptors including African Harrier-Hawk and Black Goshawk (*Great Sparrowhawk*), which seem to do well in the abundant exotic tree plantations in this area. After about 12.7 km, you reach a road junction (S2° 00.384 E29° 29.509) where there is a good

Mukura holds some Albertine Rift endemics like Regal Sunbird. ©Keith Barnes

view of the southern end of the forest, which lies about 1 km to the east of the road. This would be a good point from which to access and explore southern Mukura. As you continue north on the dirt road, the forest recedes into the distance about 2 km east of the road. Finally, about 15 km after leaving the paved road, you arrive at the northern end of Mukura, where the forest reaches to within about 200 m of the road (GPS S1° 58.793 E29° 29.477).

There are no formal trails or facilities of any kind at Mukura. Visiting naturalists will have to bushwhack their way around, taking advantage of livestock trails and the all-too-frequent man-made openings in the forest. From the last GPS point mentioned above, about 15 km after leaving the paved road, you can see a series of three forested hills to the east of the road. To reach them, walk down across agricultural fields for about 150

m, cross a small stream at the valley bottom, then bushwhack your way up the hills and into the forest. One point to aim for is the top of one of the tallest of these hills, at over 2600 m (GPS S1° 58.639 E29° 29.655). Continuing southeast from this cluster of hills, there is forest for at least a kilometer. For the moment, there is still excellent habitat in this whole area, which is the best place to search for most of Mukura's interesting bird species. Listen out for Ruwenzori Turaco, the elusive Barred Long-tailed Cuckoo, Mountain Sooty (*Black*) Boubou, and African (Ruwenzori) Hill Babbler. The midstory and canopy can hold species such as Black-tailed (*Montane*) Oriole, Stripe-breasted Tit, Common Bulbul, Yellow-whiskered Greenbul, Eastern (Olive-breasted) Mountain-Greenbul, White-browed Crombec, Red-faced Woodland-Warbler, Chestnut-throated, Ruwenzori (*Collared*), and Black-faced (*Mountain Masked*) apalises, African Yellow White-eye, and Strange Weaver, many of which form mixed flocks. White-eyed Slaty-Flycatcher and Dusky-brown (*African Dusky*) Flycatcher are both common and conspicuous. In the understory lurk beauties that include White-starred Robin and Archer's Robin-Chat. Check any flowering plants carefully for sunbirds including Blue-headed, Stuhlmann's (*Ruwenzori Double-collared*), Northern Double-collared, Regal, Bronze, and Collared. Watch the sky for Augur Buzzard and White-headed Sawwing. The western side of Mukura Forest's northern end is bounded by a small stream, which runs in the valley to the east of the road. The moist thickets along this stream, as well as some man-made canals that are fed by this stream, are good places to look for the scarce Kandt's (*Black-headed*) Waxbill. Such moist, brushy habitats are also

good places to look for Chubb's Cisticola, Green-backed (*Gray-backed*) Camaroptera, Abyssinian (*Olive*) Thrush, Baglafecht Weaver, Bronze Mannikin, and Streaky Seedeater. If you follow the small stream southeast until you are about 1 km from the main road and 1 km from the trio of forested hills mentioned above, you will reach a beautiful small wetland (⬛ S1° 58.884 E29° 30.182). At least one pair of Grauer's Swamp-Warblers is resident here. If you camp a night in Mukura, listen for Montane (*Rwenzori*) Nightjar and African Wood-Owl. Further explorations of Mukura would be certain to turn up interesting species. The southern part of the forest is particularly inviting, though reaching it would require a longer walk from the main road. However, in its current state, Mukura is not that likely to hold any species that are not present or more easily found in Nyungwe.

The *toruensis* subspecies of White-eyed Slaty-Flycatcher doesn't have a "white eye" at all. ©Ken Behrens

TIME

One morning of birding is sufficient to cover the northern end of the forest and locate most of the species mentioned above. However, a couple of days could easily be spent exploring this beautiful and rarely visited forest patch. The authors would be delighted to hear about new discoveries at this site – or for that matter at any of the sites covered in this book.

DIRECTIONS

Reaching Mukura is not too difficult but does require careful attention to these directions. A GPS will prove very useful. Drive about two hours from Kigali on the road to Kibuye, which is now completely paved. Several kilometers before the junction with the gravel road that runs north to Gisenyi and about 15 km before the town of Kibuye, there is a dirt road that heads north to Mukura Forest (GPS of intersection: S2° 03.040 E29° 26.743). This road is signed to various places including "Umurenge wa Wukura," "Adehamu", and "Ecole Primaire de Rwimpiri". It is just east of the 52-km post on the main paved road. Follow this dirt road north and east for about 8 km to an intersection signed for a local government building (GPS of intersection: S2° 00.728 E29° 28.341). Turn right, and continue for about 3.7 km until you reach the middle of a village, where there is another intersection (GPS S2° 00.384 E29° 29.509). From this point, you can see the southern reaches of Mukura Forest to the southeast, about 1 km away. Continue straight on at this intersection and drive a further ~4 km to where there is a good view of the northern part of Mukura Forest (GPS S1° 58.793 E29° 29.477). The directions in the "Birding" section start from this point.

A naturalist interested in visiting Mukura could stay at a simple hotel in Kibuye just over one hour's drive from the forest. Even better is to camp near the forest. There is a good campsite along the road about 400 m south of the point at which you have a good view of the northern forest (GPS of campsite: S1° 59.041 E29° 29.595). If you camp here, expect a lot of attention from local people, who rarely see foreign visitors. ◆

Gishwati Forest

The story of Gishwati Forest mirrors that of Mukura. It was once part of a huge contiguous forest block that connected Mukura and Volcanoes until it too was chopped into isolation; it has now dwindled to a couple of small remaining patches. In the 1980s, the World Bank even financed an ill-conceived project to convert 4000 ha of the forest into a *Eucalyptus* plantation. During the genocide, much of the northern part of Gishwati was designated as a camp for displaced people. Large portions of forest had to be cut for firewood and many of the camp residents have settled in this area for good, slash-and-burning much of what was left of an already dwindling forest to make room for farms. Today,

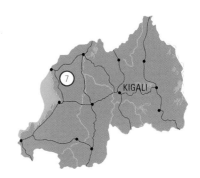

there is even less forest left here than at Mukura. Amazingly, there are still chimpanzees and Virungas golden (*gentle*) monkeys in this forest, along with a variety of interesting birds. Despite its grim history, there are reasons for optimism at Gishwati. The US-based Great Ape Trust has begun a

The haunting calls of its "holdout" chimps often emanate from the remnant forest of Gishwati. ©Ken Behrens

Augur Buzzard is one species that persists even in the heavily human-modified parts of western Rwanda.
©Ken Behrens

project here called *Forest of Hope* that is being continued by a local association. It aims to reclaim illegally occupied areas of the forest, replant native trees, educate children in local schools about the value of the forest, and to appoint wardens to enforce the area's protected status. An ecotourism program is also being considered. Reforestation efforts have already managed to increase the forested area by 67% and the number of chimps has grown from 13 to 20. This forest may even be designated as a national park in the near future. For the moment, Gishwati will mainly be of interest to dedicated explorers or those with a romantic interest in seeing a site redolent of Rwanda's past biological riches. But if the restoration of the forest continues successfully, this may become a prime destination in the future, perhaps a viable alternative to Nyungwe for those interested in chimp tracking.

KEY SPECIES

Mammals: Chimpanzee and Virungas golden (*gentle*) monkey.

Birds: Handsome Francolin (uncommon), Ruwenzori Turaco, Montane (*Rwenzori*) Nightjar, Stripe-breasted Tit, Black-faced (*Mountain Masked*) and Ruwenzori (*Collared*) apalises, Neumann's (*Short-tailed*) Warbler, Doherty's Bushshrike, Ruwenzori Batis, Red-throated Alethe, Purple-breasted, Blue-headed, Stuhlmann's (*Ruwenzori Double-collared*), and Regal sunbirds, Strange Weaver, Kandt's (*Black-headed*) Waxbill, Dusky Crimson-wing.

OTHER SPECIES OF INTEREST

Mammals: L'Hoest's and silver (*gentle*) monkeys, serval (rare), African golden cat (rare), southern tree hyrax, black-fronted duiker.

Birds: African White-backed Vulture, Mountain Buzzard, Black-billed Turaco, Narina Trogon, Red-chested Cuckoo, White-headed Woodhoopoe, Green-backed Woodpecker, White-headed Sawwing, Mountain Sooty (*Black*) Boubou, Doherty's Bushshrike, Gray and Black cuckooshrikes, African Paradise-Flycatcher, White-tailed Blue-Flycatcher, Black-tailed (*Montane*) Oriole, Slender-billed and Yellow-whiskered greenbuls, White-browed Crombec, African (*Dark-capped*) and Mountain yellow-warblers, Cinnamon Bracken-Warbler, Black-throated and Chestnut-throated apalises, Chubb's Cisticola, Banded Prinia, African (Ruwenzori) Hill Babbler, Bronze and Green-headed sunbirds, Thick-billed Seedeater, Oriole Finch, Yellow-bellied Waxbill.

HABITAT

The little forest that remains is tall, dense, and moist, similar to the western slopes of Nyungwe NP, albeit somewhat more degraded by selective logging. The surrounding area is not as heavily cultivated as most of Rwanda, but instead has many open fields used for grazing domestic animals.

MAMMALING/BIRDING

Although Gishwati Forest was once vast, there is today very little remaining forest – some maps, nevertheless, still show a huge swath of forest extending all the way from the Ruhengeri-Gisenyi highway south and west to the Kibuye-Gisenyi highway. The most accessible patch, which supports a few chimps, is located along the Kibuye-Gisenyi road and currently appears to be no larger than 2.5 km². There are a few further fragments tucked into the hills elsewhere, but accessing them requires a long trek, and they are unlikely to hold any bird species other than those found in Volcanoes and Mukura.

The main forest block is located on the Kibuye-Gisenyi gravel road, about 30 km south of Gisenyi and about 60 km north of Kibuye. If approaching from the north, you will reach the northwest corner of the forest (☐ S1° 48.942 E29° 21.077) about 24 km after leaving the paved road (and about 30 km from Gisenyi). From this point, you can park and proceed on foot downhill and follow a stream that marks the northern boundary of the forest. The stream disappears into the forest after about 600 m, although you can continue along the forest edge. This way of accessing the forest offers a chance at more open-country birds such as Little Bee-eater, Black and White-headed

Gishwati still supports Afro-montane species like Gray Cuckooshrike. ©Ken Behrens

sawwings, Mackinnon's Shrike (*Fiscal*), Chubb's Cisticola, and Streaky Seedeater. Watch overhead for Palearctic migrants including a variety of raptors and European Bee-eater.

Continuing south on the main road from the parking point described above, the road follows the western boundary of the forest for 1.5 km. Beautiful moss-laden trees stretch out over the road, a wonderful relief from the endless cultivated fields and villages usually experienced when travelling around Rwanda. This whole stretch offers excellent and easy birding. One particularly good spot (GPS S1° 49.494 E29° 21.075) lies about 1.1 km south of the parking point. Another option for accessing the forest is a trail that starts about 300 m south of the parking point (GPS of trailhead: S1° 49.074 E29° 21.183). This lovely trail makes a loop of about 5 km through the forest, crossing a couple of small streams along the way. This is the best option for those who want to see deep forest species such as Neumann's (*Short-tailed*) Warbler and Red-throated Alethe, and offers probably the best overall birding in Gishwati.

Gishwati lies at a slightly lower elevation than both Mukura and the most productive parts of Nyungwe and does not seem to support as many Albertine Rift endemic birds. Nonetheless, there are plenty of interesting species to look for. Watch for Purple-breasted Sunbird and other sunbirds on any flowering plants, particularly along the main road. The main road is also good for White-tailed Blue-Flycatcher.

Seeing chimpanzees would require a lot of luck, patience, or a healthy helping of both, as the remaining individuals here are extremely wary. However, you have a good chance of hearing the primal and alluring calls of these members of our family tree while in Gishwati. The forest association is developing an ecotourism program that will include chimpanzee tracking and so it may be possible to experience these remarkable holdouts in the near future. The Albertine Rift endemic Virungas golden (*gentle*) monkey also persists here and may also be made accessible via the efforts of the association.

TIME

A couple of hours could be spent exploring Gishwati but you are highly unlikely to turn up any species that are not present in Nyungwe NP. If you choose to take the lake road along Lake Kivu from Nyungwe NP to Volcanoes NP (Cyangugu-Kibuye to near Gisenyi-Ruhengeri), you will pass by Gishwati, which can make a perfect stop for a picnic or for stretching your legs.

DIRECTIONS

From Gisenyi, take the main paved highway east towards Ruhengeri for about 6 km before turning south onto a dirt road (GPS of intersection: S1° 41.943 E29° 19.105). Drive south for about 24 km until you reach the northwest corner of the main forest patch (GPS S1° 48.942 E29° 21.077). From here you can access the forest edge by walking across the fields to the east or by continuing along the main road to the south. Camping in the forest along the main road would be possible, although expect a lot of attention from local people. ◆

Buhanga Forest

About 10 km and a 30-minute drive south of Ruhengeri, and well south and east of the main part of Volcanoes NP, lies a tiny patch of natural vegetation known as Buhanga Forest. This patch of forest has historically been protected as a traditional sacred site and was recently integrated into Volcanoes NP. Although Buhanga is tiny – about 31 ha (77 acres) and with only around 400 meters of trails – and is heavily affected by human activity, it offers surprisingly good birding, with a different line-up of species from Volcanoes proper or Nyungwe. It serves as a tiny taste of what Rwanda's mid-elevation forests might have been like hundreds of years ago, before virtually all of the forest between Volcanoes and Nyungwe was cleared. This is a good place to see Spot-flanked and Double-toothed Barbets, White tailed Blue

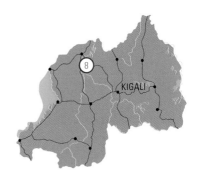

Flycatcher, Yellow-throated Greenbul, Gray-capped Warbler, Brown-backed Scrub-Robin, and Green-headed Sunbird, among other interesting birds. Buhanga supports a couple of species right at the edge of their ranges, namely Black-collared Barbet and Nubian Woodpecker. Perhaps most interestingly of all, there are two May records of presumably migrating African Pittas here! There is no doubt that this is one

Buhanga's White-browed Robin-Chats are highly vocal thicket residents. ©Ken Behrens

of those sites whose birding potential is vastly out of proportion to its small size and is an excellent site for filling in some time before or after gorilla tracking in Volcanoes.

SPECIES OF INTEREST

Mammals: (*Black-necked*) rock hyrax.

Birds: Tambourine Dove, Black Cuckoo, White-browed Coucal, Yellow-rumped Tinkerbird, Spot-flanked, Double-toothed, and Black-collared barbets, Scaly-throated Honeyguide, Nubian Woodpecker, Brown-throated Wattle-eye, Mackinnon's Shrike (*Fiscal*), Yellow-throated Greenbul, Yellow-breasted Apalis, Gray-capped Warbler, White-chinned Prinia, Brown-backed Scrub-Robin, White-browed Robin-Chat, African Paradise-Flycatcher, White-tailed Blue Flycatcher, Green-headed Sunbird, Western (*African*) Citril, Holub's Golden-Weaver, African Firefinch, Black-crowned Waxbill.

HABITAT

A scrubby little patch of degraded mid-elevation (1600 m) forest with a few huge figs (*Ficus thonningii*), dragon trees (*Dracaena steudneri*), and lots of lianas. The tangles in the center of the forest are impressively deep.

MAMMALING/BIRDING

From the main road, drive about 300 m down a small track to reach the parking area. Along this track, watch for Arrow-marked Babbler and Mackinnon's Shrike (*Fiscal*). From the parking area (**GPS** S1° 34.207 E29° 38.149), there is only one trail, wide and well-built on lava that gives this site a strange and rather Indiana Jones-esque feel! The main trail runs about 100 m, then splits. The left fork loops south and east, while the right fork winds its way westwards. Both trails dead-end after a further 100 meters. The right-hand trail ends at a broad rock platform and wall that is a good spot to scan for more open-country birds. Although it would be utterly impossible to get lost here, you are normally required to be accompanied by a park guide, who is often the guard stationed in the parking lot. In any case, it is best to talk with the Volcanoes NP staff at the main park headquarters north of Ruhengeri before visiting Buhanga.

Gray-capped Warbler and White-browed Robin-Chat are both common and vocal in the understory but luring them out into the open can be a challenge. They especially favor the dense thicket at the center of the forest, where the trail becomes tunnel-like as it penetrates the undergrowth. Red-capped Robin-Chat also occurs in Buhanga, although it is uncommon and perhaps seasonal. Tambourine Dove is also common in these thickets. Scrutinize any flowering plants for sunbirds including Green-headed, Scarlet-chested, Bronze, Collared, and Variable. Cuckoos abound – look and listen for Black, Red-chested, Klaas's, and Dideric cuckoos, as well as White-browed Coucal. Scaly-throated Honeyguide is also part of the brood-parasite mix here; listen for its rising trilling call, which is much like the call of Grauer's Warbler that you might hear in Nyungwe NP. Barbets are amazingly abundant in this forest. Look especially on dead snags along the right-hand trail or on any fruiting trees. When the big figs in the forest are in fruit, you might come across a barbet feeding frenzy. Double-toothed, Black-collared, and Spot-flanked barbets, and Yellow-rumped Tinkerbirds can all be seen. Nubian and Cardinal

White-tailed Blue-Flycatcher at full attention. ©Antero Topp

woodpeckers also favor the same snags. The area where the trail splits (📷 S1° 34.231 E29° 38.088) seems to be the best for two of Buhanga's most interesting species: Yellow-throated Greenbul and White-tailed Blue Flycatcher. The noisy "yapping" calls of the resident group of the former do much to establish the character of this forest. Along the right-hand trail there is a patch of junipers, which marks the area favored by a resident pair of Brown-backed Scrub-Robins.

In this degraded forest, it is not hard to keep an eye on the sky, where you might see Hooded Vulture, White-headed Sawwing, and Angola or Red-rumped swallows. Other species to search for in Buhanga are Broad-billed Roller, Brown-throated Wattle-eye, Tropical Boubou, African Paradise Flycatcher, African (*Dark-capped*) Yellow-Warbler, White-chinned Prinia, Green-backed (*Gray-backed*) Camaroptera, African Yellow White-eye, Dusky-brown (*African*

Gray-capped Warbler is another conspicuous component of the Buhanga soundscape. ©Keith Barnes

Dusky) Flycatcher, African Thrush, Violet-backed Starling, Western (*African*) Citril, Baglafecht Weaver, Holub's Golden-Weaver, and African Firefinch. This isolated patch of habitat also attracts migrants such as the common Willow Warbler and, exceptionally, African Pitta, as mentioned in the introduction. There have been some other odd records, such as Red-headed Bluebill, which highlight this tiny forest's continued ability to attract interesting birds. There are few large mammals, but (*black-necked*) rock hyrax can sometimes be seen on the weird lava walkways and outcrops of Buhanga.

When driving from Ruhengeri, watch fields along the way for species including Abdim's Stork, Sacred and Hadada ibises, and Yellow Bishop. The town itself hosts birds such as Hooded Vulture, Pied Crow, and Northern Gray-headed Sparrow.

TIME

You are unlikely to want to spend more than a couple of hours birding this small patch of habitat.

DIRECTIONS

Near the center of Ruhengeri town (which is also called Musanze), there is a large intersection where the roads west to Congo, northeast to Uganda, and south to Kigali all meet. This junction has a large sign for "Volcanoes NP – 12 Km", and lies about 500 m south of the other major junction in Ruhengeri, where the road to Volcanoes NP splits from the road to Uganda. A mere 40 meters northwest of this main junction (on the road to Congo), a smaller road branches off (**GPS** of intersection: S1° 30.224 E29° 38.102) and heads south towards Buhanga Forest. At this smaller intersection there are signs, amongst others, for a Rwanda Military Academy and for "Isar Musanze". Drive 8.1 km southwest and south on this road to where a small and currently unsigned track provides access to Buhanga Forest (**GPS** S1° 34.165 E29° 38.328). Drive 300 m west on this narrow track to reach the parking area. This track may be impassable during heavy rain, in which case you should park on the main road and walk in. The entrance fee at the time of writing was a steep $40 per person and a guide is obligatory. If you just show up, the ranger on duty at the parking area may be able to accompany you, but making advance arrangements with RDB in Kigali or at the Volcanoes NP headquarters is recommended. Camping is allowed at Buhanga for an extra $20 and the national park has camping equipment available. ◆

Volcanoes National Park

This national park was Africa's first when it was declared in 1925. It protects a chain of towering volcanoes that runs along Rwanda's northern border with Uganda. Although its pedigree, beautiful scenery, and pristine montane environments would be enough to make this one of Africa's great parks, it is the presence of mountain gorillas that makes Volcanoes NP one of the world's premier destinations for those interested in natural history. Some 99% of the people who see gorillas in the wild see them either here or in Bwindi Impenetrable NP in adjacent Uganda. De-

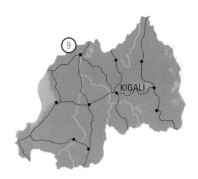

spite some debate, most people agree that Volcanoes offers the best tracking experience for Africa's most accessible mountain gorillas. Your chance of suc-

Volcanoes is not as good as Nyungwe for birding, but does support some beautiful species like Cinnamon-chested Bee-eater. ©Keith Barnes

cess here is near 100% and you have an excellent chance of an intimate encounter that goes beyond a mere sighting, during which time you can look into their soulful eyes, observe their amazingly human hands and feet, and follow them for an hour of their gentle daily routine of walking and feeding. The wonder of seeing gorillas is difficult to explain to someone who has not experienced it. With most wildlife experiences, you feel that you are the one watching as the wild creature goes about its normal life, mostly unaware of your presence. With gorillas, however, you feel that they are watching you as carefully and as thoughtfully as you are watching them. If you are only going to visit one natural place in Rwanda, it should be Volcanoes in order to see and be seen by the magnificent mountain gorilla.

Although the vast majority of visitors only come to track the mountain gorillas, there is much more to see in Volcanoes. There is good birding, although it pales somewhat in comparison to Nyungwe to the south. Albertine Rift Endemics such as Ruwenzori Turaco, Grauer's Swamp-Warbler, and Archer's Robin-Chat can be seen. Although Nyungwe is also much better for monkeys and other mammals, Volcanoes does support species absent or scarce in Nyungwe such as African savanna elephant and two further species that are more easily seen here than anywhere else in the world: Virungas golden (*gentle*) monkey and Virunga (*African*) buffalo. There is excellent hiking, with trails that climb several of the tallest volcanoes and give a chance to experience Afro-alpine habitats and associated species such as Red-tufted (*Scarlet-tufted Malachite*) Sunbird. The park's eight huge volcanic peaks form the watershed between the Nile and Congo River systems. The tallest is

Archer's Robin-Chat is one Albertine Rift endemic that is fairly common in Volcanoes. ©Josh Engel/Field Museum

Karisimbi, which at 4507 m is one of Africa's highest mountains.

KEY SPECIES

Mammals: "Mountain" eastern gorilla, Virungas golden (*gentle*) monkey, Virunga (*African*) buffalo.

Birds: *Note that most of the bird species mentioned here are Albertine Rift endemics that are more easily seen in Nyungwe NP. Some of the species listed here as "rare" or "uncommon" are listed so by virtue of their inaccessibility. There may be parts of Volcanoes where they are common, but these areas are difficult to access.* Handsome Francolin (rare), Ruwenzori Turaco, Montane (*Rwenzori*) Nightjar, African Long-eared Owl (very rare), Western (*Green*) Tinkerbird (rare), Doherty's and Lagden's bushshrikes (both rare), Mountain Sooty (*Black*) Boubou, Stripe-breasted Tit, Red-faced Woodland-Warbler, Grauer's Swamp-Warbler, Ruwenzori (*Collared*) and Black-faced (*Mountain Masked*) apalises, Archer's Robin-Chat, Red-throated Alethe (uncommon), Stuhlmann's (*Ruwenzori Double-collared*), Regal, Red-tufted (*Scarlet-tufted Malachite*), and Blue-headed sunbirds (all uncommon), Strange Weaver, Dusky (rare) and Shelley's (extremely rare) crimson-wings.

OTHER SPECIES OF INTEREST

Mammals: Spotted hyena (rarely seen), African savanna elephant (rare), Nile bushbuck, black-fronted duiker.

Birds: Mountain Buzzard, Rameron (*Olive*) Pigeon, Dusky Turtle-Dove, Brown-necked Parrot, Scarce Swift, Black-billed Turaco, Tullberg's (uncommon) and Olive woodpeckers, Gray Cuckooshrike, Black-tailed (*Montane*) Oriole, White-tailed Crested-Flycatcher (rare), Eastern (Olive-breasted) Mountain-Greenbul, White-browed Crombec (uncommon), Chestnut-throated Apalis, Chubb's Cisticola, Cinnamon Bracken-Warbler, Mountain Yellow-Warbler,

Cape Robin-Chat is often seen in the open areas on the fringes of Volcanoes NP. ©Ken Behrens

African (Ruwenzori) Hill Babbler, Mountain Illadopsis (rare), White-starred Robin, Cape and White-browed robin-chats, Abyssinian (*Olive*) Thrush, Sharpe's (rare), Waller's, and Slender-billed starlings (the latter two uncommon), Malachite Sunbird, Yellow-crowned Canary, Western (*African*) Citril, Thick-billed Seedeater, Black-headed (*Yellow-backed*) Weaver, Yellow-bellied Waxbill.

HABITAT

Considering that the mountain massifs of Nyungwe and Volcanoes are separated by only 150 km, one might expect their habitats to be quite similar. But this is not the case. Whereas the majority of Nyungwe is blanketed in dense montane forest, most of Volcanoes is scrubby and open, covered in bamboo (*Arundinaria alpine*), sub-alpine bushland, Afro-alpine grassland and heath, or open meadows. This is partly due to a difference in elevation; Volcanoes is much higher on average and includes peaks that tower far above Nyungwe's humble Mount Bigugu. At these elevations tall trees simply won't grow. However, altitude does not seem to account for all of the differences. Even most of the lower-lying parts of Volcanoes do not support tall, dense forest like that of Nyungwe. There are a few patches of such forest, notably on the southern slopes of Mount Bisoke. There are also extensive patches of *Hagenia-Hypericum* forest, mostly at moderate elevations. There are some montane bogs and marshes such as those adjacent to Lake Ngezi. The mix of largely open habitats in Volcanoes seems perfect for gorillas, which range all the way

from the park's boundary fence below up to the rims of the volcanoes above. In fact, the browsing habits of gorillas may play a role in keeping parts of Volcanoes open and unforested. Volcanoes is not so attractive for birds and with the exception of a couple of Afro-alpine species, there is very little here that is not more easily found in Nyungwe.

MAMMALING/BIRDING

The vast majority of visitors to this park come to track gorillas and do nothing else. So, here we will discuss tracking and then other possible activities.

GORILLA TRACKING

Gorilla tracking is the main activity in Volcanoes and the whole park is set up to facilitate it. RDB does a remarkable job of making sure that the tens

You don't just watch gorillas. They also watch you. ©Keith Barnes

MOUNTAIN GORILLAS

Gorillas are some of the most remarkable mammals on Earth and an experience with these, our close relatives, is sure to be a highlight for any naturalist visiting Rwanda. This is the largest member of the primate order, a fact that contributes to the awe-inspiring nature of any encounter. Female gorillas average about 90 kg, while males average about 190 kg, with the biggest individuals reaching almost 220 kg. Male gorillas are only about 50–70 kg larger than the biggest male humans, but they are ten times stronger than the most powerful athletes! The immense power of male gorillas is one of the main determining factors in gorilla society. Gorilla's social structures consist of harems in which one mature male has exclusive breeding rights over a group of females. In exchange, he protects the members of his harem and their offspring. The powerful male gorillas are such good protectors that they allow members of their group to feed on the ground securely; they are among the most terrestrial of primates. Males will kill the offspring of other males if given the chance, although this only happens rarely. Even though group territories overlap, male gorillas generally prefer to avoid rather than fight other males. They frequently give signals including hooting and chest drumming to avoid unexpected encounters. When confrontations do occur, whether with other male gorillas or potentially dangerous intruders such as humans, predators, (giant) forest hogs, or buffalo, male gorillas give intimidating displays of roaring, chest-beating, plant-smashing, and charging, before finally resorting to physical confrontation. The dominant male gets the first pick of any scarce resource, arbitrates disputes between females in his harem, and sets the feeding pace for his group. Remarkably, dominant males seem to notice when there is an injury in their group and to slow the group's pace so that the injured member can keep up.

Gorillas can live for 50–60 years but few males live beyond 35 due to the rigors of gaining and maintaining a harem. Males become mature and strong enough to create or take over a harem by about the age of 15, although gaining their own harem is a project that can take years. Sometimes, lone females gravitate to solo males and form a new group. This initial pair forms a strong bond and the females that arrive later accept their lower status in the group hierarchy. Gorillas reproduce slowly; females give birth to one young about every four years and have a maximum of 10 offspring during their lifetimes. There is a strong bond between females and their young, as well as between the harem's male and his females. Nevertheless, the females of a given group do not share a strong bond and may change groups several times over the course of their lifetime.

According to most scientists, there is only one species of gorilla in Africa, which is usually divided into three subspecies: western lowland, eastern lowland, and mountain. These subspecies were isolated by the expansions and ▶

contractions of the central African rainforest belt, the same dynamic that also contributed to the speciation of many Albertine Rift bird and mammal endemics. Despite the seeming suitability of the habitat, there are no gorillas in the center of the Congo basin. The western lowland gorilla has the largest distribution and a population estimated at 40,000 and lives in the western part of the Congo basin, from Nigeria into DRC. The eastern lowland gorilla is found in a small area of the eastern Congo basin below the Albertine Rift Mountains, and has a population of only about 4000. The mountain gorilla is the rarest subspecies, with only around 880 individuals remaining. It is found in the Albertine Rift Mountains of Rwanda, Uganda, and eastern DRC. Mountain and eastern lowland gorillas are endangered, while the western lowland is considered vulnerable. Although the mountain is the least common of the three, the vast majority of tourists who see a gorilla see this subspecies since well-organized tracking programs exist in Uganda and Rwanda.

There are a lot of differences between mountain and lowland gorillas. One of the most obvious is the long blue-black coat of the mountain as opposed to the shorter and browner coat of the lowland. On mature male gorillas, the saddle becomes gray or white, giving rise to the popular term "silverback". The mountain also has larger and less exclusive groups, in which the dominant silverback male is more tolerant of younger males. These big groups tend to support more females as well. The territories of the mountain are smaller – 4–8 km^2 as opposed to 20–25 km^2 for the lowland. All gorillas are herbivores, although they will add certain vitamins and minerals to their diet by eating invertebrates, their own dung, and mineral-rich soil. Studies have shown that the mountain eats fewer plant species than the lowland but that their main food species seem to grow much faster, thereby allowing larger and more tolerant groups to live in smaller territories. The favorite food species of the mountain include wild celery, thistle, stinging nettle, *Galium* vines, and blackberries. Their diet is so rich in succulent herbs that they rarely need to drink. Lowland gorillas tend to eat more fruits and wild ginger, and they climb trees more often to reach fruit.

All gorillas prefer open areas to thick forest. They like old clearings, landslides, valley bottoms, and similar habitats that support dense herbaceous growth at ground level. Gorillas even maintain patches of open habitat by destroying saplings

One of the things that gorillas share with humans is an individually distinct and extremely expressive face. Much like humans, their facial expressions are the best indication of their behavior.

of thousands of visitors who track gorillas each year have a smooth and enjoyable experience, while keeping the gorillas' welfare as their primary concern. There are 10 habituated troops of gorillas in Volcanoes NP and only one group of a maximum of eight people is allowed to visit each troop each

Encountering a group of gorillas in a bamboo glade, the experience of a lifetime for some. ©Ken Behrens

day, the limiting factor in the availability of tracking permits. For more on the habituated gorilla groups, see the box on page 136.

All the visitors who are tracking gorillas meet at the national park headquarters at 7 a.m., where they are divided into groups by the national park staff on the basis of an estimation of their fitness. Each group then receives a briefing from their main tracker and then drives to the parking area that is closest to the last known whereabouts of the gorilla troop they will track. Your experience will vary considerably depending on which group you are assigned to. Some can be a 15-minute drive and short walk from the headquarters, while others might be a 2-hour drive and 3-hour walk away. However, one of the advantages of tracking gorillas in Rwanda is that even the visitors that have to go the farthest are normally back for a late lunch, whereas in Uganda track-

ing gorillas can be an all-day slog. Very occasionally, a gorilla group does something unexpected that converts the tracking in Rwanda into an all-day affair

All groups are accompanied by a main tracker who explains what to expect, assistant trackers, and several armed soldiers from the Rwandan army, who are there to protect visitors from the Virunga (*African*) buffalo or from the remote chance of trouble from an incursion of bandits from nearby DRC. Porters are usually available to carry your daypack: consider hiring one even if you have no desperate need of assistance since it provides work for local people and helps them see their gorilla neighbors as a blessing rather than an inconvenience. After driving to a parking area, there is usually a walk ranging from 500 m to 2 km across fields and through exotic tree plantations to the boundary fence of the park (which was built to re-

Everything about gorillas is wondrous, from head to toe. ©Ken Behrens

duce the number of Virunga (*African*) buffalo leaving the forest to raid agricultural fields). Here you enter thick montane scrub or bamboo, with occasional patches of forest. Depending on the whereabouts of your gorilla troop, you might be following good trails or bushwhacking through thick undergrowth. Your assistant trackers and some of the army personnel usually split off to find the gorillas, keeping in touch with the main tracker via radio. Sooner or later, you will come into contact with your group of gorillas.

Once you find your gorilla group, you can approach them remarkably closely. Although you are not supposed to get any closer than seven meters, it is usually the gorillas that violate this rule and approach you! Keep in mind that many human diseases are communicable to gorillas and so do try to respect the 7-meter rule; consider covering your mouth and nose with a bandana while watching the gorillas

(see "Sneezed to Extinction?" side box on page 28). Your national park trackers will provide guidance on how to safely approach and view gorillas and when to back off so as to protect them. Each group is technically allowed a maximum of one hour with the great apes, although this is often extended by 15 or 30 minutes, depending on the mood of the group and the tracker. After your hour, you head back to the parking area and your vehicle, often by a different path, depending on where the gorillas have led you. Few people are disappointed by this experience and most consider it among the most remarkable they have ever had. As you return to your vehicle, friendly local people selling gorilla T-shirts or trinkets will almost certainly approach you. Buying something from them is another way of ensuring that local people remain positive about their role as neighbors to the gorillas and represents a small but worthwhile contribution to the conservation of these amazing animals.

The birding during gorilla tracking is rarely very interesting for two reasons: firstly, the habitat in Volcanoes is generally not very productive and is dominated by bamboo and scrub and, secondly, your trackers and fellow group members are very focused on seeing gorillas and are usually reluctant to stop for other sightings. Nonetheless, you can rack up a few interesting birds during a gorilla tracking experience. Around the national park headquarters, there are Klaas's Cuckoo, Speckled Mousebird, Mackinnon's Shrike (*Fiscal*) (check the wires behind the HQ), Bronze Mannikin, and sunbirds, especially Bronze. Between the parking areas and the national park boundary fences lie cultivated fields, remnant patches of scrub, and exotic plantations.

These hold a few birds, including Augur Buzzard, Red-eyed Dove, Chubb's Cisticola, Cape Robin-Chat, Abyssinian (*Olive*) Thrush, Yellow-crowned Canary, Streaky Seedeater, Baglafecht Weaver, Yellow Bishop, Bronze Mannikin, and Pin-tailed Whydah. Once inside of the national park, the birds you find will depend on the habitat around your gorilla group. Most of the mountain slopes are covered in bamboo and open patches of herbaceous vegetation, neither of which are very good for birds. If there are any flowers, watch for Stuhlmann's (*Ruwenzori Double-collared*) and Regal sunbirds. Chubb's Cisticola is very common in all the more open habitats. Mountain Yellow-Warbler and Cinnamon Bracken-Warbler are common in any thicket habitats. If you luck into some scrubby montane vegetation or a little patch of forest,

A couple of the national park's namesake volcanoes. ©Ken Behrens

THE GORILLA GROUPS OF VOLCANOES NP

Gorillas have small harem social structures in which one mature "silverback" male enjoys exclusive breeding rights over a group of females. In exchange, this silverback protects the group from predators and other gorillas. Young "blackback" males also form part of a gorilla group and the presence of other silverback males will sometimes be tolerated. Rwanda's gorillas are the best studied in the world and most of our knowledge of gorillas comes from here. It is interesting that despite the existence of tens of thousands of lowland gorillas, the endangered mountain gorilla, with a population in the hundreds, is so much better known. Although there are currently 10 habituated groups of gorillas in Volcanoes, gorilla social structure is far from static and groups can fall apart or split, and new silverbacks can even take over an existing group.

Susa-A Group. Family size: 28 members (including 3 silverbacks)

There are lots of superlatives about Susa, the world's most famous gorilla group and the one studied by Dian Fossey. It is the biggest known group of gorillas in the world (it numbered 42 at its peak) but has recently split into two groups. Susa includes the oldest known habituated gorilla, Poppy, who was born in 1976, plus a rare pair of twins. The group's name comes from the Susa River that flows within their home range. The pre-split Susa was infamous for being difficult to track but the new Susa-A group usually stays at lower elevations within the park.

Karisimbi Group (Susa-B). Family size: 15 members

This is the group that split off from Susa. It seems to have established its home range high on the slopes of Karisimbi Volcano, which means that it is often difficult or impossible for tourists to reach these gorillas. If you are assigned to track Karisimbi, expect an all-day trek!

Sabyinyo Group. Family size: 8 members

This group is usually found close to the national park boundary on the gentle slopes between Mount Sabyinyo and Mount Gahinga. The powerful Guhonda, weighing in at around 220 kg and the largest known gorilla in the world, is the leader of this group.

Agashya Group (formerly known as Group 13). Family size: ~25 members

This was one of Rwanda's first habituated gorilla groups. The old name of "Group 13" came from the fact that the group comprised 13 members. However, it has now grown to an impressive 25 individuals. Agashya, the group's silverback, is known for his impressive ability to snatch gorillas from other groups and assimilate them into his own.

▶

Amahoro Group. Family size: 17 members

Amahoro means "peaceful" in reference to the tranquil temperament of the group's silverback, Ubumwe. Perhaps because of its peacefulness, this group has lost group members to the Umubano group. Tracking Amahoro can be difficult.

Umubano Group. Family size: 11 members

Umubano was formed by the silverback Charles, who attempted to take over Amahoro, failed, and eventually founded his own group. Like Amahoro, Umubano is usually found between Karisoke and Bisoke Volcanoes. These groups are usually more difficult to track than the Sabyinyo and Agashya groups, but easier than Susa-A and Karisimbi.

Hirwa Group. Family size: 9 members

This group, whose name means "lucky one" is relatively new and was formed in 2006 by a silverback from the Susa group. Despite being relatively small and new, this group has been holding its own among the longer-established groups.

Kwitonda Group. Family size: 18 members (including 2 silverbacks)

This interesting group was first habituated in the Democratic Republic of Congo. In 2005, they crossed into Rwanda, where they have remained ever since. The group, named after its silverback, Kwitonda, whose name means "the humble one", has earned a reputation for being fairly difficult to track.

Bwengye Group. Family size: 11 members

This recently formed group spends most of its time on the slopes of Karisoke. They had a stretch of very bad luck, when six of their infants died, but their fortunes have improved in the last few years. Visiting this group usually requires a tough trek.

Ugenda Group. Family size: 11 members (including 2 silverbacks)

The name of this group means "being on the move" as they are famous for ranging widely within the Karisimbi area.

the most likely Albertine Rift endemic species are Ruwenzori Turaco, Ruwenzori (*Collared*) and Black-faced (*Mountain Masked*) apalises, Archer's Robin-Chat, and Strange Weaver. The most likely other mammals during gorilla tracking are squirrels, Virunga (*African*) buffalo, and Nile bushbuck.

African savanna elephants are present, but rarely seen.

Volcanoes supports the rare and beautiful Virungas golden (*gentle*) monkey. It is an Albertine Rift endemic that is mainly found in bamboo. There are two habituated troops that that can be visited: Kabatwa at the base of Sabyinyo Volcano and Musanga at the base of Karisimbi. Tracking these monkeys can be arranged at the park headquarters and is usually a half-day activity, for which there is an additional fee.

MOUNT BISOKE AREA

This extinct volcano is 3,711 m (over 12,000 ft.) above sea level and is the anchor in the center of Volcanoes NP. This mountain and its slopes make the most interesting destination for a visiting naturalist interested in an excursion other than gorilla tracking. Although the birding here is not as good as in Nyungwe NP, the habitat is different and some hiking here will enhance your trip to Rwanda. This is particularly true of a hike up to the rim of Bisoke itself, where you can experience some beautiful Afro-alpine habitat unlike anything that exists in Nyungwe.

To hike anywhere in the Bisoke Area you have to be accompanied by a park guide. You may find the park staff startled to meet someone who has interests beyond gorillas but they will be willing to accommodate your desires. Since you will be with a ranger, the directions given here do not need to be very detailed. Men-

Afro-alpine habitat on the top of Mount Bisoke. ©Ken Behrens

tion to the park staff the key names of places mentioned in this site account and they should understand what you want to do and how to get you there.

Lake Ngezi lies on the northern slopes of Bisoke. This lake and the surrounding marshes are mainly of interest to birders as a reliable site for the Albertine Rift endemic Grauer's Swamp-Warbler. Reaching the lake requires a hike of about 2 km, with ~200 meters of elevation gain. Start from one of the parking areas along the eastern side of Bisoke (including Sarrere, Bisati, and #6). Your park guide will know which one is prefer-

able depending on the current state of the access roads. Regardless of where you park, you'll have a hike of 500 m–1 km across agricultural fields to reach the park boundary (S1° 26.745 E29° 30.238). Scramble over the park boundary wall and proceed for just over 1 km to the lake. There are a couple of potentially confusing junctions on this trail but your guide will know how to get you to Ngezi. Despite mainly scrubby and open habitat along the way, this is still one of the better places in Volcanoes to see Afro-montane forest species, including a good variety of Albertine Rift endemics. Watch and listen out for Mountain Buzzard, Rameron (*Olive*) Pigeon (often in flight), Ruwenzori Turaco, Red-chested Cuckoo, Olive Woodpecker, Mountain Sooty (*Black*) Boubou, Northern Puffback, Black Sawwing, African Paradise-Flycatcher, Stripe-breasted Tit, Eastern (*Olive-breasted*) Mountain Greenbul, Red-faced Woodland-Warbler, Mountain Yellow-Warbler, Chestnut-throated, Ruwenzori (*Collared*), and Black-faced (*Mountain Masked*) apalises, White-starred Robin, Archer's Robin-Chat, Stuhlmann's (*Ruwenzori Double-collared*) and Regal sunbirds, and Strange Weaver. This area is one of the best in Rwanda for the scarce Brown-necked Parrot – watch especially for flocks in flight. Around the lake, any marsh vegetation can have Grauer's Swamp-Warbler. One reliable spot to check lies just off the trail (S1° 26.445 E29° 29.672). Waterbirds are scarce on the lake itself, but scan for Red-knobbed Coot.

Some of the best forest habitat in Volcanoes is on the southern slopes of Bisoke, which is also the area where

Although Strange Weaver is more common in Nyungwe, it can also be found in Volcanoes. ©Josh Engel/Field Museum

Dian Fossey worked and was eventually murdered. There is a memorial to her and a trail that provides access. To reach this area, park at one of the same parking areas that give access to Lake Ngezi (including Sarrere, Bisati, and #6). Proceed to the park boundary. There are a couple of different routes, depending on which parking area you use. After entering the forest, follow the trail southwest. In about 800 m, you reach a junction (📍 S1° 28.123 E29° 29.989) where a trail heads up to the top of Mount Bisoke. There is good forest and good birding in this area, and in patches along the next 1.8 km of trail on the way to the Fossey Memorial (📍 S1° 28.393 E29° 29.077), as well as along the first stretch of the trail to Bisoke. Interesting species recorded here include Rameron (*Olive*) Pigeon, Black-billed and Ruwenzori turacos (the latter more common), Mountain Sooty (*Black*) Boubou, Black-tailed (*Montane*)

Oriole, African Paradise Flycatcher, Stripe-breasted Tit, Mountain Yellow-Warbler, Chestnut-throated Apalis, African (Ruwenzori) Hill Babbler, African Yellow White-eye, Dusky-brown (*African Dusky*) Flycatcher, Archer's Robin-Chat, and Bronze, Stuhlmann's (*Ruwenzori Double-collared*), and Regal sunbirds.

If you decide to make the trek up Bisoke, turn north at the intersection mentioned above (📍 S1° 28.123 E29° 29.989) and hike 1.5 km (about 600 m of climbing) before you reach the crater rim. The forest and most bird species disappear at about 3200 m. After passing through the bamboo zone, you finally reach the Afro-alpine grassland and moorland habitat on the crater rim. There are very few birds here. Focus your efforts on any flowering plants, as both Red-tufted (*Scarlet-tufted Malachite*) and Malachite sunbirds occur in this habitat. There is a trail all the way around the crater rim. The

DIAN FOSSEY, BILL WEBER, AND AMY VEDDER: PIONEERS IN GORILLA RESEARCH AND CONSERVATION

Dian Fossey is one of the best-known figures in the history of conservation. She began her work with gorillas after meeting Louis Leakey, who suggested the project to her and helped in its early stages. Her first study site was in eastern DRC, but she was forced out of that country by political instability in the 1960s. She set up Karisoke Research Center in the western part of Rwanda's Volcanoes NP as an alternative study site and spent the rest of her life working here. Aside from being a gifted scientist who made many discoveries about mountain gorillas, Fossey became famous for her very direct methods of conservation and her skill in bringing attention to the gorillas' plight. Several times she witnessed the horrifying results of young gorillas being collected for foreign zoos. Since gorillas fight to the death to protect the young within their group, collecting one or two young might require slaughtering 10 or more adults. Fossey was opposed to gorilla tourism as she saw diseases being transmitted from humans to gorillas and also believed that tourist activities interfered with the animals' natural behavior. As Fossey's love for the gorillas grew, so did her disgust at the corruption or indifference of the agencies charged with protecting them, and the heartlessness of the poachers who targeted them. She set up patrols that destroyed traps, captured poachers, and, some say, went as far as to burn the homes of poachers or to kidnap their children. Despite her efforts, the gorillas within her study group were still killed. In 1985, amid growing controversy about her methods and opposition from various forces within Rwanda, Dian Fossey was mysteriously murdered in her home at the Karisoke Research Center. She was buried at the study site, alongside several gorillas that had been victims of poachers. Visitors to Volcanoes NP today can visit the site and see a memorial at her grave and the remnants of her house. Although she was certainly controversial, Dian Fossey undoubtedly led a remarkable life and did a huge amount to aid the cause of mountain gorilla conservation. To learn more about her, read her book *Gorillas in the Mist* or watch the movie of the same title. Among the several books written about Fossey, one of the best is a biography by Farley Mowat called *Woman in the Mists*.

Amy Vedder and Bill Weber started studying gorillas under Dian Fossey, but quickly developed different methods from their more famous boss. They attempted to engage local people in conservation efforts, rather than treating them as the enemy. When the Rwandan government was planning to convert a critical portion of Volcanoes NP into cattle pasture, Weber and Vedder convinced them to start an eco-tourism program as a more profitable alternative that would leave the gorilla habitat intact. This program, one of the first of its type in the world, has been remarkably successful. Although the situation of the mountain gorilla is still perilous, the population is more stable now than ▶

in previous decades. One aspect of this program is the establishment of the *Kwita Izina* naming ceremony for the young gorillas born each year. This ceremony parallels the venerable ceremony held by Rwandan people for naming their own children. It engages the local community – not to mention celebrities and politicians from far and wide – and provides an excellent platform for publicizing the gorillas' situation. The likes of Bill Gates and Ted Turner have made the pilgrimage to Rwanda to participate. To learn more about the work of Vedder and Weber, read their book *In the Kingdom of Gorillas*.

Red-faced Woodland-Warbler is another of the AREs that is most readily seen in Volcanoes. ©Ken Behrens

Malachite Sunbird can be found on the heights of Volcanoes NP. ©Ken Behrens

The inconspicuous Thick-billed Seedeater is found at the edges of montane forest. ©Ken Behrens

east side has had both sunbirds (S1° 27.660 E29° 29.018). On a clear day, the view down into the crater, north towards Uganda, to the flanking volcanoes, and south into the cultivated, hilly, mid-elevations of Rwanda are spectacular. There are trails that access the other volcanoes in the national park, although most are more strenuous than Bisoke and none of them offers more interesting bird habitat.

TIME

Gorilla tracking is normally a half-day activity, although it can extend well into the afternoon for those visiting a more distant group of gorillas. Another day or more could be spent in Volcanoes NP looking for Virungas golden (*gentle*) monkey and Virunga (*African*) buffalo, exploring the Mount Bisoke area, or taking one of the many other hikes that are possible within the national park. Buhanga Forest, a tiny patch of habitat south of the town of Ruhengeri, is considered part of the national park but is covered in a separate site account on page 123. This forest makes a good birding excursion of a couple of hours.

DIRECTIONS

The town of Ruhengeri (or Musanze) is the largest town in the Volcanoes area. Driving here from Kigali takes a couple of hours. The park headquarters (S1° 25.932 E29° 35.672) is about 12 km north of Ruhengeri and is clearly signed. An extensive network of roads and parking areas on the southern flanks of the national park provides access for gorilla tracking and other activities.

At writing, the price of a gorilla-tracking permit stood at $750 per person. These permits should be arranged months or even a year ahead, especially during the peak periods such as the European and American summer vacation season. There is a new website that shows the availability of gorilla permits, a useful tool when planning a trip (http://www.volcanoessafaris.com/contact-us/before-you-go/gorilla-permit/). There are two Virungas golden (*gentle*) monkey groups that can be visited. At the time of writing, permits for tracking cost $100 per person.

Other activities such as hiking to Mount Bisoke or Lake Ngezi also require visitors to be accompanied by an armed ranger due to the presence of dangerous animals such as the Virunga (*African*) buffalo. Arrange these activities at the park headquarters. At writing, a hike to Bisoke or the Dian Fossey memorial costs $75, while a "natural walk" costs $45. A five-day program to climb the four biggest volcanoes is even offered at $1500 per person.

This is Rwanda's prime tourist attraction and as such there are more options for accommodation here than anywhere else outside of Kigali. One of the cheapest and most convenient places to stay is the Kiningi Guest House, located 300 m from the park headquarters. Budget hotels are also available in the town of Ruhengeri. Fairly luxurious options (about $350 for a double room) include Gorilla's Nest Lodge, Mountain Gorilla Lodge, and La Bambou Lodge. For extreme luxury ($500-800 for a double), there are Sabyinyo Community Lodge (Silverback Lodge), Jack Hanna's House, and Volcanoes Lodge. Camping is allowed in Buhanga Forest. ◆

Rugezi Marsh

This marsh lies about 15 km east of the eastern side of Volcanoes NP (NW Rwanda). It stretches for some 20 km along a valley that drains into Lake Bulera via the Rusumo Falls. Historically, it must have been an incredible wetland paradise, teeming with birds and all sorts of other wildlife, before virtually the entire marsh was converted to agriculture in recent decades. Fortunately, though, there is some hope for the future. Several years ago, the government of Rwanda carefully marked out the historical extent of the marsh and placed a moratorium on any cultivation within these bounds. Natural vegetation is quickly regenerating and although the papyrus that once must have been common in this valley is still largely missing, it will undoubtedly take root in the near future.

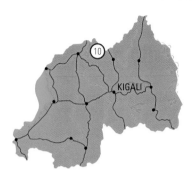

In its current state, this is far from an essential birding destination but could prove an interesting stopover for visitors travelling between Volcanoes NP and Kigali. The marsh and surrounding scrub and exotic plantations support an interesting mix of species that includes Mountain Buzzard, Gray Crowned-Crane, Blue-headed Coucal, Carruthers's Cisticola, Grauer's

Carruthers's Cisticola is readily found in Rugezi Marsh. ©Ken Behrens

Swamp-Warbler, and Crimson-rumped Waxbill. It will be exciting to see which species reappear at this site in the future. In the past, White-winged Swamp-Warbler occurred together with its congener Grauer's Swamp-Warbler, as well as Papyrus Yellow-Warbler, Papyrus Canary, and White-collared Oliveback.

KEY SPECIES

Birds: Carruthers's Cisticola, Grauer's Swamp-Warbler.

OTHER SPECIES OF INTEREST

Birds: African Marsh-Harrier, Mountain Buzzard, Gray Crowned-Crane, Blue-headed Coucal, Lesser Swamp-Warbler, Little Rush-Warbler, Chubb's and Winding cisticolas, African Thrush, Slender-billed Starling, Black-throated Canary, Black-headed (*Yellow-backed*) Weaver, Yellow Bishop, Fan-tailed Widowbird, Black-crowned and Crimson-rumped Waxbills.

HABITAT

The valley bottom is full of marsh vegetation, mainly *Miscanthidium* and non-papyrus *Cyperus*. There are small, isolated stands of papyrus, particularly at the western end of the marsh. The surrounding hills are heavily populated and mainly covered in cultivated fields and exotic tree plantations, although some scrub remains.

BIRDING

Though the marsh stretches for many kilometers, this account will focus on the northern sector of the marsh, which is closest to Ruhengeri and Volcanoes NP.

En route to the marsh from Ruhengeri to the west or Kigali to the south, you pass through the densely populated, heavily cultivated landscapes typical of much of Rwanda. There are remnant patches of scrub and wetland, extensive exotic tree plantations (mainly *Eucalyptus*), and even more extensive cultivated fields. Though far from natural, these landscapes can be beautiful and are far from birdless: Augur Buzzard, Black Kite, Hooded Vulture, Red-eyed Dove, Little Swift, Wire-tailed, Angola and Red-rumped swallows, Pied Crow, Northern (*Common*) Fiscal, Streaky Seedeater, Baglafecht and Village weavers, and Northern Gray-headed Sparrow can be seen almost anywhere in the Rwandan countryside. There are also abundant wetland areas, particularly along the northern shores of Lake Bulera. Here you can find Hadada and African Sacred ibises, Yellow-billed Stork, Red-knobbed Coot, Black-headed Heron, Gray Crowned-Crane, African Pied and Cape wagtails, and Yellow Bishop. Scrubby areas that retain some indigenous plant species play host to Klaas's Cuckoo, Dusky Turtle-Dove, Common Bulbul, Chubb's Cisticola, Gray-capped Warbler, Dusky-brown (*African Dusky*) Flycatcher, White-eyed Slaty-Flycatcher, Mackinnon's Shrike (*Fiscal*), Bronze Sunbird, Black-throated Canary, Western (*African*) Citril, Black-crowned Waxbill, and Bronze Mannikin. Scrubby areas of remnant montane vegetation adjacent to exotic tree plantations are often the most productive spots as they come the closest to true montane forest.

The first place where a visitor arriving from Ruhengeri will reach the marsh proper is near a large bridge (▣ S1° 25.289 E29° 49.956) that crosses the stream just before it drains out of the marsh and into Lake Bulera via Rusumo Falls. The cliff-like vicinity of the bridge and falls sometimes attracts interesting species such as Mottled Swift and Slender-billed Starling. Just southeast of the bridge is one of the marsh's largest remaining patches of papyrus. Here, although it is easy to park your vehicle and walk down into the marsh (S1° 25.322 E29° 50.007), be prepared for soggy conditions. Though far from pristine, this is a good place for general marsh and wetland birding. Look for species including Black-headed Heron, African Sacred Ibis, African Marsh-Harrier, Green Sandpiper (boreal winter), Malachite Kingfisher, Northern (*Common*) Fiscal, Plain Martin, Red-rumped and Angola swallows, Lesser Swamp-Warbler, Little Rush-Warbler, Winding Cisticola, Whinchat (boreal winter), Bronze Sunbird, Streaky Seedeater, Fan-tailed Widowbird, and Common Waxbill. There is a small colony of Black-headed (*Yellow-backed*) Weavers here in season. Adjacent *Eucalyptus* plantations support species such

as Mountain Buzzard, Dusky Turtle-Dove, and Lesser Honeyguide.

About 60 meters north of the bridge, you can turn east onto a gravel road that gives access to the vast stretch of Rugezi Marsh (of intersection: S1° 25.245 E29° 49.941). Drive for 2.5 km on this road to a place where the road runs very close to the edge of the marsh (S1° 25.018 E29° 50.790). This spot is good for both Winding and Carruthers's cisticolas, plus Fan-tailed Widowbird, Crimson-rumped Waxbill, and other common wetland species. White-browed Robin-Chat and Yellow-bellied Waxbill can be found in adjacent scrub.

Continue on the gravel road for a further 600 m to a place where a small trail runs down into the marsh (S1° 25.196 E29° 51.059). This is also a good place for Carruthers's Cisticola. If you continue driving southeast and south on the main gravel road, you will parallel the marsh for about 15 km. There are many opportunities

Rugezi Marsh stretches for many kilometers. ©Ken Behrens

to walk down into the marsh and try your luck; nevertheless, the habitat is still re-generating and is fairly uniform overall and so you may quickly stop finding new species. About 10 km from the turn-off from the paved road, a vast stretch of marsh is visible to the west (S1° 26.650 E29° 52.499). Geographically, this seems to be the heart of the marsh and at one stage may have been the core of a phenomenal wetland wilderness. This area will certainly be worth exploring as the marsh vegetation re-generates. From here you can continue on the gravel road parallel to the marsh and eventually reach the main paved road that goes south to Kigali. A more sensible strategy for the quickest onwards journey either to Ruhengeri or Kigali is to turn around and retrace your tracks to the bridge and the paved road.

TIME
An hour or two will suffice for most, although interesting discoveries may await those willing to invest more time.

DIRECTIONS
At the northern end of Ruhengeri, there is an intersection where the main Congo-Uganda road meets the road north to Volcanoes NP (well-signed). From this intersection, take the tarred highway east towards the Uganda border. Drive about 20 km to an intersection where a smaller but still paved road heads east (of intersection: S1° 22.787 E29° 44.761). This smaller road is signed for "Lac Bulera". Drive east on this road, which winds along the north shore of Lake Bulera. After 23 km, you will reach an intersection where a gravel road heads off to the east, just north of a fairly large bridge (S1° 25.289 E29° 49.956). The birding directions start from here. No entrance fees are charged here, although visitors should be sensitive to local property rights, especially if exploring the fields and plantations above the marsh. ◆

Fan-tailed Widowbird, a marsh denizen. ©Ken Behrens

Route from Kigali to Akagera NP

Although the landscape between Kigali and Akagera NP has been heavily modified by humans and holds very few non-domestic mammals, it is still home to some interesting birds. There are several places worth a stop that will break up the drive to the national park and which may well produce a few bird species that you fail to encounter elsewhere in Rwanda on a given trip.

KIGALI

KEY SPECIES
Birds: Ruaha (*White-headed Black*) Chat.

OTHER SPECIES OF INTEREST
Birds: Yellow-billed Duck, Little Grebe, Gray Crowned-Crane, Long-crested Eagle, African Rail, Ross's Turaco, Eastern (*Gray*) Plantain-eater, Tambourine Dove, Blue-headed Coucal, Pearl-spotted Owlet, Common Scimitar-bill, Gray Kestrel, Red-necked Falcon (rare), Black-headed Gonolek, Orange-breasted (*Sulphur-breasted*) Bushshrike, Mackinnon's, Red-backed, and Rufous-tailed (*Isabelline*) shrikes (latter two in boreal winter), White-headed Sawwing, White-winged Black-Tit, Gray-capped Warbler, Red-faced and Trilling cisticolas, Black-lored Babbler, Swamp Flycatcher, Brown-backed Scrub-Robin, Red-chested Sunbird, Vieillot's (*Black*), Northern Brown-throated, Grosbeak, and Red-headed weavers, Fan-tailed Widowbird, White-collared Olive-back (rare), Black-crowned and Black-cheeked (*Black-faced*) waxbills.

HABITAT
Mainly villages, cultivation, and *Eucalyptus* plantations. There are remnant patches of scrub, marshes, and a few ponds.

BIRDING
When heading to Akagera, it takes a while to escape the sprawl of Kigali. Just as the city begins to subside, you

Gray Kestrel is uncommon throughout most of its African range, but can reliably be found in Rwanda. ©Lee Hunter

enter Kabuga, a fairly large satellite town. Just north of Kabuga lies a small series of ponds (🔲 S1° 57.199 E30° 14.474) that are worth birding. Possible species here include Yellow-billed Duck, Sacred Ibis, Little Egret, African Openbill, Gabar Goshawk, Green Sandpiper (boreal winter), Blue-headed Coucal, Black-headed Gonolek, Chubb's Cisticola, Black-headed (*Yellow-backed*), Compact (uncommon), and Grosbeak weavers, and Fan-tailed Widowbird.

Continuing east along the main road for 3.5 km past the ponds, there is a large rookery right in the village of Rugende (🔲 S1° 56.754 E30° 16.148): Black-headed Heron, Sacred Ibis, Yellow-billed Stork, and Pink-backed Pelican all nest here.

Driving for around another 44 km brings you to a major T-intersection in the village of Kayonza (🔲 S1° 54.127 E30° 30.434). Here you can turn left to reach the northern gate of Akagera NP and all of northeast Rwanda or right to reach the park's southern gate and southeast Rwanda. If you turn right and head south towards the more frequently-used southern gate of Akagera NP, watch in 13.3 km for a big tree on the east side of the road that has held a Black Goshawk (*Great Sparrowhawk*) nest (🔲 S1° 58.867 E30° 33.317). In general, this route is good for raptors including Augur Buzzard, African Harrier-Hawk, Long-crested Eagle, and Lanner Falcon. Watch out for Eurasian (*Common*) Kestrel nesting in villages.

Another 3.2 km further on (16.5 km total from the Kayonza intersection), you reach another intersection (🔲 S2° 00.525 E30° 33.509) where you should to turn east towards the

national park. Drive 8.5 km to the small village of Rwinkwavu, where there is a bridge that crosses a wet valley (🔲 S1° 57.818 E30° 35.425) with a dammed pond just to the west of the road. This area is the best birding spot along the Kigali to Akagera route and is well worth some time. You could even spend a very productive full morning birding here. There is an interesting mix of montane birds (some of which are rare or absent in Akagera), as well as widespread scrub and wetland birds, and some true savannah species. The key places to check are the dam to the west, the marsh and scrub in the valley to the east, and the drier thorn scrub on the hillsides to the east, a good patch of which extends for up to 1 km from the bridge. There is also a larger pond about 1.2 km down the valley, east of the bridge, that can be worth a scan (🔲 of southern side of pond: S1° 57.654 E30° 36.020). You can wander around all these habitats and bird them at will.

The dam and other wetlands around Rwinkwavu are surprisingly good for wetland birds including Little Grebe, Purple Heron, African Openbill, Gray Crowned-Crane, (*African*) Wattled Lapwing, African Darter, Eurasian (*Common*) Moorhen, Black Crake, African Rail, Blue-headed Coucal, Swamp Flycatcher, Fan-tailed Widowbird, and Black-crowned and Common waxbills. Species more typical of the scrub and drier savannah covering the slopes above the valley include Red-necked Francolin (*Spurfowl*), African Gray Hornbill, Bare-faced Go-away-bird, Ross's Turaco, Blue-spotted Wood-Dove, Tambourine Dove, African Pygmy-Kingfisher, Cardinal Woodpecker, Black-headed

Gonolek, Orange-breasted (*Sulphur-breasted*) Bushshrike, Mackinnon's, Red-backed, and Rufous-tailed (*Isabelline*) shrikes (the latter two boreal migrants), Gray-backed Fiscal, Yellow-throated Greenbul, Red-faced and Trilling cisticolas, Tawny-flanked Prinia, Gray-capped Warbler, Black-lored Babbler, White-browed Robin-Chat, Brown-backed Scrub-Robin, African Thrush, Rueppell's (*Rüppell's*) Glossy-Starling, Bronze, Mariqua (*Marico*), and Red-chested sunbirds, Western (*African*) Citril, Brimstone and Yellow-fronted canaries, Black-cheeked (*Black-faced*) Waxbill, Yellow Bishop, Green-winged Pytilia, and Pin-tailed Whydah. This place is also weaver heaven. Vieillot's (*Black*) Weaver, quite local in Rwanda, has a colony in a tree above the road near the dam. Black-headed (*Yellow-backed*), Spectacled, and Village weavers nest around the lake, while Northern Brown-throated, Grosbeak, and Red-headed weavers and Holub's Golden-Weaver are also found in the area. Overhead, watch for African Fish-Eagle, Wahlberg's Eagle, Gray Kestrel, White-rumped Swift, Angola Swallow, Lesser Striped-Swallow, Rock Martin, and White-headed Sawwing. Long-crested Eagle sometimes nests near the bridge and some rare species like Red-necked Falcon and White-collared Oliveback have even been recorded.

The final 17 km of the drive to the park pass through some degraded savannah that still holds a lot of birds. It can be worth stopping and walking into the bush if you see a lot of activity or a feeding flock of birds. Ruaha (*White-headed Black*) Chat is common, especially around buildings and even in the village of Akagera

Red-chested Sunbird occurs in wet scrub on the way to Akagera. ©Lee Hunter

(GPS S1° 56.288 E30° 40.078). Many of the species of the dry savannah habitat, described in the Akagera NP site account below, can be found along this stretch, including Black-breasted Snake-Eagle, Lilac-breasted Roller, Pearl-spotted Owlet, Eastern (*Gray*) Plantain-eater, Common Scimitar-bill, Gray-backed Fiscal, White-winged Black-Tit, Arrow-marked and Black-lored babblers, Red-faced Crombec, Sooty and Familiar chats, Scarlet-chested and Mariqua (*Marico*) sunbirds, and Red-billed Quelea. Around the southern park gate itself (☐ S1° 53.940 E30° 40.915), watch for the uncommon Gray Kestrel.

To head to the northern gate of Akagera NP, turn left and head north at the Kayonza intersection (☐ S1° 54.127E30° 30.434). In about 5 km, you will see the southeastern arm of Lake Muhazi and some good-looking marsh habitat (☐ S1° 52.010 E30° 29.860). Over the next 13 km, there are many opportunities to view the lake and several large marshes. This area is worth a few quick stops and scans, although the wetlands inside Akagera NP tend to be far more productive. Forty-seven kilometers past Lake Muhazi, you reach a junction (☐ S1° 28.269 E30° 23.973) where you should turn right/east onto a dirt road that accesses the national park. After driving for 10 km down this dirt road, watch to the south of the road for a long, narrow pond (☐ S1° 25.068 E30° 27.782) that is worth scanning for herons, egrets, cormorants, and other waterbirds. The final 11.5 km to the Akagera NP northern gate pass through savannah that is becoming increasingly populated and degraded but that still holds some birds including (*African*) Wattled Lapwing, Gray-backed Fiscal, White-headed Saw-wing, Pied Crow, Trilling Cisticola, Yellow (boreal winter) and African Pied wagtails, Yellow-fronted Canary, and Black-headed (*Yellow-backed*) Weaver. Shoebill has been seen at least once in a small wetland just outside the park near the north gate.

TIME

These stops can account for an hour or a couple of hours on the way to or from Akagera NP. Although Rwink-wavu is quite a good spot and a longer visit would produce a lot of birds, most birders prefer to invest more time in Akagera NP itself.

DIRECTIONS

Driving from Kigali to the southern gate of Akagera NP takes about 3 hours without stops. The drive to the northern gate takes about an hour longer. ◆

The rather localized Northern Brown-throated Weaver is common at many different sites in Rwanda. ©Ken Behrens

Akagera National Park

This large national park (1122 km²) runs along much of Rwanda's eastern boundary with Tanzania. It offers a range of mammal and bird species and a safari experience that are completely different from the more frequently visited Albertine Rift mountain sites in western Rwanda. This park is more like archetypal Africa, with sweeping savannah vistas, lakes and woodlands teeming with colorful and conspicuous birds, and good numbers of big mammals. Akagera supports over 50 species of mammals. Some of the top species here include leopard, "Masai" giraffe, Uganda topi, African savanna elephant, Cape (*African*) buffalo, "Boehm's" plains (*common*) zebra, and roan antelope. There are plans to reintroduce black (*browse*) rhinoceros (last seen in 2007) and lion in the near future. Although with some 525 species

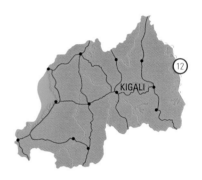

Akagera formerly contended for the highest bird list of any protected area in Africa, its area has been reduced by 60% in recent decades and its bird list has declined to around 480. Nevertheless, it is still one of the continent's most diverse parks for birds. The top birds are the unique Shoebill, rare Ring-necked Francolin, and highly localized Red-faced Barbet. Other highlights include some species that reach the northern edge of their Afrotropical range here, namely Purple-crested Turaco, Crested Barbet, Souza's Shrike, Tabora (*Long-tailed*) Cisticola, and Miombo Wren-Warbler. The park also offers perhaps Rwanda's best papyrus birding, with specialties that include Papyrus Gonolek, Greater Swamp-Warbler, and Papyrus Canary.

This is a park where you could spend weeks exploring while finding new things and simply savoring the pristine and beautiful landscape. One of the benefits of being off the well-beaten track is that it often feels as if you have Akagera to yourself, and it is much less crowded than the famous savannah parks in Kenya, Tanzania, and southern Africa. Although Akagera has been much neglected and

The gaudy Black-headed Gonolek. ©Keith Barnes

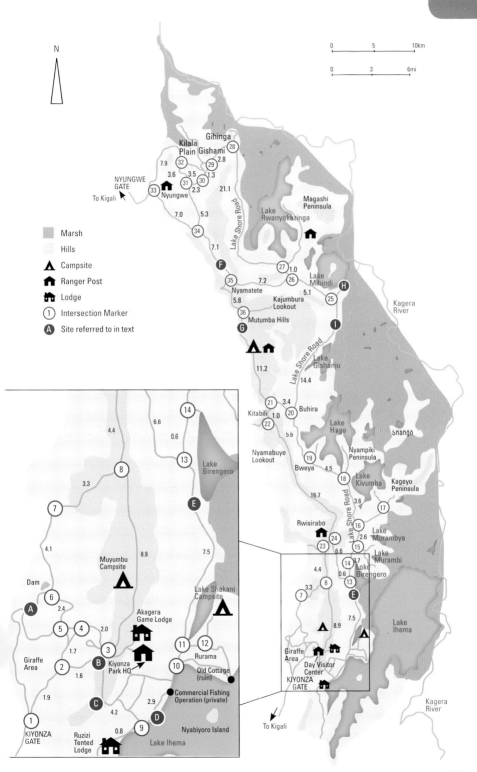

Legend

- Marsh
- Hills
- Campsite
- Ranger Post
- Lodge
- ① Intersection Marker
- Ⓐ Site referred to in text

Shoebill, king of the papyrus. ©Kevin Bartlett

abused in the past, the current outlook is bright. In 2010, a partnership between the Rwanda Development Board and the international non-profit African Parks was formed to manage and promote this national park. Infrastructure has been improved (including construction of a new lodge and a fence along the western border) and anti-poaching activities have increased.

KEY SPECIES

Mammals: Uganda topi

Birds: Ring-necked Francolin (rare), Shoebill, Madagascar (*Squacco-*) Pond-Heron (rare and seasonal), White-backed Night-Heron (rare), Brown-chested Lapwing (seasonal), Forbes's Plover (rare), Bronze-winged Courser, Purple-crested Turaco, Crested and Red-faced barbets, Souza's Shrike (rare), Greater and White-winged swamp-warblers, Miombo Wren-Warbler, Carruthers's and Tabora (*Long-tailed*) cisticolas, Ruaha (*White-headed Black*) Chat, Papyrus Canary (rare).

OTHER SPECIES OF INTEREST

Mammals: Olive baboon, vervet monkey, silver (*gentle*) monkey, northern lesser and thick-tailed greater galagos, yellow-winged bat, lesser elephant shrew, golden (*common*) and side-striped jackals, common dwarf (*dwarf*) mongoose, spotted hyena, rusty-spotted (*blotched*) genet, serval, leopard, aardvark (very difficult to see), African savanna elephant, plains (*common*) zebra, hippopotamus, bushpig, common warthog, "Masai" giraffe, Cape (*African*) buffalo, Cape bushbuck, Lake Victoria sitatunga (very difficult to see), common eland, Sudan oribi, Bohor reedbuck, Defassa waterbuck, common impala, roan antelope.

Birds: *Almost all of the species shown as occurring in eastern Rwanda in the range maps in* Birds of East Africa *by Stevenson and Fanshawe occur in Akagera. A high proportion of these species are of national interest as this is the only fully intact savannah-type site remaining in the country. This list highlights some of the scarcer and more desirable species from African or region-wide perspectives. Coqui, Red-winged (rare), Shelley's, and Hildebrandt's*

Uganda topi has a small range that includes Akagera NP, where it is quite common. ©Ken Behrens

francolins, Blue Quail, Saddle-billed Stork, Goliath Heron, Rufous-bellied Heron, Palm-nut Vulture, (*Western*) Banded Snake-Eagle, Pallid and Montagu's harriers (boreal winter), Ovampo (*Ovambo*) Sparrowhawk (rare), Ayres's Hawk-Eagle, Denham's and Black-bellied bustards, Gray Crowned-Crane, Water Thick-knee, Long-toed and Senegal lapwings, Lesser Jacana, Hottentot (*Black-rumped*) Buttonquail (rare), Temminck's Courser, Greater Painted-Snipe, Ross's Turaco, Bare-faced Go-away-bird, Thick-billed Cuckoo (rare), Spotted and Verreaux's eagle-owls, Black-shouldered, Swamp, Freckled, Square-tailed, and Pennant-winged nightjars, Blue-naped Mousebird, Giant Kingfisher, Blue-breasted Bee-eater, Lilac-breasted and Broad-billed rollers, Crowned Hornbill, Spot-flanked, Black-collared, and Double-toothed barbets, Wahlberg's and Scaly-throated honeyguides, Bennett's, Green-backed, and Bearded woodpeckers, Gray Kestrel, White Helmetshrike, Marsh Tchagra, Black-headed and Papyrus gonoleks, Gray-headed Bushshrike, Gray-rumped Swallow, White-winged Black-Tit, African Penduline-Tit, Yellow-throated Greenbul, Moustached Grass-Warbler, Fan-tailed Grassbird (*Broad-tailed Warbler*), Singing, Trilling, Stout, Croaking, and Wing-snapping cisticolas, Gray-capped Warbler, Greencap (*Green-capped*) Eremomela, Black-lored Babbler, Southern Black-Flycatcher, Ashy and Swamp flycatchers, Brown-backed Scrub-Robin, Gray-winged Robin-Chat, Collared Flycatcher (rare in boreal winter), Sooty Chat, Mocking Cliff-Chat, Splendid and Rueppell's (*Rüppell's*) glossy-starlings, Violet-backed Starling, Red-billed and Yellow-billed oxpeckers, Green-headed, Green-throated, Red-chested, Purple-banded, and Copper sunbirds, Striped Pipit (rare), Cabanis's Bunting (rare), Slender-billed and Black-necked weavers, Lesser Masked-Weaver, Cardinal Quelea, Fawn-breasted Waxbill, Orange-winged Pytilia (rare), Parasitic Weaver (rare).

HABITAT

The habitats within Akagera NP are the most complex and varied of any site covered in this book and, for ex-

A re-introduced population of African savanna elephant thrives in Akagera. ©Ken Behrens

ample, over 250 species of tree can be found here. In this section we can only touch on the park's diversity and give a broad overview of its main habitat types. In general, there are hills in the western portion of the park, which slope down to a series of wetlands and lakes along the whole eastern side of the park, which is also the border with Tanzania.

Wooded grasslands in which *Acacieae* and *Combretum* are the dominant tree species cover most of this park's gently rolling hills. In general, the trees become sparser as the elevation increases. On the highest hills, especially in the northwest of the park, trees become infrequent and broad stretches are almost pure grassland, dominated by three grass species: redgrass (*Themeda triandra*), thatching grass (*Hyparrhenia filipendula*), and fragrant oil grass (*Cymbopogon afronardus*). The southern hills

are lower-lying and generally support a greater diversity of trees, with less lush grass between. Historically, before the park was reduced by 60%, there was more montane habitat in its western portions, which supported certain bird species that are no longer present within the park's current boundaries.

The whole eastern and much of the central portion of the park is crisscrossed by a series of wetlands, lakes, and rivers that form a contiguous network from north to south. These wetlands are bordered by a band of lush broadleaved woodland, thicket, and gallery forest. This is where the park's vegetation is most complex and diverse, with important tree species including *Albizia*, white thorn (*Senegalia polyacantha*), and figs (*Ficus* spp.). Even within this denser habitat, there are frequent grassy openings. Towards the west, at the bottoms of the hills,

Sunrise in the Mutumba Hills, with the vast Kagera wetlands and Tanzania off in the distance. ©Ken Behrens

Black-bellied Bustard stalking through the rainy season grass. ©Ken Behrens

The normally shy Coqui Francolin can become extroverted during the breeding season. ©Keith Barnes

the broadleaved woodland grades into the drier thorny savannah.

The broadleaved woodland and thorny savannah in the south are different from that in the north. The south of the park is drier, the two habitats are not as strongly differentiated, and both habitats have a miombo (*Brachystegia*) element that produces a slightly different mix of bird species than in the north of the park.

The most conspicuous plant in the great chain of wetlands along the eastern boundary of Akagera is papyrus (*Cyperus papyrus*), which often occurs in huge monospecific stands. Other common marsh genera here include *Cladium*, *Miscanthidium*, and non-papyrus *Cyperus*. Swampy brush occurs where the lush woodland meets the marsh. In some places there are extensive mudflats and floodplains, which can be heavily grassed when wet or become bare and dusty when dry. One of the largest and most impressive floodplains is Kilala, near the park's northern gate.

MAMMALING/BIRDING

This is a huge park in which you could spend a large amount of time. Those keen for a quick mammal "fix" should focus their attention on the Kilala Plain in the north. The easiest way to access this area is via the park's northern Nyungwe gate. Another good sector for mammals is the "giraffe area" near the park's southern gate. The Mutumba Hills in the northwest are covered in very open savannah that is also good for mammal viewing, although it is a longer drive from the Nyungwe gate than the Kilala Plain. Birders are faced with a wider and tougher array of choices since most of the park is excellent for birds! Several interesting miombo-type birds are found mainly or exclusively in the southern third of the park, centered on the park headquarters. This is also a good area for Red-faced Barbet. Lake Birengero offers the best chance for Shoebill, while Lakes Ihema and Shakani are excellent for waterbirds and species associated with lakeside woodland and gallery forest. So birders with limited time should focus their efforts on the southern part of the park, which is also where the park's two lodges lie. But the central and northern portions of the park can also provide rich rewards for the venturesome birder.

A wetland duo: a hippo with a Long-tailed Cormorant. ©Ken Behrens

MAMMAL OVERVIEW

Although Akagera has lost some of its mammal species such as black (*browse*) rhinoceros and lion, it is still an excellent site for mammals. The classic African savannah mammals complement well Nyungwe's chimps and Volcanoes' gorillas. The most conspicuous mammals are the antelopes. Defassa waterbuck is the most common, with a population estimated to be in excess of 1000. These large shaggy-looking antelope favor the park's lakes and wetlands. The slim and elegant common impala is the next commonest antelope and can be found throughout the park. The angular and beautifully colored Uganda topi is common and widespread but does seem partial to the floodplains such as Kilala. Sudan oribi is a smaller and shyer antelope species that is found mainly in bushed grassland and Akagera is one of the best places in Africa to see this widely but sparsely distributed species. Cape bushbuck is found mainly in thick brush and this common but shy species relies on stealth for survival. Bush duiker is similar in habitat and behavior. The slim and fawn-colored Bohor reedbuck shares the wetland and lakeside habitat used by waterbuck. Common eland is the largest African antelope, with the biggest males weighing up to a ton. This species can be found in small numbers in the park, especially in the grasslands on the Kilala Plain and Mutumba Hills in the northwest of the park. Blue wildebeest occurs in small numbers, mainly keeping to open, grassy areas. The beautiful roan antelope is rare throughout much of its African range; indeed it takes some luck to find this uncommon species in Akagera but it is often sighted in the southern sectors of the park. Rocky hills hold a few klipspringer that are likely to be golden klipspringer (see "Species of interest" section). Lake Victoria sitatunga is fairly common in marshes and swampy scrub but the dense nature of its habitat and its shyness make it extremely difficult to see.

Sudan oribi is a scarce grassland-loving antelope. ©Ken Behrens

Akagera's lakes support some immense Nile crocodiles. ©Keith Barnes

The heavyweights of the park are the African savanna elephant, Cape (*African*) buffalo, and hippopotamus. They are all best searched for around the park's lakes and wetlands and all range widely, albeit only at night in the case of the hippo. Elephants occurred naturally in the park but were extirpated in the 1960s. In 1975, elephants were re-introduced and their current population is estimated at around 120 individuals. Three of the re-introduced elephants were hand-reared and one, nicknamed "The Chief", became rather too familiar with humans. This elephant became a scourge to the communities neighboring the park and was famous for his love of the local banana beer: the construction of a western border fence was undoubtedly celebrated by the local brewers! Black (*browse*) rhinoceros was introduced in 1957 and thrived for decades, and its population reached over 50 in the late 1970s. Unfortunately, poaching in the early 1980s decimated the population and

the last confirmed sighting was in 2007. Fortunately, plans to re-introduce rhinos in the near future are being considered.

Akagera holds an introduced population of "Masai" giraffe, which is fairly common in the park. The "giraffe area" in the south and Kilala Plain in the north are the best places to see them. Common warthog is not rare and can be found throughout. Bushpig is probably not uncommon but being rather shy it prefers dense woodland and gallery forest where it is hard to spot. "Boehm's" plains (*common*) zebra is also common, with a population estimated at around 500. The giraffe area, Mutumba Hills, and Kilala Floodplain are good areas for zebra.

Predators are not seen as frequently here as in parks such as Masai Mara and Serengeti. Lions and wild dogs have been extirpated or driven across the border into Tanzania, although plans are afoot to re-introduce lions. Leopard and serval are present in the park, but typically are shy and hard to see. The loud vocalizations of spotted hyena are easily heard at night but seeing these animals by day requires some luck. Golden (*common*) and side-striped jackals are present but not often seen. Akagera holds several mongoose species, with common dwarf (*dwarf*) being the most frequently sighted. Look for these highly sociable little predators around termite mounds. Spotlighting at night gives the best chance of seeing many nocturnal mammal species including white-tailed mongoose, rusty-spotted (*blotched*) genet, African civet, wild cat, and maybe even the near-mythical aardvark and pangolin.

Akagera doesn't have Nyungwe's diversity of primates, but does host lots of olive baboons and vervet monkeys, which are found throughout the park's wooded and forested areas. Silver (*gentle*) monkeys also live in Akagera and are mainly found in gallery forest. Night drives often turn up thick-tailed greater and northern lesser galagos, commonly called bushbabies.

Akagera's lakes hold large numbers of Nile crocodiles, some of which are impressively huge. Water monitor is a huge and elaborately patterned lizard that can also be found along the shores of the park's wetlands.

BIRD OVERVIEW

Akagera is a typical mixed woodland and grassland savannah park in which you will find most of your target birds by keying in to general habitat rather than by checking specific stakeouts. These first few paragraphs are designed to instruct birders on what birds they can expect in each of the park's habitats. Of course, there are no set rules when it comes to habitat preferences and birds have wings and often do unexpected things. Nonetheless, by improving your understanding of African savannah habitats you are likely to find a lot more birds than someone who rushes between stakeouts or simply wanders through the landscape. Some of the birds mentioned for each habitat below are common, while others are scarce. Just because a species is mentioned for a certain habitat does not necessarily mean that it is easy to find, even if you are in a prime slice of that habitat. The subsequent sections on the southern and northern parts of the park focus mainly on species that are more localized and not necessarily found throughout a given habitat in the park.

Crowned Lapwings thrive on floodplains.
©Ken Behrens

Lizard Buzzard is just one of a bounty of raptors found in Akagera. ©Ken Behrens

The huge Martial Eagle is the top avian predator in savannah environments. ©Ken Behrens

Little Bee-eater can be found throughout much of Rwanda. ©Ken Behrens

Open *Combretum/Acacieae* savannah habitat covers the largest portion of the park. This habitat will henceforth be referred to as "dry savannah". Birds in this habitat often form large feeding flocks that can contain many species. Whistling or playing the call of Pearl-spotted Owlet often brings in individual birds or sometimes even whole flocks as this diurnal bird-eating owlet is much-loathed by small savannah birds. When imitating the owlet's call, remember to do so sparingly and try not to inflict undue stress on responding birds. Frequent members of savannah bird parties that are likely to react allergically to owlet calls include Yellow-fronted Tinker-

Akagera is one of the best places in the world for the localized Red-faced Barbet. ©Christian Boix

Search the shoreline of Akagera's lakes for Water Thick-knees. ©Keith Barnes

bird, Cardinal Woodpecker, Chinspot Batis, Brubru, Black-backed Puffback, Black Cuckooshrike, African Black-headed Oriole, White-winged Black-Tit, African Penduline-Tit, Common Bulbul, Red-faced Crombec, migrant warblers from Eurasia such as Willow and Icterine, Croaking Cisticola, Yellow-breasted Apalis, Green-backed (*Gray-backed*) Camaroptera, Tawny-flanked Prinia, Buff-bellied Warbler, Yellow-bellied Eremomela, Pale Flycatcher, Red-backed (*White-browed*) Scrub-Robin, Scarlet-chested, Mariqua (*Marico*), and Purple-banded sunbirds, Golden-breasted Bunting,

The scarce Rufous-bellied Heron is regularly seen in Akagera. ©Ken Behrens

Yellow-fronted and Black-throated canaries, Black-cheeked (*Black-faced*) Waxbill, and Red-cheeked Cordon-bleu. Other species that occur widely in the park's dry savannah but with little or no tendency to join flocks include Gabar Goshawk, Laughing Dove, Emerald-spotted Wood-Dove, Ross's Turaco, Blue-naped Mouse-bird, Striped Kingfisher, African Gray Hornbill, Slate-colored Boubou, Flap-pet Lark, African Thrush, Greater Blue-eared Glossy-Starling, and Red-billed Quelea. This dry savannah habitat is the first one encountered when entering the southern gate and covers the hills throughout the giraffe area, park headquarters, and Akagera Game Lodge zone. This is also the habitat around the park's northern gate, although the savannah there is moister overall. Most of the park's less-travelled western routes, from the headquarters towards the Rwisirabo ranger station, up to the Nyamabuye

Lookout, and the Mutumba Hills, pass through this habitat. Generally, the higher and more exposed portions of these western hills are grassier and less wooded, and the next paragraph addresses the birds that prefer these grasslands.

Akagera's dry savannah is far from monotonous and ranges from almost pure grassland with only scattered trees to quite dense woodland in transition to the broadleaved woodland. Certain species prefer the more open, grassy portions of savannah, namely, Coqui, Red-winged, and Shelley's francolins, Harlequin Quail, Black-bellied Bustard, Small (*Common*) Buttonquail, Gray-backed and Northern (*Common*) fiscals, Rufous-naped Lark, Gray-rumped Swallow, Fan-tailed Grassbird (*Broad-tailed Warbler*), Stout Cisticola, Whinchat (boreal winter), African (*Common*) Stonechat, Sooty Chat, Plain-backed Pipit, and Yellow-throated Longclaw. Most of these spe-

Lilac-breasted Roller is one of Africa's most beautiful birds. ©Ken Behrens

Shelley's Francolin is a shy species of open grassland. ©Ken Behrens

(African) Wattled Lapwing showing off its wattles. ©Keith Barnes

cies prefer the fairly arid hilltop grassland found in the west of the park, although some also occur down into grassy woodland openings and floodplains. Some species such as Long-billed Pipit, Familiar Chat, and Cinnamon-breasted Bunting use grassland, but only when there is a significant component of exposed rocks or bare rocky ground. The best example of grassland habitat is probably the Mutumba Hills but it can be found in many other places in the western hills, including around the Muyumbu campsite.

The park's other major woody habitat is the matrix of broadleaved woodland, thicket, gallery forest, and grassy openings found along the shores of the wetlands and lakes in the park's lower-lying areas. Sometimes this habitat is referred to as "groundwater forest" but for convenience it will henceforth be referred to as "lush woodland". It is the most complex and also the most diverse in terms of birds. Species best searched for in this lush woodland include Hildebrandt's Francolin, (*Western*) Banded Snake-Eagle, African Goshawk, Little Sparrowhawk, Black Goshawk (*Great Sparrowhawk*), Crowned Hawk-Eagle (*African Crowned Eagle*), African Hobby, Red-eyed Dove, Blue-spotted Wood-Dove, Tambourine Dove, African Green Pigeon, Eastern (*Gray*) Plantain-eater, Yellowbill, African Pygmy-Kingfisher, Woodland Kingfisher, Broad-billed Roller, Crowned Hornbill, Yellow-rumped Tinkerbird, Black-collared and Double-toothed barbets, Lesser, Scaly-throated, and Greater honeyguides, Golden-tailed, Green-backed, and Bearded woodpeckers, Brown-throated Wattle-eye, Tropical Boubou, Black-headed Gonolek, Sulphur-breasted and Gray-headed bushshrikes, African Paradise-Flycatcher, Greencap (*Green-capped*) Eremomela, African Yellow White-eye, Ashy Flycatcher, White-browed Robin-Chat, Splendid and Rueppell's (*Rüppell's*) glossy-starlings, Collared, Green-headed, and Bronze sunbirds, Cabanis's Bunting, Baglafecht, Black-necked, and Spectacled weavers, and Holub's Golden-Weaver. Lush woodland can be found all along the shores of Akagera's lakes and wetlands. The majority of the Lake Shore Road, running from intersection 9 all the way up to intersection 28 in the north of

Red-necked Francolin (*Spurfowl*) is Akagera's most common francolin. ©Keith Barnes

the park, passes through this habitat. Specific places to access this habitat include the area between intersection 9 and the fishing camp, the Shakani campsite area, the road adjacent to Lake Birengero, and the road to the "Hippo Beach" from intersection 25, to name but a few.

Many species thrive in both dry savannah and lush woodland. Some of these are only found in the denser, lower-lying dry savannah and the drier and sparser lush woodland, while others are found throughout both habitats, from the driest dry savannah to the most moist and densest lush woodland, which is essentially gallery forest. Species commonly found in both habitat types include Helmeted Guineafowl, Red-necked Francolin (*Spurfowl*), African Harrier-Hawk, Lizard Buzzard, Shikra, Ring-necked Dove, Meyer's (*Brown*) Parrot, Bare-faced Go-away-bird, Levaillant's, Red-chested, Black, African, Klaas's, and Dideric cuckoos, White-browed Coucal (which also thrives in the marshes), Pearl-spotted Owlet, Speckled Mousebird, Gray-headed Kingfisher, Little Bee-eater, Lilac-breasted Roller, Green Woodhoopoe, Common Scimitar-bill, White Helmetshrike, Black-crowned Tchagra, Fork-tailed Drongo, Singing and Trilling (very common) cisticolas, Black-lored and Arrow-marked babblers, Southern Black-Flycatcher, African Thrush, Violet-backed Starling, Western (*African*) Citril, Brimstone Canary, Red-headed and Village weavers, Green-winged Pytilia, and Red-billed Firefinch.

Patches of grassland and thicket that are especially rank and usually found within lush woodland are the best place to seek out certain species including Marsh Tchagra, Moustached Grass-Warbler, African (*Dark-capped*) Yellow-Warbler, Cardinal Quelea, Black-winged (*Red*) Bishop, White-winged, and Fan-tailed widowbirds, Fawn-breasted and Black-crowned waxbills, and Pin-tailed Whydah. This kind of rank habitat is found throughout the lush woodland from intersection 9 to 28 but becomes

(*Western*) Banded Snake-Eagle is an uncommon denizen of lush woodland and gallery forest. ©Keith Barnes

Woodland Kingfisher, just one of an array of kingfisher species that occur in Akagera. ©Ken Behrens

more frequent in the slightly wetter northern reaches of the park. One especially good area to try is south of intersection 25, described below as a likely site for Blue Quail. The wet and swampy scrub that occurs where lush woodland meets papyrus and other types of wetland is particularly attractive to species such as Giant Kingfisher, Yellow-throated Greenbul, Gray-capped Warbler, Swamp Flycatcher, Red-chested and Copper sunbirds, Black-headed (*Yellow-backed*) and Grosbeak weavers, Crimson-rumped and Common waxbills, and Bronze Mannikin. Most of these species will range into both lush woodland and wetland (especially papyrus) but seem to spend most of their time where these two habitats meet.

Akagera's vast wetlands are one of the park's most outstanding features and are one of the largest protected wetlands in East Africa. Species to look for throughout the lakes, rivers, and wetlands include White-faced and Fulvous whistling-ducks, Comb (*Knob-billed*) Duck, Egyptian and Spur-winged geese, Red-billed Duck (*Teal*), Hottentot Teal, African Open-bill, Abdim's, Wooly-necked, Saddle-billed, and Yellow-billed storks, Great and Long-tailed cormorants, African Darter, Great White Pelican,

Hamerkop, Gray, Black-headed, Goliath, Purple, Squacco, Rufous-bellied, and Striated herons, Great, Intermediate, Little, and Cattle egrets, Black-crowned Night-Heron, Glossy, Sacred, and Hadada ibises, African Spoonbill, African Fish-Eagle, and Malachite and Pied kingfishers. Southern Pochard and Great Crested Grebe are best scanned for on extensive stretches of open water. All along the eastern side of the park, from Lake Ihema up to Lake Rwanyakazinga, wetland habitat can be found.

Certain bird species are found throughout the park's marsh habitat, both in the tall papyrus swamps and in the lower *Cladium* and *Miscanthidium* marshes: Little Bittern, African Marsh-Harrier, Black Crake, Purple Swamphen, Allen's Gallinule, African Jacana, Long-toed Lapwing, African Reed-Warbler, Lesser Swamp-Warbler, Little Rush-Warbler, Winding and Carruthers's cisticolas, and Slender-billed and Northern Brown-throated weavers. Papyrus Gonolek (common), Greater Swamp-Warbler (uncommon), White-winged Swamp-Warbler (fairly common), and Papyrus Canary (rare) are all specialties that are confined to the papyrus swamps.

The flat ground covered in short grass that is typical of floodplains attracts several species including Spur-winged Plover (*Lapwing*), Senegal, Crowned, and (*African*) Wattled lapwings, Temminck's Courser, Banded

Yellow-billed Oxpecker on a plains (*common*) zebra. ©Ken Behrens

Yellow-throated Longclaw is common in the grasslands of Akagera. ©Sam Woods

Martin, African (*Grassland*) and Plain-backed pipits, and Red-billed (*Black-chinned*) Quailfinch. The giraffe area south of intersection 6 and the Kilala Plain in the north are prime examples of this habitat, which is common elsewhere adjacent to the eastern wetlands.

Fairly bare stretches of lake shoreline are prime areas for searching for Water Thick-knee, Cape Wagtail, plus several species of migrant shorebirds. This habitat can be found in certain places along the shore of Lake Ihema, including the short loop around intersections 10, 11, and 12, as well as in many other places.

A handful of species are mainly found around human structures: Black Kite, Ruaha (*White-headed Black*) Chat, Northern Gray-headed Sparrow, and Village Indigobird. The two species of oxpeckers, Red-billed and Yellow-billed, are best searched for in the vicinity of large mammals: Red-billed tends to be found on smaller mammals such as warthogs and antelope,

while Yellow-billed prefers sizeable mammals including Cape (*African*) buffalo and giraffe.

This is an excellent park for raptors. Keep an eye on the sky for Black-shouldered Kite, Black Kite, African Fish-Eagle, White-backed, Lappet-faced, and White-headed vultures, Rueppell's (*Rüppell's*) Griffon (*Vulture*), Black-breasted and Brown snake-eagles, Bateleur, Augur Buzzard, Tawny, Wahlberg's, and Martial eagles, African Hawk-Eagle, Eurasian (*Common*) and Gray kestrels, and Peregrine and Lanner falcons.

Swifts and swallows spend most of their time on the wing and can be seen almost anywhere; most species prefer to nest near wetlands and are most frequently seen around the lakes. Watch almost anywhere for Alpine, Mottled, Common, White-rumped, and Little swifts, African Palm-Swift, Plain Martin, Bank, Barn, Angola, Wire-tailed, and Red-rumped swallows, Lesser Striped-Swallow, Common House-Martin, and White-headed Sawwing.

Defassa waterbuck is the most common antelope in Akagera. ©John Wilkinson

Large numbers of boreal migrants from Europe and Asia pass through or spend the winter in Akagera. Species that are most likely in savannah and lush woodland are Common Cuckoo, European Roller, Red-backed, Rufous-tailed, and Lesser Gray shrikes, Wood, Eastern Olivaceous, Icterine, and Garden warblers, and Spotted Fly-catcher. Wetlands and grasslands host White Stork, Blue-cheeked and European bee-eaters (migrant groups of which can appear in the sky anywhere in the park), Sedge Warbler, Great Reed-Warbler, Whinchat, Northern Wheatear, and Western Yellow Wagtail. Virtually all of the migrant shorebirds known from Rwanda have been recorded from the wetlands of Akagera. Migrant raptors include European Honey-Buzzard, Eurasian Marsh-Harrier, Pallid and Montagu's harriers, Common (Steppe) Buzzard, Steppe, Lesser Spotted, and Booted eagles, Lesser Kestrel, and Eurasian Hobby.

SOUTHERN AKAGERA

The southern third of Akagera is the most frequently visited portion of the park and has most visitor facilities, including a day visitor center, the park's headquarters, two lodges, two campsites, and an extensive network of well-maintained gravel roads for exploration. The mammals here are not quite as good as those in the north (especially in the Kilala Plain) but are nonetheless still good, especially in the giraffe area. The birding is excellent. The savannah has more of a miombo element here than in the north of the park and supports several species at the far northern limits of their ranges. Purple-crested Turaco and Crested Barbet are fairly common in the dry savannah. Miombo Wren-Warbler is less common and conspicuous but not rare and a frequent member of feeding flocks. Tabora (*Long-tailed*) Cisticola is common here and also occurs in the north of the park, albeit less frequently. Souza's Shrike is an enigmatic resident that seems to occur at very low densities in the dry southern savannah.

Birding stops prior to the southern Kiyonza gate of Akagera can be productive, especially at the small village of Rwinkwavu (covered under site 11). Watch especially for Ruaha (*White-headed Black*) Chat around any villages. There is fairly good savannah habitat for about 1km before reaching the gate (S1° 53.940 E30° 40.915). About 300 m after passing through the Kiyonza gate, turn left onto a side road (of intersection: S1° 53.791 E30° 40.966) that will take you to a couple of loops through the giraffe area. There is excellent dry savannah throughout much of this area (see the "Bird Overview" above for a review of the species possible in this habitat). Just south of junction 6 there is a flat, short-grassed floodplain that can be interesting **A** (S1° 51.863 E30° 40.800), although it may be impossible to drive here when it is wet. This open area is good for mammals like giraffe, Bohor reedbuck, Uganda topi, and common warthog, often with one or both species of oxpeckers in attendance. Brown-chested Lapwing, a scarce migrant from West Africa that mainly occurs from July to December, has been recorded here. Also look for Bronze-winged Courser around dawn and dusk, plus Denham's and Black-bellied bustards, Harlequin Quail, Crowned and (*African*) Wattled lapwings, and African (*Grassland*) and Plain-backed pipits. The small dam in the northern part of the floodplain is a good place to wait at dusk for Square-tailed, Swamp, and Pennant-winged nightjars.

Looping back to the main road via junctions 5 and 2 or 5, 4, and 3, you arrive at the park's day visitor center **B**,

It takes serious luck to find the very low-density Souza's Shrike in Akagera, at the far northern edge of its range. ©Christian Boix

a good place to get information about the park. Park guides are available for hire here, although they are not compulsory. They can be very helpful in navigating, guiding you to good spots for mammals, and sometimes for birding as well. About 1.5 km east of here there is the park headquarters and the Akagera Game Lodge (GPS of lodge: S1° 52.450 E30° 42.917). Although the lodge and HQ are surrounded by dry *Acacieae*, *Combretum*, and *Brachystegia* savannah, in the immediate vicinities there are some exotic trees and irrigation supports a lusher microhabitat that attracts species that are more typical of the lush woodland around Lake Ihema that lies below. Fruiting *Ficus* trees or *Euphorbias* in the lodge grounds, along with the surrounding dry woodland, are one of the best stakeouts in the park for the highly localized Red-faced Barbet. Other species that favor the lush oasis around the lodge include Meyer's (*Brown*)

Parrot Purple-crested Turaco, Spot-flanked Barbet, Bennett's Woodpecker, Blue-naped Mousebird, Black-backed Puffback, African Pied Wagtail, Mocking Cliff-Chat, Familiar Chat, Green-cap (*Green-capped*) Eremomela, Red-faced Crombec, Tabora (*Long-tailed*) Cisticola, Southern Black-Flycatcher, Pale Flycatcher, Angola Swallow, White-winged Black-Tit, African Penduline-Tit, Scarlet-chested Sunbird, Rueppell's (*Rüppell's*) Glossy-Starling, Violet-backed Starling, Red-headed, Village, and Baglafecht weavers, Green-winged Pytilia, Bronze Mannikin, and Village Indigobird. Little Swift, Lesser Striped-Swallow, Red-rumped Swallow, and Rock Martin all nest on the human structures in this area. The lodge's hilltop location makes it an excellent place to scan for swifts, swallows, and migrating bee-eaters and raptors, perhaps even with a cold drink in hand! Scarce species including Ayres's Hawk-Eagle,

Brown-chested Lapwing is a scarce migrant from West Africa and the Congo Basin that occurs in Akagera mainly from July to December. ©Keith Barnes

Night excursions can turn up the remarkable Pennant-winged Nightjar. ©Ken Behrens

Striped Pipit, Souza's Shrike, and Orange-winged Pytilia have all been seen within 300 m of the lodge. The enigmatic Ring-necked Francolin has even been recorded on the ridges and knolls around the lodge, but beware of the presence of similar Shelley's, Red-winged, and Coqui francolins. Listen carefully for the Ring-necked's odd and distinctive call.

The sector of the park immediately west of the park HQ and Akagera Game Lodge – in other words, intersections 1 to 6 – is excellent for night drives. There are chances for nocturnal mammals such as white-tailed mongoose, thick-tailed greater and northern lesser galagos (including some odd melanistic individuals), scrub hare, elephant shrew, spotted hyena, African civet, rusty-spotted (*blotched*) genet, and occasionally jackals and leopard. The potential for nocturnal birds is excellent. Pennant-winged Nightjar, which is undoubtedly one of the most thrilling birds in Africa, is frequently

seen. Freckled Nightjar is often recorded, especially around rocky outcrops. Square-tailed and Swamp nightjars tend to prefer open grassy hilltops, as around the Muyumbu Campsite. Black-shouldered and European nightjars are sometimes recorded, the latter only during the boreal winter. African Scops-Owl is fairly common, while Spotted and Verreaux's eagle-owls are occasional. One specific place to look for Spotted Eagle-Owl is the small gravel quarry 260 m south of intersection 3 (GPS of quarry: S1° 52.902 E30° 42.500). Although do-it-yourself night drives were permitted in the past, they are now forbidden and visitors are asked to return to their lodge or campsite by 6 pm. Night drives are offered by the national park in a park vehicle and at writing cost $40 per person for a 2–3 hour drive. If you have specific places you'd like to visit or certain species to target, make sure to discuss this with the park staff when arranging the night drive.

From intersection 3 near the HQ and Akagera Game Lodge, you can go north to explore a large area of dry savannah and grassland. Look for Crested Barbet, especially along the first kilometer of this route. Drive 3.6 km to the Muyumbu Campsite (GPS S1° 50.980 E30° 43.275). This is a good area for general dry savannah birding, with species like African Hawk-Eagle, Ross's Turaco, Common Scimitar-bill, Yellow-fronted Tinkerbird, Red-faced Barbet, Gray-backed Fiscal, African Black-headed Oriole, Flappet Lark, Plain-backed Pipit, Sooty Chat, Croaking and Tabora (*Long-tailed*) cisticolas, and Yellow-breasted Apalis. Rwanda's first record of Green-backed Eremomela recently came from near Muyumbu. The campsite is an excellent place for night birds, namely Square-tailed, Swamp, and Freckled nightjars, and African Scops-Owl.

To reach the lakes that lie below and their associated marshes and lush woodland, head down the hills from the lodge towards intersection 9, losing 300 m of elevation along the way. The place where the road makes a couple of sharp bends while descending the escarpment **C** (GPS S1° 53.730 E30° 42.635) is good for Purple-crested and Ross's turacos. Also look out here for flowering *Albizia* trees that can attract sunbirds including Variable, Green-throated, Mariqua (*Marico*), and Purple-banded. At intersection 9 (GPS S1° 54.132 E30° 43.366) you reach the Lake Shore Road and can turn south (right) to Ruzizi Tented Lodge or north (left) to the rest of the park. Ruzizi offers good lush woodland and wetland birding all around the lodge, with species such as Giant Kingfisher, African Green Pigeon,

Brown-throated Wattle-eye, Black-headed Gonolek, White-browed and Red-capped robin-chats, Ashy Flycatcher, and Red-chested Sunbird.

Driving north from intersection 9 a stop in the strip of lakeside lush woodland **D** (GPS S1° 53.523 E30° 43.957), which is quite narrow here, can be productive for most of the species mentioned for lush woodland habitat in the "Bird Overview" above, while wetland species can be seen on the lake itself. Species that have been recorded in this area include Yellow-rumped Tinkerbird, Carruthers's Cisticola, Gray-capped Warbler, Gray-winged Robin-Chat, Ashy Flycatcher, Shelley's (Kakamega) Greenbul, and Black-necked Weaver. Gray-rumped and Angola swallows can sometimes be seen swooping over the adjacent open areas.

The national park offers boat trips on Lake Ihema. They visit an island with a large waterbird breeding colony that may hold Great and Long-tailed cormorants, African Darter, Black-crowned Night-Heron, Cattle, Little, Intermediate, and Great egrets, Squacco, Goliath, and Black-headed herons, and African Openbill. The boat trip also offers a chance to see some impressively huge Nile crocodiles, hippos, and sometimes other large mammals. Boat trips can be arranged at the day visitor center or HQ. At writing, prices were $30 per person for a trip for a day trip and $40 per person for a dusk trip. Dusk trips have occasionally scored the rare and very shy White-backed Night-Heron in the past.

After driving 2 km north from intersection 9, you arrive at a fishing village (GPS S1° 53.312 E30° 43.994) where Marabou Storks often lounge about. If you continue another 1 km, you arrive at intersection 10 ( S1° 52.842 E30° 44.183). Turn right to make a short loop that gives views of a productive stretch of the shoreline of Lake Ihema. Only 700 m down the loop road, check the lakeside for a small weaver colony that often hosts Slender-billed Weavers (S1° 52.967 E30° 44.517). Scan the shoreline for Water Thick-knees and a variety of mammals including African savanna elephant, Cape (*African*) buffalo, and Uganda topi, which can be found around all of the park's lakes. After looping around, you arrive at intersection 12 (S1° 52.547 E30° 44.568). Turning right/north will bring you to Shakani campsite (S1°52.216 E30°44.795), which offers an excellent mix of lush woodland and wetland, including papyrus,

and a corresponding variety of birds. This is a good area to get out of the car and do a bit of ranging on foot but beware of the large mammals present here: hippopotamus, buffalo, and elephant are common, and there are also huge crocodiles in these lakes. Birds to look for here include Spur-winged Plover (*Lapwing*), Long-toed Lapwing, Red-chested Cuckoo, Brown-throated Wattle-eye, Papyrus and Black-headed gonoleks, Yellow-throated Greenbul, White-winged Swamp-Warbler, Ashy Flycatcher, Collared Sunbird, Holub's Golden-Weaver, and Golden-breasted Bunting.

Back on the main road, at intersection 11 (S1° 52.511 E30° 44.277), you can turn to the north to continue towards Lake Birengero. The first 2 km of this route stay close to the western shore of Shakani, which can

Tabora (*Long-tailed*) Cisticola is fairly common in the park, especially in the southern sector. ©Ken Behrens

be scanned for additional waterbirds. After leaving Shakani, drive about 3 km to where you start to see Lake Birengero through the woodland to the east ⓔ. This papyrus-fringed lake is the best place in Rwanda to look for Shoebill, although it has always been hard to find here and seems to be more difficult every year. Any place that offers a good view is worth scanning and it can be worth stopping even when there is no view; walk cautiously, birding as you go, for 200 m eastwards through the woodland to reach the lakeshore and then scan from there. The Shoebills seem to prefer the far side of the lake, up to 1 km away, so a scope is often essential for getting decent views. When arriving from the south, stop at the first place that offers a clear view of the lake ⓔ (GPS S1° 49.147 E30° 44.536) where Shoebills have been seen many times. Walking about 150 m east brings you to an excellent swath of papyrus that holds a full suite of papyrus specialty birds, including the elusive Papyrus Canary, plus waterside scrub birds such as White-chinned Prinia and Red-chested Sunbird. Also look for Crowned Hawk-Eagle (*African Crowned Eagle*) in the excellent lush woodland, especially just to the north of ⓔ.

Midway along the western shore of Birengero at intersection 13 (GPS S1° 48.753 E30° 44.472) you can turn west and leave lush woodland and enter vast stretches of rarely visited dry savannah and grassland. Continuing north on the main road 600 m, you reach intersection 14 (GPS S1° 48.434 E30° 44.303). Drive east on a short access road through lush woodland to reach an excellent vantage point for

Shoebill and all manner of other wetland birds. White-headed Sawwing and (*Western*) Banded Snake-Eagle are two other uncommon species that have been recorded here.

Visiting the sites described so far, from the Kiyonza gate through the park's headquarters, down to Lake Ihema, and north to Lake Birengero, will make for at least one very full day, and several days could easily be spent in this sector of the park alone. Intrepid visitors with more time on their hands can continue north to explore Lakes Murambi, Kivumba, and Hago, the adjacent lush woodland, and the dry savannah on the hills to the west. The mammal and bird overview sections above will be helpful for those targeting certain species in this central area. Driving all the way through the park in one day to exit the northern Nyungwe gate is possible but would be very rushed, especially for birders. Even those focused on mammals will probably find that doing less driving and spending more time stopping and scanning in promising spots will turn up more of their quarry than this kind of marathon drive.

NORTHERN AKAGERA

Despite being less frequently visited and having fewer visitor facilities (just one campsite), the park's northern sector still offers rich rewards to those who visit. Those keen to see mammals will be entranced by the Kilala Plain, Rwanda's own miniature version of the Serengeti or Masai Mara.

Although it is possible to drive through from the southern end of the park, most visitors will arrive from the west and enter at the northern Nyungwe gate (GPS S1° 27.040 E30°

The Mutumba Hills are scenically beautiful and great for large mammals. ©Ken Behrens

32.592). Check the weavers nesting around the gate: most will be Village Weavers, but the uncommon Lesser Masked-Weaver has been recorded here. Park guides are available for hire at the Nyungwe ranger post and are very helpful in navigation and in showing you the best recent areas for mammals. Contracting rangers is not compulsory.

From the Nyungwe gate, turn north and drive for 6 km to where you see the flat, grassy expanse of the Kilala Floodplain to your north and east. This area is one of the highlights of Akagera NP as it usually holds high concentrations of large mammals and has an epic scenic beauty that is more often associated with Kenya or Tanzania than with Rwanda. To explore the plain, follow the existing tracks; off-roading is strictly forbidden, although it does occur and continues to be a problem. Watch for plains (*common*) zebra, "Masai" giraffe, Cape (*African*)

buffalo, Sudan oribi, Bohor reedbuck, Defassa waterbuck, Uganda topi, and common eland. On the bird front, this is a good area for Gray Crowned-Crane, Pallid and Montagu's harriers (during the boreal winter), Black-bellied Bustard, Senegal and Crowned lapwings, Banded Martin and other swallows (especially migrants on passage during boreal spring and fall), Yellow-billed Oxpecker, and Zitting Cisticola, as well as other grassland floodplain species. Shoebill has even been sighted a few times in the wetter portions of the plain.

If you turn south rather than north at the Nyungwe gate and ranger station, you will quickly climb onto the savannah and grassland-covered hills that dominate the northwestern sector of the park. After passing junction 34 about 9 km from the Nyungwe gate there is a strip of thicker woodland that runs for about 3 km along a valley bottom to the west of the road. One

The Kilala Plain is a beautiful place that is usually full of big mammals, almost like Rwanda's miniature version of the Ser

particularly good spot is about 12 km from the gate ❻ (📷 S1° 31.032 E30° 36.884). Look for Red-faced Barbet perching in the trees along this lush strip, along with Striped Kingfisher, Black-collared Barbet, Singing Cisticola, Tawny-flanked Prinia (which is not particularly common in Akagera), Greencap (*Green-capped*) Eremomela, and Green-winged Pytilia.

Continue south for around 2 km to junction 35, where you turn right/

west onto a road that steeply climbs into the heart of the Mutumba Hills region. From here onwards, the road is rough in spots and a 4x4 vehicle becomes necessary. Within 1 km of the turn, watch for Fan-tailed Grassbird (*Broad-tailed Warbler*). The next 10 or so kilometers pass through sparse dry savannah and open grassland. This whole area is good for Cape (*African*) buffalo, Sudan oribi, common eland, and plains (*common*) zebra. It is also

Behrens

1800 m and is the highest point in the park. Look for Coqui and Shelley's francolins, Brown Snake-Eagle, Lizard Buzzard, Martial Eagle, Black-bellied Bustard, Brubru, Rufous-naped Lark, Stout (abundant), Siffling (scarce), and Wing-snapping (in the wetter grassland) cisticolas, Sooty Chat (common), Yellow-throated Longclaw (common), and Cinnamon-breasted Bunting. If you spend the night at Mutumba, listen and watch for Swamp Nightjar, and savor what is likely to be an unforgettable sunset and sunrise.

Towards the eastern side of Akagera's northern sector lies Mohana Plain on the shores of Lake Rwanyakazinga. This is an excellent place for a variety of big mammals including Cape (*African*) buffalo and Uganda topi. Another interesting place to visit in the northeast of Akagera is the "Hippo Beach" or *Plage aux hippos* **H** on the shore of Lake Mihindi. This spot is a slow 50–60 km drive from the Nyungwe gate, but makes a convenient stop for those driving through the park. To reach the Hippo Beach, drive to intersection 25 (▨ S1° 32.726 E30° 43.270) and continue eastwards on a side road about 2.2 km to an open spot on the lakeshore (▨ S1° 32.105 E30° 44.165). This is indeed a great place to see hippos, which spend their days in the shallow water just offshore. The sights and sounds of a pod of hippos seen at close range are not easily forgotten. This is also a decent birding spot, with good papyrus and general wetland birding: look for Eurasian Marsh-Harrier (boreal winter), Papyrus Gonolek (common here), Greater Swamp-Warbler, and Slender-billed Weaver.

Blue Quail has been seen in an interesting area with lush patches of grass-

scenically beautiful, with sweeping views over to the eastern wetlands and across the border into Tanzania. The Mutumba Hills campsite (▨ S1° 36.112 E30° 38.772) lies in this stretch and is the only place to sleep in the northern sector of the park. The vicinity of the camp – especially the ~2 km of the main road to its north **A** – offers some of the best birding in the area. The main road runs along the top of Mount Mutumba at just over

land within lush woodland that can be reached by driving 4.3 km south of intersection 25 on the main road ❶ (GPS S1° 34.770 E30° 43.288). If you fail to find Blue Quail in this particular spot, it is worth exploring the whole area as there is a lot of similar habitat interspersed with the lush woodland in the north of the park.

TIME

A lightning-fast tour could take in the highlights of the southern part of the park or the Kilala Plain in one day, but those wanting to savor this exquisite park should plan to spend five days to a week here. Three days are enough for seeing a good proportion of the park's mammals and birds. A birder's approach will depend on how much time they have spent elsewhere in Africa. Those who are new to the continent will want to spend more time and locate a higher proportion of the park's huge bird list. Birders who have already spent some time birding the continent, especially elsewhere in East Africa, may want to make a shorter visit that is focused on Red-faced Barbet, miombo specialties, and/or papyrus specialists (including Shoebill). Regardless of your plans, bear in mind that driving through the park from one gate to another takes a full day and would mean a rush that would be too much for most people.

DIRECTIONS

Driving to the southern Kiyonza gate of Akagera from Kigali takes 2–3 hours on a good paved road. Reaching the northern Nyungwe gate takes about an hour longer. There is some birding along the way to both gates (see site 11).

There are three accommodation options inside the park: Ruzizi Tented Lodge, Akagera Game Lodge, or camping at one of the three campsites. Ruzizi is an upmarket lodge situated on the shores of Lake Ihema. Bookings can be made through African Parks (e-mail: ruzizi@african-parks.org; tel.: +250 (0)787113300). Akagera Game Lodge is on a hill near the park headquarters. Book with the lodge directly (e-mail: akagera01@yahoo.de; tel.: +250 (0)785201206). Both lodges are in the southern part of the park. The Muyumbu and Shakani campsites are also situated in the south of the park and both are excellent for birding. Muyumbu is on a hill in the *Acacieae/Combretum* savannah, while Shakani is on the shore of Lake Shakani. The third campsite, Mutumba Hills, is in the northwest of the park. Though the open savannah and grassland at Mutumba are good for birding, this campsite is not as diverse for birds as the other two campsites. It compensates for this by offering good chances of large mammals (buffalo, common eland, Uganda topi, Sudan oribi, and others) right from the campsite, plus some of the most spectacular views in the park. There is no need to book for the campsites, unless you want to rent the park's camping equipment, in which case you need to book and the park staff will set up your tent before you arrive. For more information on Akagera, visit the African Park's website: www.african-parks.org/Park_2Akagera+National+Park%2C+Rwanda.html. ◆

Mashoza Parike Woodland and Abudada Dam

About 7 km northwest of the town of Kibungo, capital of Ngoma District, there is a very small tract of degraded but still productive lush woodland. It lies in the village zone or *umudugudu* of Mashoza and the locals, who have protected it as a place to collect firewood call it *Parike* (from the French "Parc"). It lies in a lush, green, farmed valley dotted with remnant fig trees. Approximately 1 km east of the woodland there is a dammed lake known as Abudada. Collectively, this valley provides some of the most productive birding on mainly agricultural land in Rwanda and the 180-odd species

recorded here demonstrate that birds and people can survive (if not thrive) alongside one another even in densely populated farming areas. Mashoza Parike is one of only a handful of

Olive-bellied Sunbird is a highly localized species in Rwanda that can be found in the Mashoza Parike.
©Ken Behrens

remaining patches of lush lowland woodland in the east of the country away from Akagera NP. This site demonstrates how rewarding such woodlands must have been before their destruction to make way for the ever-increasing human population. It holds an interesting mix of species and is something of a missing link between the true montane forests of Nyungwe NP and elsewhere in the west, and the savannah and woodland now mainly confined to Akagera NP. This mix includes desirable forest species such as Narina Trogon, Luehder's (*Lühder's*) Bushshrike, Gray-winged and Snowy-crowned robin-chats, Mountain Illadopsis, and Black-billed and Black-necked Weavers. Mashoza Parike is also a reliable site for the locally scarce Olive-bellied Sunbird. Abudada Dam has yielded such birds as Little Bittern, Lesser Moorhen, Purple Swamphen, Marsh Tchagra, and the ever-scarce White-collared Oliveback. The woodland has been given some degree of protection and an ecotourism project may be set up here in the near future, which would be well worthy of support.

SPECIES OF INTEREST

Birds: Yellow-billed and Comb (*Knob-billed*) ducks, Red-necked Francolin (*Spurfowl*), African Openbill, Little Bittern, African Goshawk, Wahlberg's Eagle (intra-African migrant), Lanner Falcon, Palm-nut Vulture, African Wood-Owl, Black Crake, Lesser Moorhen, Purple Swamphen, Blue-headed Coucal, Levaillant's Cuckoo (seasonal), African Green-Pigeon, Narina Trogon, African Pygmy-Kingfisher, Tambourine Dove, Purple-crested and Ross's turacos, Eastern (*Gray*) Plantain-eater, Double-toothed, Crested, and Spot-flanked barbets, Green-backed and Golden-tailed woodpeckers, African Black-headed Oriole, Brown-throated Wattle-eye, Marsh Tchagra, Black-headed Gonolek, Orange-breasted (*Sulphur-breasted*) and Luehder's (*Lühder's*) bushshrikes, Black Cuckooshrike, White-headed Sawwing, White-tailed Blue-Flycatcher, Rueppell's (*Rüppell's*) Glossy-Starling, Violet-backed Starling,

A Double-toothed Barbet duo on the woodland edge. ©Ken Behrens

Mountain Illadopsis, Yellow-throated and Yellow-whiskered greenbuls, Black-lored Babbler, Gray Apalis, Red-faced, Chubb's, and Trilling cisticolas, White-chinned Prinia, Gray-capped Warbler, African (*Dark-capped*) Yellow-Warbler, Sedge and Marsh warblers (boreal migrants), Little Rush-Warbler, Red-capped, Snowy-crowned and Gray-winged robin-chats, Olive-bellied, Red-chested, Green-headed, and Copper sunbirds, Cape Wagtail, Thick-billed Seedeater, Black-billed, Black-necked, Northern Brown-throated, Slender-billed, Vieillot's (*Black*), and Compact weavers, Black-winged (*Red*) and Yellow bishops, Fan-tailed Widowbird, White-collared Oliveback, Green-winged Pytilia, Black-and-White Mannikin, Red-headed Bluebill, Peters's Twinspot (rare), Black-crowned, Crimson-rumped, Fawn-breasted, and Yellow-bellied waxbills, African Firefinch.

HABITAT

Mashoza Parike is a small, degraded, broadleaved native woodland, approximately 800 m long by 300 m wide at its widest point. There is invasive *Lantana* in places where the forest has been opened by woodcutting. The woodland is fringed by agricultural land with some mature fig trees, rice paddies, small areas of scrub, and exotic *Eucalyptus*, fir trees, and banana plants. The nearby Abudada Dam has aquatic plant cover at its shallow eastern end and is fringed by a variety of exotic and native trees (including figs, *Acacieae*, and others).

BIRDING

Follow the "Directions" below to get to Abudada Dam. Scan the open water, the shores, and the vegetation east of the lake from the road above the dam. Species such as African Jacana, Black Crake, White-faced Whistling-Duck, Yellow-billed Duck, and Black-headed Heron are usually present, while Knob-billed Duck, Spur-winged Goose, Little Bittern, Intermediate Egret, and Lesser Jacana – all less common – are possible here. A telescope will be very useful here but less practical when birding elsewhere at this site. After you have thoroughly checked the lake, backtrack to the west up the road on which you arrived. Walk down the road for 250 m and then turn left onto the first small path that you encounter in the village as the road winds up the hill. This small path will bring you back to the lakeside, where weavers such as Black-headed (*Yellow-backed*), Slender-billed, and others, are usually in evidence. The dam is on the western side of the lake and is where, in a couple of mature *Acacieae* trees, Green-backed, Cardinal, and Golden-tailed woodpeckers are often seen, along with Ross's and Purple-crested turacos. The stream that runs out of the dam is flanked by thick vegetation that is very productive for species such as Gray-capped Warbler, White-collared Oliveback, and boreal migrants including Marsh and Sedge warblers.

Continuing west, there is a major road that you should cut across while keeping the stream on your left. Once across the main road, continue walking west on a small footpath that runs along the north side of the valley. Carefully check the scrub in this area for a variety of species such as Marsh Tchagra and sunbirds (Bronze, Red-chested, Collared, and others) and listen for the startling, loud, whistled calls of the resident Black-headed Gonoleks. This valley often produces locally uncommon species such as Double-toothed and Spot-flanked

Search the thick parts of the Mashoza Parike woodland for Brown-throated Wattle-eye. ©Lee Hunter

barbets, White-tailed Blue-Flycatcher, and Grosbeak Weaver. Scan the sky for raptors all the time, including Wahlberg's Eagle, Bateleur, Augur Buzzard, and Palm-nut Vulture. In any reeds along the stream look for Black-winged (*Red*) Bishop, warblers, cisticolas and Fan-tailed Widowbird.

About 700 m west of the lake, you reach the Mashoza Parike woodland (GPS of center of woodland: S2° 6.585 E30° 30.588). Continue along the path, which curves around the north side of the woodland and bird its flanks as you walk. Although any of the numerous tracks into the woodland can be explored, the best path is obvious after about 500 m, roughly at the center of the northern side of this small patch. Any other paths will often be overgrown but can be productive if you don't mind a few *Lantana* scratches! Inside the woodland,

you should hear Gray Apalis and the gloriously varied refrains of Snowy-crowned Robin-Chat (one of Africa's most serious contenders for the nightingale's crown). Look for Olive-bellied and Copper sunbirds and Black-necked Weaver in the more degraded clearings. Regardless of which paths you explore, walk slowly and quietly; although this woodland is small, there are some excellent birds to be found here. Keep an eye out for Yellow-rumped Tinkerbird, Brown-throated Wattle-eye, White-chinned Prinia, Collared Sunbird, Peters's Twinspot, and Red-headed Bluebill. Small paths in the interior give your best chance for the skulkers like Gray-winged, Red-capped, and Snowy-crowned robin-chats, Mountain Illadopsis, and Luehder's (*Lühder's*) Bushshrike. Other species present here should include Yellow-whiskered and Yellow-throated greenbuls, Black-billed Weaver, and the occasional Narina Trogon. The best path into the woodland loops back to rejoin the boundary path after around 200 m ( of intersection: S2° 6.480 E30° 30.544).

Adjacent to the south side of the forest are rice paddies that are worth scanning for assorted herons and egrets, Hamerkop, African Openbill and Yellow-billed Storks, kingfishers, and the occasional pair of Gray Crowned-Cranes. Keep an ear open for the Little Rush-Warbler's distinctive song and watch the sky for migrating European Bee-eaters and hirundines in spring and autumn.

TIME

These sites are most productive in the early morning and late evening. One hour exploring the dam followed by 2–3 hours in the woodland should suffice. A whole day could easily be spent here if adjacent valleys or less trodden paths through the wood are also explored.

DIRECTIONS

Although this site lies only a few kilometers off of the main paved route, getting here is a little tricky and it pays to follow the directions carefully. A GPS is highly recommended, as is plugging the waypoints below into Google Earth in order to fully understand and visualize the directions.

From Kabarondo (where the dirt road to southern Akagera NP meets the main north-south road in eastern Rwanda) drive about 10 km south to the village of Remera. If you are coming from the south, drive about 8 km north from the Kibungo junction to reach Remera. In Remera there is one

main turn-off to the west (at S2° 5.020 E30° 33.408), a dirt track that stays in reasonable condition all-year-round but can be sticky after heavy rain. Zero your odometer here. Take this road until the prominent fork 800 m from the turn-off (S2° 5.179 E30° 33.084) and follow the fork left. The road straightens out and then at 2 km from the village (1.2 km from the first fork), it forks again; keep left again. After around 5.3 km (at S2° 6.394 E30° 31.316), a small fork turns left down a small hill. Take this fork, and after another 300 m, turn left again. From here, you can see the dam ahead, while the forest is along the valley to your right (west of the lake). Drive 400 m through a small village until you reach a Y-intersection. Turn left, and drive another 800

Mashoza is one of the places where the scarce Palm-nut Vulture has been recorded in Rwanda. ©Ken Behrens

m until you are immediately above the eastern side of the lake. This is a fairly good place to park (at S2° 6.985 E30° 31.430). Try not to block the road and expect a crowd of curious children! The birding directions above start from here.

It is possible to visit this site on foot from the main paved highway, a round trip that entails 12–15 km of hiking and at least a half-day walking. This might be an attractive option for backpacking birders. Although you could walk the driving route described above, there is a shorter route for those who are on foot. Start from the Kibungo turn-off on the main highway, which is about 8 km south of the turn to the woodland described in the driving directions. From the Kibungo turn-off, head northwest for 1.3 km on the main road until you reach Kabare Secondary School. Turn left here onto a small track that takes you past Kabare A Primary School (at S2° 7.623 E30° 32.785). Continue on the same track straight down the hill, ignoring turns to the left and right and continuing in a westerly direction. Pass into a *Eucalyptus* woodland (at S2° 7.35030° E32.225) where the road zigs and zags. At the bottom of the wood you'll see the dam in the distance ahead of you. Continue on the same path for about 1.2 km more until you reach the eastern side of the lake. The directions given above in "Birding" start from this point. ◆

Purple-crested Turaco is usually not difficult to locate in Mashoza Parike, Akagera NP, and elsewhere. ©Ken Behrens

Papyrus Swamps of Southeastern Rwanda

Aside from the well-known national parks, most natural habitat in Rwanda has been converted into agricultural land. However, one major type of natural habitat outside of the parks has often managed to survive intact. Rwanda has extensive tracts of papyrus swamp (technically a marsh, but often referred to as "swamp"), a habitat that provides specialist species, varied and colorful waterbirds, and even several notable mammals. A natural history trip to Rwanda would hardly be complete without enjoying the wildlife of this characteristically African habitat. Despite some areas of papyrus enjoying government protection, the increasing value of sugar cane and rice as cash crops is leading to more and more papyrus being converted into agricultural use. Nonetheless, good tracts remain in many places: close to Kigali (see site 1), in the southeast of the country (covered in this site account), and along Rwanda's eastern fringe where the papyrus in Akagera NP (site 12) is still in good condition.

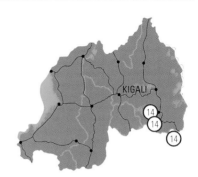

This section covers the papyrus swamps in southeast Rwanda, all part of one large swath of wetland that runs all the way up to Kigali. This stretch is still almost contiguous despite being assaulted by agriculture at many points. The quality of the habitat tends to get better the farther south you go, although even close to Kigali, there are some good species. Some of the best bird species include the stunning (both visually and vocally) Papyrus Gonolek, one of several papyrus specialties, along with the shy White-winged Swamp-Warbler and

very rare Papyrus Yellow-Warbler. Rufous-bellied and Black herons, Lesser Jacana, and Allen's Gallinule are some of the other desirable species still found here. Shoebill, the king of the papyrus, has alas not been recorded here for many years, and persists only in small numbers in Akagera NP and possibly on the northern shores of Lake Rweru, where large tracts of mostly pristine papyrus still remain. The fringes and overgrown cultivation adjacent to papyrus swamps are often very productive, holding species such as Splendid Glossy-Starling and White-collared Oliveback.

KEY SPECIES
Birds: Greater and White-winged swamp-warblers, Papyrus Yellow-Warbler (rare), Carruthers's Cisticola, Papyrus Gonolek, Papyrus Canary.

OTHER SPECIES OF INTEREST
Mammals: Hippopotamus, Lake Victoria sitatunga, African clawless otter, silver (*gentle*) monkey.

Birds: Pink-backed Pelican, Little Bittern, Rufous-bellied, Goliath, and Black herons, Madagascar (*Squacco*) Pond-Heron, Marabou Stork,

Rush-Warbler, Red-faced, Trilling, and Winding cisticolas, Gray-capped Warbler, Swamp Flycatcher, Black-lored Babbler, Red-chested Sunbird, Splendid Glossy-Starling, Spectacled, Grosbeak, Red-headed, Slender-billed, and Northern Brown-throated weavers, Holub's Golden-Weaver, Lesser Masked-Weaver, Fantailed and Red-collared widowbirds, Yellow and (*Southern*) Red bishops, White-collared Oliveback, Fawn-breasted, Crimson-rumped, and Black-crowned waxbills, Black-and-white Mannikin.

HABITAT

Permanently waterlogged valleys with river channels fringed by aquatic vegetation dominated by papyrus (*Cyperus papyrus*) sedges. Shallow lakes can often be found within the papyrus. The marshes are bordered by various kinds of cultivation, including rice paddies, wet scrub, and in some cases, patches of degraded woodland.

MAMMALING/BIRDING

The wildlife watching is similar at all of the sites described in this section and so this first paragraph will consist of a general treatment of the mammals and birds of the southeastern papyrus swamps, while the subsequent paragraphs will give details of access and specific places to visit at each site.

Papyrus swamps are often difficult to bird. During the middle of the day, the hot sun usually forces the wildlife to keep a low profile and so dawn is by far the best time to visit. Since Rwanda is on the equator, the sun rises at 6 am all year and dawn is a fleeting affair. Don't forget to don mosquito repellent before you set off. The vivacious dawn chorus will include Blue-headed Coucal, Papyrus Gonolek, White-winged Swamp-Warbler, and African Reed-

The sensational Papyrus Gonolek livens up its marshy habitat. ©Ken Behrens

African Openbill, Glossy Ibis, Spur-winged Goose, Comb (*Knob-billed*) Duck, Fulvous Whistling-Duck, African and Eurasian (boreal winter) marsh-harriers, African Fish-Eagle, Osprey (boreal winter), Peregrine Falcon, Allen's Gallinule, Gray Crowned-Crane, Water Thick-knee, Long-toed Lapwing, Purple-crested and Ross's turacos, Levaillant's and Dideric cuckoos, Blue-headed Coucal, Square-tailed Nightjar, Giant Kingfisher, African Pygmy-Kingfisher, Blue-cheeked (boreal winter) and Blue-breasted bee-eaters, Spot-flanked Barbet, Golden-tailed and Green-backed woodpeckers, Black-headed Gonolek, Brown-crowned and Marsh tchagras, Common House-Martin (boreal winter), White-headed Sawwing, Cape and Yellow (boreal winter) wagtails, Yellow-whiskered Greenbul, African (*Dark-capped*) Yellow-Warbler, Lesser Swamp-Warbler, African and Great (boreal winter) reed-warblers, Sedge, Marsh, and Icterine warblers (all boreal migrants), Little

Warbler, as well as both Winding and Carruthers's cisticolas (learn the differences in the calls of these two similar congeners). Birds commuting between roosting and feeding sites just after dawn include ducks and geese, above all Yellow-billed and Comb (*Knob-billed*) ducks, Fulvous and White-faced whistling-ducks, Spur-winged Geese, Great, Intermediate, Little, and Cattle egrets, and Goliath, Purple, Black-headed, Black, Striated, and Rufous-bellied herons (the first three common, and the latter three uncommon). Ponds and lakes are likely to have active gallinules such as Purple Swamphen, Black Crake, and

Red-knobbed Coot, as well as the rarer Allen's Gallinule and possibly migrating crakes in spring and autumn. Keep an eye out for Papyrus Gonoleks patrolling territories at this time of day and also for marsh-harriers (both African and Eurasian), which do a good job – along with the occasional Peregrine Falcon – of flushing up the many species buried in the marsh. Listen for the characteristic display flight of Carruthers's Cisticola and carefully scan any areas of bushes among the papyrus for weavers and waxbills, which often feed on the fringes of the swamp. Scan for bee-eaters, bearing in mind that Little is commoner than

Malachite Kingfisher occurs in wetlands throughout Rwanda. ©Ken Behrens

Blue-breasted, and listen for the very similar calls of Blue-cheeked and European bee-eaters overhead, mainly during boreal fall and spring migration. If you spot movement among the reed beds, it could be silver (*gentle*) monkeys, African clawless otters, or even Lake Victoria sitatunga. Investigating tracks and roads into the papyrus will often yield rewards. Hirundines are plentiful, especially migrant species, and they can often be found flocking around bridges.

Ngoma-Bugesera Bridge: Travel south from Kigali, crossing the Nyabarongo bridge detailed in Site 1, and continue on the good paved road through Nyamata and on towards the Burundi border. Watch for a turn-off to the left for the village of Gashora, about 20km south of Nyamata. This turn is also signed for La Palais Hotel, a popular weekend getaway from Kigali. Turn left and drive along this unpaved road for 5–6 km into Gashora. Turn right at an intersection in the town center (GPS S2° 12.514 E30° 14.487) and drive for about 1.8 km to a bridge just outside the town. Explore along the bridge and causeway to the east, keeping an eye out on both sides. A track that is sometimes drivable for several kilometers runs north from the bridge road (from GPS: S2° 12.442 E30° 15.524) and is worth checking out, although with care as this road is in poor condition. If you continue east on the main road, there will be footpaths heading both north (easy) and south (treacherous after rain!) along the shores of the fast-flowing river. The trail heading north continues for a long way and so you should retrace your steps when you have gone far enough.

Kabaya: If you are driving from Tanzania towards Kigali or if you have visited Mashoza Parike Woodland and have time for another birding venue, this area of marsh was still productive at the time of writing (despite being rapidly converted into rice paddies). It lies on the border between Ngoma and Kirihe Districts in southeast Rwanda and the main road from the Tanzanian border (at Rusumo, see be-

Swamp Flycatchers are partial to papyrus swamps. ©Ken Behrens

low) to Kigali runs right past. If you have no private transport, a number of buses also travel along this road and drivers will be happy to stop on the command of *Hagarara*! The best place to start exploring is on the north side of the village of Kabaya (S2°16.130 E30° 32.841). There is a small track that leaves the main road here and heads west through the wetlands towards a small village on the other side of the valley. You will see rice paddies to the north and papyrus swamps to the south. Once across the wetlands, you can continue around the western fringe of the papyrus where footpaths and a small hill provide vantage points over the wetland.

Bare: Along with a tiny tract of degraded broad-leaved woodland, some of the best papyrus swamp birding in southeast Rwanda can be accessed through this village. Getting here is fairly complicated. Unless you have a local guide with you who can ask the way, you should probably engage the services of a motorcycle-taxi driver and follow them in your vehicle or get on the back of the bike if you have no transport of your own. From the turn-off to Kibungo village (S2° 8.235 E30° 33.421), drive south into and through Kibungo, past the hospital, and continue as the road turns to dirt. At a junction about 3 km south of the center of Kibungo (S2° 11.140 E30° 31.988), take the right fork heading southwest. Then, in 2.2 km, at another junction (S2° 11.071 E30° 30.914), take the road to the left (south) and continue to Bare. From this left turn, it should take about 30 minutes on a fairly poor road to arrive in the town. Once in Bare (S2° 16.352 E30° 29.367), you can take

Though drab in non-breeding plumage, the male (*Southern*) Red Bishop is a sight to behold in its breeding colors. ©Ken Behrens

the road to the east (through S2° 16.420 E30° 29.456), which descends in about 4 km to a river crossing and a good area of papyrus (S2° 17.620 E30° 30.040) where all the key species are found. Alternatively, take the road south about 4 km (through S2° 16.649 E30° 29.219) to the end of the Bare peninsula, where there is a small tract of degraded but still productive broad-leaved woodland (S2° 18.096 E30° 29.002) and a small lake. Footpaths allow you to explore this area well, which may be worthwhile as it harbors a lot of species in addition to the papyrus specialties.

Rusumo: Rusumo is a village that lies on the Kagera River on the Rwanda/Tanzania border. There is some good papyrus swamp just upstream

African Fish-Eagles patrol Rwanda's lakes and wetlands. ©Ken Behrens

(southwest) of the village and there is also an interesting track north of the village that can be explored either on foot or by vehicle. From Rusumo village (GPS S2° 23.014 E30° 46.727), there is a footpath that heads south towards the edge of the papyrus. After walking for about 700 m there is some reasonable habitat that holds many papyrus species (GPS S2° 23.345 E30° 46.692). If you are feeling adventurous, continue northwest along the edge of the swamp about 800 m to where you will find the edge of an excellent and extensive patch of papyrus (GPS S2° 23.112 E30° 46.365). Another place worth birding lies just north of the village of Rusumo. Leave the main paved road towards the east side of the village (GPS S2° 22.980 E30° 46.854) and follow a track first west and then north around a large hill and then up to the hilltop (GPS S2° 22.673 E30° 46.924) where the views are excellent and the birding is often good.

Look out along the way for Striped Pipit and Moustached Grass-Warbler. This steep gorge is also a good place for raptor watching, especially during migration, due to the powerful thermals generated by the wind as it passes through the valley. There is a resident pair of Peregrine Falcons in the area, a fairly rare bird in Rwanda, and this is also the only location in eastern Rwanda where White-necked Raven is regularly seen.

TIME

The first 2–3 hours of the day are usually the most productive, although late afternoon can also be quite good. In general, three hours will provide a good sample of the habitat and species at any of the specific sites covered in this account.

DIRECTIONS

See under "Mammaling/Birding" section. ◆

Makera Forest

Makera Forest (not to be confused with Mukura in western Rwanda) is the only tract of native forest remaining in southeast Rwanda. It is small (0.6 km^2) but given its location on the edge of the Akagera papyrus system close to the Tanzanian border and the habitat type (groundwater forest), it is a precious refuge and remnant of the much more extensive gallery forest that would have lined this river valley in the past. Makera is well off the beaten track and reaching it requires some effort. Not surprisingly, it is little studied and may hold either resident or vagrant species that are currently unknown in Rwanda. Thus, a visit here should be considered exploratory and of scientific importance. Interesting records should be sent to the authors and forwarded to the African Bird Club Rwanda representative. Despite being protected, selective cutting both for firewood and timber continues. If nothing changes, Makera will eventually diminish or disappear and another precious Rwandan refuge will be lost forever.

SPECIES OF INTEREST

Mammals: Silver (*gentle*) Monkey.

Birds: Long-crested Eagle, Eastern (*Gray*) Plantain-eater, Meyer's (*Brown*) Parrot, Yellow-rumped Tinkerbird, Slate-colored Boubou, White (*White-crested*) Helmetshrike, African Black-headed Oriole, Yellow-throated and Yellow-whiskered greenbuls, Gray Apalis, Trilling Cisticola, Rueppell's (*Rüppell's*) Glossy-Starling, Holub's Golden-Weaver, Black-headed (*Yellow-backed*) Weaver, (*Southern*) Red Bishop, Yellow-fronted Canary.

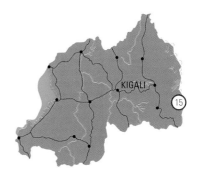

HABITAT

A partially degraded tract of groundwater forest, including yellowwoods (*Podocarpus*), many of which have been removed, and palms. There are also tracts of papyrus nearby. The small patches of degraded *Acacieae* woodland around the forest are unprotected and are likely to be chopped down in the near future.

BIRDING

Once you arrive at the village near Makera Forest, as described below under "Directions", park your car and begin your exploration on foot. Take mosquito repellent as mosquitoes are active here during the day. There are several footpaths leading 100 m across the fields between the village and the forest. Walk along the edge until you find one of many tracks entering the forest, used for firewood collection and the removal of larger trees for timber (both illegal). A guard is employed to supposedly protect the forest and he will probably find you before you enter the forest. If you do not speak Kinyarwanda, you will need an interpreter or good mimicry to explain what you are doing. There was no es-

Search inside of Makera Forest for yapping groups of Yellow-throated Greenbul. ©Ken Behrens

tablished entrance fee as of 2010. It is difficult to get lost along these paths, but you may want to take a GPS reading at the point you enter the forest as a precaution.

Foraging flocks are likely to contain Yellow-rumped Tinkerbird, Lesser Honeyguide, African Black-headed Oriole, Yellow-throated and Yellow-whiskered greenbuls, African Paradise Flycatcher, Gray Apalis, Green-backed (*Gray-backed*) Camaroptera, African Yellow White-eye, Collared Sunbird, and others. In the swampier parts of the forest, keep an eye and ear out for an unidentified greenbul species seen in 2010 that may be White-throated Greenbul, a species still unconfirmed in Rwanda.

On the north side of the forest, small hills harbor remnants of drier *Acacieae* woodland that are good for species such as Eastern (*Gray*) Plantain-eater, Meyer's (*Brown*) Parrot, Slate-colored Boubou, White (*White-crested*) Helmetshrike, Trilling Cisticola, and Rueppell's (*Rüppell's*) Glossy-Starling. The papyrus fringes should harbor most of the papyrus specialties (including Papyrus Gonolek and White-winged Swamp-Warbler), as well as more widespread wetland species like Black-headed Heron, African Jacana, Wood Sandpiper (boreal winter), Spur-winged Plover (*Lapwing*), Woodland and Malachite kingfishers, Western Yellow Wagtail, (*Southern*) Red Bishop, and Black-headed (*Yellow-backed*) Weaver.

TIME

Although the forest is small, if you manage to reach this remote site, it is worth exploring the whole forest, which can take the best part of a day. For those with limited time, it is easy to bird the two main trails in a half-day.

DIRECTIONS

The forest is located about 30 km northwest of Kirehe town and 32 km north of Rusumo town on the Tanzania border ( of forest: S2° 6.448 E30° 50.869). You will almost certainly need either local knowledge or a GPS – and perhaps even printouts from Google Earth or Maps to get here. The access road is unpaved and best attempted in a 4x4, especially during the wet season. After leaving the main paved road, it can easily take an hour to reach Mukura Forest, given the poor road quality.

From the main paved road, which leads north to Akagera and eventually to Kigali, take the Nyakarambi turn-off (□ S2° 17.449 E30° 44.411). This junction is about 12 km north of the Rusumo border crossing into Tanzania. Travel northeast through Nyakarambi village and 8.3 km after leaving the paved road, turn left (□ S2° 15.171 E30° 48.244) and then quickly left again (□ S2° 14.950 E30° 48.343) towards Kamamo. Continue due north, past Kamamo village on your right. Two kilometers after the second left turn, turn right (□ S2° 13.904 E30° 48.357) and follow the main road as it twists first northeast, then sharply southeast, then north-

east again. From the second twist to the northeast, you will see papyrus swamps to the east. From here it is about 12 km north to Makera on an easy-to-follow road. The forest here is on your right, just east of the main road and a village (□ of village: S2° 6.758 E30° 50.728). Park anywhere here, take one of the paths across the fields, and explore the forest along numerous well-trodden trails that lead into its heart. From Nyakarambi to Makera the total journey is about 27 km.

To use local knowledge, consult the motorcycle-taxi riders at Nyakarambi, Kirehe, or Rusumo, who may know Makera, and will definitely know the village of Kamamo, halfway there. One could be engaged to show the way, or to drive you if you have no vehicle. From Kamamo, there is only one road north along the side of the river valley and papyrus swamps, which runs the 15 km to Makera. ◆

African Jacana is found in the wetlands adjacent Makera, and in most of Rwanda's wetlands. ©Ken Behrens

Mammal taxonomy and nomenclature follows the *Handbook of the Mammals of the World* (HMW) published by Lynx Edicions (2009–2013) for the families already completed by this encyclopedia and *The Kingdon Field Guide to African Mammals* (1997) for species not covered by HMW. Where taxonomy differs between HMW and Kingdon, we follow HMW, placing the alternative Kingdon name in parentheses and *italics*.

For birds, this section (as the rest of the guide) follows the latest *Clements Checklist of Birds of the World* (2007, with revisions through 2013) published by Cornell University Press. There are a few species that are split or named differently in the region's best field guide, *Birds of East Africa,* by Stevenson and Fanshawe (2002), whose alternative names are in parentheses and *italics*.

Threatened species status as designated by the IUCN are Critically Endangered, Endangered, Vulnerable, or Near Threatened. Species in **bold** are Albertine Rift endemics (AREs). We also highlight several races or subspecies that may be split in the future. Alternate names of some potential splits are given in parentheses, but not italics.

This icon **O** next to a species name means that a photo of the species is included in the section.

L'Hoest's monkey is commonly seen along the roadside in Nyungwe NP. ©Keith Barnes

SPECIALTY MAMMALS

CHIMPANZEE

This great ape is even more closely related to humans than gorillas. Seeing the lively and aggressive chimps offers a rather different perspective on the human family tree than an encounter with the generally docile gorillas. Nyungwe NP and the adjacent Cyamudongo Forest, which is administered as part of the park, offer a good chance of seeing chimps. Although there are many more chimps in the forest proper, they are often easier to see within the confines of Cyamudongo, where a habituated troop often allows close approach and observation. Nevertheless, it is always best to arrange a tracking permit and a skilled tracker with RDB before arriving in Rwanda.

"MOUNTAIN" EASTERN GORILLA

Along with the orangutan, chimpanzee, bonobo, and western gorilla, the eastern gorilla is one of the great apes and one of the closest living relatives to humans. The local race of gorilla, *beringei*, is endemic to the Albertine Rift forests of the Virungas and Bwindi. It seems that *beringei* separated from eastern lowland gorillas (*graueri*) about 400,000 years ago after these two races had separated from western gorilla (*gorilla*) around 2 million years ago. However, their specific status remains somewhat controversial. Some authorities (e.g. Kingdon) consider them to be one polytypic species. Western (nominate) and eastern (*graueri + beringei*) are sometimes considered two species such as in HMW; but occasionally all three taxa are considered separate species. Notwithstanding these scientific digressions, seeing gorillas in the wild is definitely one of the top wildlife-watching experiences on offer anywhere on the planet. Rwandan gorillas were extensively studied and made famous by Dian Fossey and her primatological colleagues between the late 1960s and early 1980s. In light of Fossey's work, an ecotourism program has developed in Volcanoes NP and has become one of the great conservation success stories of recent decades. Money generated through gorilla tracking has contributed to the increasing population of this critically endangered taxon and numbers of these "mountain" eastern gorillas continue to rise (880 at the last census).

ANGOLAN (*PIED*) COLOBUS

This is the most common monkey in Nyungwe NP and can be encountered almost anywhere. The local subspecies *ruwenzorii* is endemic to the Albertine Rift. Although official tracking is available from the national park, you are likely to bump into this species without need of any special effort to see it; even the small patch of forest on the Gisakura Tea Estate sometimes holds a troop. However, near Uwinka there is a huge "super-troop" of around 400 individuals, one of the largest monkey troops in the world. If your aim is to see this troop, sign up for the official tracking and let the park guides know that this is your goal.

GUEREZA (*COLOBUS*)

The *occidentalis* race of this widespread monkey historically occurred in northwest Rwanda. One would expect to see it at Volcanoes NP as it has been recorded in the adjacent Mgahinga (Uganda) and Virungas (DRC) National Parks. However, it is possible that not enough lowland forest for this species remains in Volcanoes. In any case, keep an eye out for this species in any low-lying forest in the northwest.

JOHNSTON'S (*GRAY-CHEEKED*) MANGABEY

The taxonomy of this monkey is quite complex. Kingdon prefers to lump all the taxa discussed here with those found farther west in central Africa under the name "gray-cheeked mangabey". The taxon *johnstoni* was originally described as a subspecies of gray-cheeked mangabey but in 2007 certain authorities on mangabeys decided to split the species, a treatment that has been followed by HMW. This species may intergrade with Ugandan crested mangabey on the Rwanda/Uganda border. Although it is known from the Virungas on the DRC side, HMW does not report it in Volcanoes NP. Johnston's mangabey seems to have less contrast between the mantle and general body color and is longer-limbed. In Rwanda, the best-known sites for Johnston's mangabey are in Nyungwe NP, where habituated groups can be tracked.

L'HOEST'S MONKEY ⊙

This good-looking ARE monkey is globally scarce but is usually easy to see in Nyungwe NP, often feeding along the sides of the main road. It also persists in Gishwati Forest and maybe in Mukura Forest too. L'Hoest's is classified as Globally Vulnerable by the IUCN.

DENT'S (*MONA*) MONKEY

This is another monkey with complex taxonomy. According to King-don, the mona monkey superspecies comprises six taxa (*mona, campbelli, lowei, denti, wolfi,* and *pogonias*) that are mostly allopatric (not overlapping) and scattered across West Africa and the Congo Basin from Senegal to Uganda and Rwanda. The race *denti* has also frequently been subsumed into the crowned monkey (*pogonias*) group. More recently, authorities such as Groves (2001) have considered the taxon *denti* to be a distinct species, a treatment followed by HMW. Within Rwanda, Dent's monkey is scarce in Nyungwe NP, where it is probably most easily seen at Cyamudongo.

OWL-FACED MONKEY

This rare and beautiful monkey occurs in Nyungwe NP and is seemingly confined to the extensive remote bamboo zone in the south. Although a habituation program has been contemplated in the past, for now this species is essentially inaccessible to visitors.

SILVER (*GENTLE*) MONKEY

This group poses another complex taxonomic issue since both this taxon (*dogetti*) and that of the Virungas golden monkey (*kandti*) have been considered part of the widespread gentle monkey (also called "blue" monkey) superspecies by authorities such as Kingdon. Groves (2001) and HMW consider it to be a good species but it hybridizes readily with several other conspecific monkeys. Silver (*gentle*) monkey occurs widely in Rwanda in almost any forest habitat and sometimes even in papyrus swamps. It is common in Nyungwe and Volcanoes NPs, and also occurs in the southeastern papyrus swamps, Akagera NP, and Makera Forest.

Carruther's mountain squirrel is endemic to the Albertine Rift. It forms an interesting link between two of Africa's major groups of squirrels. ©Trevor Hardaker

VIRUNGAS GOLDEN (*GENTLE*) MONKEY

This is another complex taxonomic issue as both this taxon (*kandti*) and that of the silver (*gentle*) monkey (*dogetti*) have been considered part of the widespread gentle monkey (also called "blue" monkey) superspecies by authorities such as Kingdon. This near-endemic monkey is heavily reliant on bamboo. It occurs in Gishwati Forest and Volcanoes and Nyungwe NPs, where it is much rarer than the silver (*gentle*) monkey. Volcanoes NP is by far the best place to see it, as two troops have been habituated and an official tracking activity is offered. Although not nearly as essential as pre-arranging gorilla-tracking permits, to avoid disappointment it is still best for those interested in pursuing this species in Volcanoes NP to arrange permits with RDB beforehand.

CARRUTHER'S MOUNTAIN SQUIRREL ⊙

This small squirrel has greenish-brown overall coloration and a barred tail, and is endemic to the Albertine Rift. It seems to be a morphological bridge between two of Africa's biggest squirrel groups: the rope squirrels (*Funisciurus*) and the bush squirrels (*Paraxerus*). It looks like a bush squirrel but is currently classified as a rope squirrel. It is fairly common in Nyungwe NP.

BOEHM'S SQUIRREL

This charming little ARE squirrel looks and acts like a chipmunk, although it is a bit more arboreal than most true chipmunks. It is common in Nyungwe NP.

RUWENZORI SUN SQUIRREL

This medium-sized gray squirrel with a barred tail is endemic to the Albertine Rift and is fairly common in Nyungwe NP.

AFRICAN CLAWLESS (*SWAMP*) OTTER

Although Kingdon considered the taxon *congicus* as a separate species (swamp otter), HMW has decided to include it within the African clawless otter group pending further taxonomic research and review. This mainly West African taxon occurs in Nyungwe NP. The Kamiranzovu Marsh is the best place, although sighting this shy species requires a serious slice of luck. The African clawless otters that occur in eastern Rwanda (e.g. Akagera NP) and elsewhere in papyrus swamps in the southeast probably represent a different race from *congicus*.

RUSTY-SPOTTED (*BLOTCHED*) GENET

Although this species is widespread across much of the Afrotropics, it is likely to undergo thorough taxonomic review soon and the taxon in East Africa (*letabae*) may well prove to be a separate species.

AFRICAN PALM CIVET

This bizarre member of the monospecific family Nandiniidae may be the carnivore equivalent of the coelacanth, with some ancient traits shared only with fossils. African palm civets are arboreal and primarily frugivorous, moving around in pairs and small groups. They occur in Nyungwe NP, although sightings are rare.

AFRICAN GOLDEN CAT

This beautiful species mainly occurs in West Africa and the Congo Basin and is extremely rare throughout Rwanda. The extremely lucky few may see it in Nyungwe NP or Gishwati Forest.

(*BLACK-NECKED*) ROCK HYRAX

Although Kingdon considers the taxon *johnstoni* a separate species ("black-necked rock hyrax"), HMW has decided to include it in the rock hyrax group pending further taxonomic research and review. This taxon can be seen in the Buhanga Forest.

VIRUNGA (*AFRICAN*) BUFFALO

Although Kingdon considers all African buffalo taxa to be conspecific, HMW takes a much more liberal view of Africa's bovines and splits them into four separate species. Both Lake Chad and forest buffalos are extralimital to Rwanda, while Cape (*African*) buffalo is the "common" buffalo found in the country's eastern savannahs. The fourth species, Virunga buffalo (*mathewsi*), has a highly restricted range and is found in extreme SW Uganda, eastern DRC, and western Rwanda. In Rwanda – and worldwide – the best place to see this highly restricted range species is Volcanoes NP. It is not clear whether the taxon that is extinct in Nyungwe was this or the more widespread Cape (*African*) buffalo.

LAKE VICTORIA SITATUNGA

Kingdon considers all sitatunga taxa to be conspecific, but HMW again takes a more liberal view and gives five species for the continent. Rwanda only harbors the Lake Victoria sitatunga (*spekii*), which is not uncommon in Akagera NP but still rarely seen. It is also found elsewhere in Rwanda but is extremely difficult to see, being found mainly in the depths of papyrus swamps.

ROAN ANTELOPE

This handsome antelope is rare throughout its African range and can be seen occasionally in the southern portion of Akagera NP.

UGANDA TOPI

Kingdon considers all topi/tsessebe taxa to be conspecific. HMW, on the other hand, recognizes seven species in Africa, of which this is the only one to occur in Rwanda. The Uganda topi has a small global range, being restricted to southwest Uganda, Rwanda, and the Rutchura Plains of DRC. It is common and easily seen in Akagera NP.

LESTRADE'S (*PETER'S*) DUIKER

Duiker taxonomy is confusing and controversial. In the past many authorities – including Kingdon – lumped the whole Peter's duiker (*callipygus*) complex together. Recently, however, some authorities have began to consider the *weynsi* subspecies of Peter's as a distinct species, "Weyne's Duiker", in which the "Lestrade's duiker" (*lestradei*) is included as a subspecies. However, HMW treats Lestrade's as a full species and therefore as a new Albertine Rift endemic mammal. The bad news is that like the other duikers in Nyungwe (eastern yellow-backed and black-fronted), this species is extremely difficult to see. This is probably the result of extensive hunting and trapping during Rwanda's tumultuous past couple of decades. With the recently increased levels of protection, it is hoped that duiker sightings in Nyungwe NP will become commoner.

BLACK-FRONTED DUIKER

This widespread central African forest duiker is represented in Rwanda by an Albertine Rift endemic taxon *kivuensis*. This subspecies is a possible future split, above all in light of recent developments in duiker taxonomy: two races previously considered part of the black-fronted complex have recently been elevated to full species level and are Albertine Rift Endemics: Itombwe (*hypoxanthos*) and Rwenzori (*rubidus*) duikers, restricted to DRC and Uganda, respectively. The black-fronted duiker is very hard to find in Nyungwe NP.

GOLDEN KLIPSPRINGER

It has recently been realized that klipspringer taxonomy is incredibly complex. What was once considered a single species has been split into 11 species in Africa by HMW. Based on the information given, it is difficult to ascertain which of these species is present in Akagera NP; it would appear to be golden klipspringer, although this needs to be verified by future research. Whichever taxon does occur here, this klipspringer is far from common in Akagera and is found only on a few rocky hilltops.

SPECIALTY BIRDS

RING-NECKED FRANCOLIN

This species, which is nowhere common, has only a small range and is considered Near Threatened. It has been recorded in Akagera NP, mostly on rocky grassland hills in the southern part of the park. Beware of the other francolins that also occur in the same habitat, including Red-winged, Shelley's, and Coqui.

RED-WINGED FRANCOLIN

This slightly larger species is uncommon in Akagera and is found in much the same habitat as Ring-necked (rocky grassland hills).

SHELLEY'S FRANCOLIN

This is another francolin that is uncommon in Akagera NP and is also found in similar habitat to the previous two species; nevertheless, this species seems to prefer slightly more lush grassland.

HILDEBRANDT'S FRANCOLIN

This large francolin is fairly common in Akagera NP. It is usually seen in and around the lush lakeside woodland and gallery forest.

HANDSOME FRANCOLIN

Coveys inhabit forest, bamboo, alpine heath, and forest edges between 2000 and 3500 m in the ARE. This species is best seen in Nyungwe by driving the paved roads, especially in the Uwinka area, early in the morning or late in the evening, when they often allow close approach if you are in a vehicle. Handsome Francolin is often heard on trails but rarely seen well. It also exists in Gishwati Forest and Volcanoes NP where it is much harder to find.

BLUE QUAIL

This beautiful quail is uncommon and sporadic in lush grassland in Akagera NP.

SHOEBILL

The Shoebill is the king of Africa's papyrus specialist species. It may have formerly been more widespread in Rwanda but is now confined to the Kagera River system, mainly within Akagera NP. Lake Birengero is the best place for Shoebill within the park, although it has been seen on the Kilala Plain and even in wetlands outside the park boundary. The Shoebill seems to be declining in Rwanda and is becoming more difficult to find. It is considered Vulnerable by the IUCN.

DWARF BITTERN

This tiny and colorful bittern is a scarce and probably seasonal visitor to wetlands. It is best searched for in and around Akagera NP.

MADAGASCAR (*SQUACCO*) POND-HERON

This rare non-breeding migrant from Madagascar occurs in Rwanda between July and September. There are records from wetlands including those in Akagera. The populations of this species are in fast decline and it is considered Endangered.

WHITE-BACKED NIGHT-HERON ◉

Rwanda is far from the best place to look for this difficult species, although there are records from Lake Kivu and Akagera NP's Lake Ihema.

(*WESTERN*) BANDED SNAKE-EAGLE

This species is scarce and lives in low densities throughout its range. The lush woodland and groundwater forest of Akagera are the best places to search for it. It rarely soars or perches conspicuously, preferring to sit in forest mid-levels and sub-canopy.

CASSIN'S HAWK-EAGLE

This mainly West African and Congo Basin species is rarely but regularly seen in Nyungwe, especially in the high stretches of forest along the main road near the Uwinka camp.

MOUNTAIN BUZZARD

This montane species of east and southeastern Africa is an East African endemic if split from the southern "Forest" Buzzard. Mountain Buzzard

White-backed Night-Heron is occasionally seen on Lake Kivu or Akagera NP's Lake Ihema. ©Christian Boix

is fairly common in Nyungwe NP, especially in the more open eastern side of the park.

BROWN-CHESTED LAPWING

This good-looking shorebird is a non-breeding migrant from West Africa and the Congo Basin. It occurs occasionally in Akagera, mainly from July to December.

HOTTENTOT (*BLACK-RUMPED*) BUTTONQUAIL

This generally rare species exists in Akagera NP but is much less common than the Small (*Common*) Buttonquail. Hottentot Buttonquail is most likely to be found in short, open, and often flooded grassland, rather than in the taller grassland and overgrown cultivation preferred by Small Buttonquail.

BRONZE-WINGED COURSER ⊙
This handsome courser is scarce throughout its large African range. It is occasionally seen in Akagera NP, especially in the giraffe area.

AFEP PIGEON
Afep Pigeon is now extremely rare in Nyungwe – if it still persists at all. Watch for it in the lower, western portions, and in the adjacent Cyamudongo Forest.

GREAT BLUE TURACO
This spectacular "cartoon character" bird is common in Nyungwe, where it occurs up to 2650 m. It also occurs in Gishwati Forest.

BLACK-BILLED TURACO
This beautiful green turaco is fairly common in Nyungwe, where it occurs up to 2400 m. It is also present in Volcanoes NP, albeit less commonly.

RUWENZORI TURACO
This handsome and rather odd turaco has recently been placed in its own genus, *Ruwenzorornis*. Pairs inhabit montane forest between 1900 and 3500 m. It is fairly common in both Nyungwe and Volcanoes NPs but may behave more furtively than other turacos. It is best located by its sharp descending call, which sounds rather squirrel-like and is quite different from the deep and resonant calls of most turacos.

ROSS'S TURACO
Ross's is fairly common and widespread in a variety of woodlands. It is vocal and fairly easy to find in the Cyamudongo tract of Nyungwe NP,

With luck, the elusive Bronze-winged Courser can be found in Akagera. ©Ken Behrens

Akagera NP, Mashoza Parike, and elsewhere. It can even be found on agricultural land if isolated fig trees remain.

BARRED LONG-TAILED CUCKOO

There is reason to believe that the race *montanus* – restricted to the Albertine Rift – is a separate species from *patulus*, the other race in eastern and southern Africa. When vocal, it is obvious that this species is fairly common in Nyungwe but it is still very difficult to see well, even when using recorded calls. This species is also present in Mukura Forest.

CONGO BAY-OWL

Despite reports from Nyungwe, this endangered and mysterious owl is unconfirmed in Rwanda. In the neighboring Itombwe Mountains, the only confirmed locality for this species, it is known to inhabit grassy clearings in montane forest at *c.* 2400 m.

FRASER'S EAGLE-OWL

Fraser's is rare in Nyungwe NP, where it is at the far eastern edge of its range. The forest surrounding the Kamiranzovu Marsh is the best place to search for it.

RED-CHESTED OWLET

This widespread but always hard-to-find owlet is uncommon-to-rare in Nyungwe NP.

ALBERTINE OWLET

This ARE is scarce in Nyungwe, where the only regular localities seem to be the lower-elevation forest around the Kamiranzovu Marsh and the higher forest along the main road west of Uwinka. Elsewhere, it is known to oc-cur between 1100 and 1700 m. Albertine Owlet is considered Vulnerable by the IUCN.

MONTANE (*RWENZORI*) NIGHTJAR ●

The nominate *ruwenzorii* subspecies is an Albertine Rift near-endemic, although there is also an isolated population in Angola. More frequently (including on the Clements list), *ruwenzorii* is treated as a race of Montane Nightjar. Elsewhere, the *guttifer* subspecies is fairly widespread in East African mountains from Malawi to Tanzania. Montane Nightjar is common at Nyungwe, especially where there are clearings in the forest on the road between Uwinka and Gisakura. It occurs in Volcanoes but is much more difficult to find.

ITOMBWE NIGHTJAR

A single specimen from DRC's Itombwe Mountains taken in 1955 is all that is known about this species.

Montane (*Rwenzori*) Nightjar is best searched for in Nyungwe. ©Ken Behrens

There are no records from Rwanda, but it is not out of the question that the wilds of Nyungwe harbor this enigmatic bird.

SCARCE SWIFT
Despite living up to its name, Scarce Swift is regularly recorded in Nyungwe NP. Watch for it in the sky almost anywhere in the park, although the slopes above the Kamiranzovu Marsh are one of the best places.

SCHOUTEDEN'S SWIFT
This species is known only from five records from the foothills of the Itombwe Mountains in adjacent DRC at altitudes of 1000 to 1500 m and has never been reliably recorded in Rwanda. The lower forests in Nyungwe and adjacent Cyamudongo Forest may harbor this species.

MOTTLED SWIFT
This large swift is patchily distributed across much of Africa and is occasionally seen in Akagera NP and elsewhere.

BAR-TAILED TROGON
This species dwells in the central and East African mountains from southern Malawi to the Albertine Rift, with isolated populations also existing in Angola and the Cameroon highlands. It is uncommon in Nyungwe and Volcanoes National Parks.

SHINING-BLUE KINGFISHER
This mainly West African and Congo Basin species has been recorded in Nyungwe but is very rare.

BLUE-BREASTED BEE-EATER
Blue-breasted Bee-eater is uncom-

Yellow-billed Barbet has become rare in Rwanda, mainly occurring in Nyungwe. It was probably more common in the past when Rwanda's middle-elevation forests were more intact.
©Ken Behrens

mon-to-rare in Rwanda and mainly occurs around papyrus swamps. It has been recorded along the Nyabarongo River south of Kigali, at most of the southeastern papyrus sites, and in Akagera NP.

CINNAMON-CHESTED BEE-EATER
This montane species is common across much of Rwanda, including Nyungwe and Volcanoes NPs and has even been recorded in Akagera NP.

WHITE-HEADED WOODHOOPOE
This highly vocal bird is fairly common in Nyungwe NP and Gishwati Forest and can be encountered almost anywhere in forest habitats in these sites.

FOREST WOODHOOPOE

This mainly West African and Congo Basin species was formerly known from Nyungwe NP but may now be extinct. Watch for it in lower parts of the park and in the adjacent Cyamudongo Forest. Any records should be documented.

BLACK-AND-WHITE-CASQUED HORNBILL

This huge and spectacular species is fairly common and vocal in Nyungwe NP. The Bururi road and the Cyamudongo Forest are good places to find this hornbill.

YELLOW-BILLED BARBET ⬤

This is a very rare species in Nyungwe NP and its occurrence – which may be seasonal – is poorly understood. It has been seen on the Kamiranzovu Trail and near the canopy walkway.

GRAY-THROATED BARBET

This species is fairly common in Cyamudongo Forest but rare in the main part of Nyungwe NP.

WESTERN (*GREEN*) TINKERBIRD

This diminutive species has an oddly disjunct range in the mountains of Cameroon, Angola, and the Albertine Rift. It is uncommon in Nyungwe and becomes very difficult to find during the dry season.

RED-FACED BARBET

Akagera NP is one of the best places in the world to see this species whose range is restricted to the Lake Victoria basin. It is fairly commonly encountered, especially around figs and other fruiting trees within drier woodland. For example, the vicinity of the Akagera Game Lodge is one of the best areas. Red-faced Barbet is considered Near Threatened by the IUCN.

DWARF HONEYGUIDE

This diminutive honeyguide is scarce and inconspicuous in Nyungwe NP between 1500 and 2400 m. Care must be taken when identifying this species since Lesser Honeyguide is common throughout Rwanda, sometimes even in the interior of the forest such as Cyamudongo. Least Honeyguide is also present in Nyungwe.

TULLBERG'S WOODPECKER

Tullberg's Woodpecker has a disjunct range in the mountains of East Africa and Cameroon-Nigeria. It can be found in Nyungwe NP, although it is uncommon and inconspicuous.

BUFF-SPOTTED WOODPECKER

This small woodpecker was formerly known from the lower elevations of Nyungwe NP and even from Akagera NP. Now, however, it is extremely rare if not entirely extirpated, so any records should be documented.

ELLIOT'S WOODPECKER

Although Elliot's is rare in Nyungwe, it can be encountered throughout the forest.

GRAY PARROT

This species is under pressure from habitat destruction and the cagebird trade throughout much of its range and Rwanda is no exception. It formerly occurred in Nyungwe NP but has become extremely rare in this park. The recent records from Gisenyi on the shores of Lake Kivu may refer to individuals crossing over from DRC to feed in the fruit trees of lakefront hotels.

Gray-throated Barbet is easily seen in Cyamudongo Forest. ©Keith Barnes

BROWN-NECKED PARROT

The part of Volcanoes NP around Mount Bisoke is a good place to look for this widespread but always scarce species.

AFRICAN BROADBILL

This chunky little bird is uncommon in Nyungwe but can be seen on the Bururi road. Listen for its very loud mechanical "*brrrrrtttt*" display created by flying in a circle and rapidly clapping its wings together.

AFRICAN PITTA

There are records of African Pitta from Nyungwe NP and Buhanga Forest (near Volcanoes NP) but it is rare and its seasonal occurrence is poorly understood. The Buhanga records almost certainly refer to migrants.

YELLOW-BELLIED WATTLE-EYE

The widespread *graueri* race is rare in Nyungwe NP.

RUWENZORI BATIS

This attractive black-and-white species is common in forest throughout Nyungwe NP and is also fairly common in forest habitat in Volcanoes NP and Gishwati and Mukura Forests.

PINK-FOOTED PUFFBACK

Nyungwe NP lies at the upper end of the elevation range for this species, which is uncommon in the park. It is most frequently recorded in lower-lying forest as around the Kamiranzovu Marsh, the Bururi road, and the Karamba Trail. It has also been recorded in the Uwinka area at much higher elevation.

MARSH TCHAGRA

This species is scarce throughout its range. It can be found in Akagera NP, around Abudada Dam, and at some of the papyrus-dominated wetlands in the southeast.

Luehder's (*Lüehder's*) Bushshrike is perhaps most easily found in Cyamudongo Forest. ©Keith Barnes

LUEHDER'S (*LÜHDER'S*) BUSHSHRIKE ●

This monotypic species has an oddly disjunct range in Nigeria and Cameroon and then from southern Sudan south to the Albertine Rift and into western Kenya. It is uncommon in Nyungwe NP, Cyamudongo Forest, and Mashoza Parike.

PAPYRUS GONOLEK

This handsome papyrus specialist is restricted to the Lake Victoria basin. It is found in most of Rwanda's papyrus swamps, including those near Kigali, in Akagera NP, and elsewhere in the southeast. Judging by its calls alone, this gonolek is surprisingly common, but it can be difficult to see well. It sometimes responds well to recordings. The IUCN considers it Near Threatened.

WILLARD'S SOOTY BOUBOU

This species was described in 2010 (Voelker *et al.* 2010) from museum skins. It has gray-to-blue-gray eyes as opposed to reddish-black-to-black in Mountain Sooty, *L. poensis*. Willard's

occurs in lower forest, mainly 1600–1950 m in Uganda and Burundi. The lower elevation ranges of Nyungwe NP have recently been shown to harbor this species and there are records from the Kamiranzovu Swamp area and from the main road near the western park entrance. It should also occur in Cyamudongo Forest. John Bates and Josh Engel of the Field Museum of Natural History and Tropical Birding posted the first recordings of this new species on Xenocanto in 2012.

MOUNTAIN SOOTY (*BLACK*) BOUBOU

The taxonomy of Africa's black boubous including Mountain Sooty, *L. poensis*, is complex (see Voelker *et al.* 2010 for more information). In classical taxonomy, the race *holomelas* was considered endemic to the Albertine Rift. However, it has been shown that many of the lower-elevation "black boubous" in the Albertine Rift are in fact Willard's Sooty Boubous (see above). Furthermore, the relationship between *poensis* from East Africa and the Cameroon mountains is more complex than it would at first appear. Our advice is you make sure that, if you hear members of this complex at various altitudes, you get a look at them (check eye color) and that you record the elevation of your record.

MANY-COLORED BUSHSHRIKE
A variety of taxa and color morphs make the taxonomy of this group confusing. In Rwanda, the ARE subspecies *graueri* is uncommon in Nyungwe NP and less common than Doherty's Bushshrike. In adjacent Uganda, a different subspecies (*batesi*) occurs in lowland forests at Kibale and this subspecies could also occur in lower forest in Rwanda.

DOHERTY'S BUSHSHRIKE
Nyungwe NP is one of the best places in Africa to see this scarce and shy species.

LAGDEN'S BUSHSHRIKE
This is the least common of Nyungwe's forest bushshrikes and is represented by the taxon *centralis,* which lacks the orange wash on the throat and breast. The Rukuzi and Bigugu Trails in Nyungwe NP are the best places to search for Lagden's. It is considered Near Threatened.

MACKINNON'S SHRIKE (*FISCAL*)
This sharp-looking shrike is fairly common in open country and edge habitat throughout most of the country at mid- to high elevations.

SOUZA'S SHRIKE
Souza's occurs in very low densities in the southern part of Akagera NP and adjacent areas. Interestingly, a *Bra-*

Black-tailed (*Montane*) Oriole is a mellifluous resident of montane forest. ©Keith Barnes

chystegia specialist farther south, Sousa's Shrike is restricted to *Commiphora/Combretum* woodland in Rwanda.

BLACK-TAILED (*MONTANE*) ORIOLE ○
This oriole is restricted to East African and Albertine Rift montane forests. It is common in Nyungwe and Volcanoes NPs, and Gishwati and Mukura Forests.

BLACK SAWWING
Black Sawwing is a complex polytypic species (having many variants or subspecies) that most authors now agree comprises a single species of 12 races. However, this species still needs work as several of these subspecies seem not to interbreed. The identity of the races that occur in Rwanda is not well

known; *mangbettorum* has been recorded, while *reichenowi* and *ruwenzori* may also be present.

WHITE-BELLIED CRESTED-FLYCATCHER
The race *toroensis*, with a bluish-gray back and less black on the throat than the nominate race, is endemic to the Albertine Rift. The nominate race occurs in the Cameroon-Nigerian mountain chain. This species is rare in Nyungwe, where it may occasionally be seen joining flocks in montane forest between 1500 and 2400 m.

WHITE-TAILED CRESTED-FLYCATCHER
This member of the fairy flycatcher family is widespread in montane East Africa and is a common flock species in Nyungwe NP and other montane forests.

DUSKY TIT
This all-dark tit occurs at the lower altitudes in Nyungwe NP, mainly on the Bururi road and around Gisakura.

STRIPE-BREASTED TIT ◉
Stripe-breasted Tit comprises three races, all endemic to the Albertine Rift. The Itombwe (*tanganjicae*) and Kabobo (*kaboboensis*) mountains in the DRC each have their own endemic races. Rwanda supports the widespread nominate race. In Nyungwe, this species is fairly common between 1800 and 3400 m, generally preferring high altitude areas such as the Bigugu Trail, the Uwasenkoko Swamp surrounds, and the main road around the Uwinka office. It is also present but uncommon in forested parts of Volcanoes NP, for example on the slopes of Mount Bisoke.

SHELLEY'S (KAKAMEGA) GREENBUL
If split (which Clements does not), Kakamega Greenbul is restricted to the mountains of Kenya, Tanzania, and the Albertine Rift. This species is uncommon in Nyungwe but is best searched for along the lower parts of the Bururi road.

Stripe-breasted Tit, a spunky Albertine Rift endemic. ©Ken Behrens

The stubby White-browed Crombec is a low-density species that is endemic to East Africa and the Albertine Rift. ©Josh Engel/Field Museum

EASTERN (OLIVE-BREASTED) MOUNTAIN-GREENBUL

The *kikuyuensis* subspecies, found in Rwanda, Uganda, eastern DRC, and Kenya, is sometimes considered a full species, "Olive-breasted Mountain-Greenbul". Whatever its true taxonomic designation, this bird is common in montane forest (e.g. Nyungwe NP, Mukura Forest, and Volcanoes NP).

LEAF-LOVE

This mega skulker formerly existed in Rwanda but has apparently been extirpated from the country. All records should be documented.

CABANIS'S GREENBUL

This drab species is uncommon and inconspicuous in montane forest, mainly in Nyungwe NP. It seems to be slightly commoner and easier to find in Cyamudongo Forest.

YELLOW-STREAKED GREENBUL

This greenbul can be quickly recognized by its incessant wing-flicking behavior. It is fairly common in Nyungwe NP and can be found throughout most of the park.

WHITE-BROWED CROMBEC ●

This is an East African and Albertine Rift montane endemic, with three disjunct races. In Rwanda, the Albertine Rift endemic race is *chloronota*. The extremely local *chapini* is known from the Lendu Plateau in adjacent DRC. This race is sometimes treated as a separate species, which unfortunately may be extinct. In Kenya and western Uganda the nominate race is found. White-browed Crombec is uncommon in Nyungwe NP and Mukura and Gishwati Forests.

NEUMANN'S (*SHORT-TAILED*) WARBLER

This species is not uncommon at Nyungwe, but as a stealthy understory inhabitant it is best located by listening for its loud and distinctive three-note call. It prefers altitudes between 1200 and 2400 m, being common on the Kamiranzovu trail and also found on the Karamba trail. Its delightful scientific genus name *Hemitesia* means "partial tesia", which refers to a group of tailless birds from Asia. Although probably unrelated, it is an appropriate name for these birds.

RED-FACED WOODLAND-WARBLER

This is one of the most common ARE birds. The nominate race, present in Rwanda, is less rufous on the face and lacks the gray on the lower breast of *schoutedeni*, which is endemic to the Kabobo Plateau in DRC. This wood-

Cinnamon Bracken-Warbler is one of the most common birds on the eastern side of Nyungwe NP.
©John Wilkinson

land-warbler is common in forest throughout Nyungwe above 1500 m and is present but less common in Volcanoes NP. It is also found in Mukura and Gishwati Forests.

PAPYRUS YELLOW-WARBLER
There are disjunct populations of this very scarce species in Zambia, western Kenya, and Burundi, Rwanda, Uganda, and DRC. It is still found in papyrus sites in southeastern Rwanda but is rare. Papyrus Yellow-Warbler is strangely rare or absent from the papyrus swamps of Akagera NP. This species was formerly found in other wetland sites including the Akanyaru and Rugezi Marshes but may now be extirpated. It is considered Vulnerable by the IUCN.

MOUNTAIN YELLOW-WARBLER
This is supposedly a monotypic species despite many scattered and disjunct mountain populations from Malawi to South Sudan. In Rwanda, it is a common resident between 1800 and 3500 m, where it skulks in rank growth. Mountain Yellow-Warbler is fairly common in Nyungwe and Volcanoes NPs and in Gishwati Forest.

GREATER SWAMP-WARBLER
This hefty warbler is uncommon in the papyrus swamps of Akagera NP and the country's other major wetlands, mainly in the east.

WHITE-WINGED SWAMP-WARBLER
Despite being a monotypic species, this warbler has a disjunct Afrotropical range between Zambia and northeast DRC. It is fairly common in any extensive papyrus swamps. It is very shy and difficult to see well but is vocal and fairly responsive to recorded calls.

GRAUER'S SWAMP-WARBLER

This endangered endemic is scarce but regular in high altitude swamps and sedges in Nyungwe NP, Volcanoes NP, Mukura Forest, and Rugezi Marsh, mostly between 1900 and 2600 m. Nyungwe is the easiest place to find this species. A large population exists in Kamiranzovu Marsh, while a few pairs are also present at the easily accessed Uwasenkoko Marsh on the main road between Butare and Uwinka. In Volcanoes NP, it can be found around Lake Ngezi.

EVERGREEN-FOREST WARBLER

The race *barakae* is an Albertine Rift endemic, occurring from the Ruwenzoris to Itombwe and southwest Rwanda. It is rare but occurs in both Nyungwe and Volcanoes NPs. It is difficult to separate visually this race from the nominate Cinnamon Bracken-Warbler and vocalizations are thus key to identification.

CINNAMON BRACKEN-WARBLER ◉

The widespread nominate race is common in forested sites including both Nyungwe and Volcanoes NPs.

RUWENZORI (*COLLARED*) APALIS

This species is a fairly common Albertine Rift endemic, preferring low-to-middle levels of the forest. It is now considered to be monotypic, although birds from Nyungwe were once considered a separate race *catoides*. This spritely little bird is common at Nyungwe but uncommon in Volcanoes NP.

BLACK-THROATED APALIS ◉

This interesting species has four disjunct races scattered between Cameroon, Kenya, and Angola. The nominate race occurs from Kenya to South Sudan and across the Albertine Rift into DRC. Black-throated Apalis is a fairly common bird in Nyungwe and Volcanoes NPs.

Black-throated Apalis is just one of an amazing six apalis species found in Nyungwe. ©Ken Behrens

BLACK-FACED (*MOUNTAIN MASKED*) APALIS

This is one of the most common Albertine Rift endemics. The nominate race present in Rwanda has less gray on the face and neck, and less green on the breast sides and flanks than *marungensis*, which is endemic to the Marungu Plateau in southeast DRC. Black-faced is common in forest throughout Nyungwe above 1500 m. It is also present though less common in Volcanoes NP and Gishwati and Mukura Forests.

BUFF-THROATED (*KUNGWE*) APALIS

Kungwe Apalis is considered Endangered by the IUCN and BirdLife International, but other authorities, including Clements, doubt its taxonomic status and treat it as a race of the widespread Buff-throated Apalis. This canopy-loving species is not uncommon at Nyungwe NP, which may be the best place in the world to see it. It seems especially partial to drier forest in the northwest of the park. Perhaps the best locality is the Karamba trail. Other places to search include the Kamiranzovu Trail, Rukuzi Trail, and some of the trails in the Uwinka area. Beware of confusion with the co-occurring Gray Apalis that is similar both in vocalizations and appearance.

CHESTNUT-THROATED APALIS

This East African and Albertine Rift endemic is sometimes treated as conspecific with Kabobo and Chapin's Apalises. It is a canopy apalis that often first gives itself with its *tiiiiirrrrrr-tiiiirrrrr* telephone-ringing call. It is common in flocks in Nyungwe and Volcanoes NPs.

WHITE-CHINNED PRINIA

This rather atypical prinia is found throughout Rwanda in a variety of edge habitats, including overgrown agricultural areas. It can be found in and around Nyungwe NP, around Lake Kivu, in Buhanga Forest, around the southeastern papyrus sites, and in Akagera NP.

TRILLING CISTICOLA

Trilling Cisticola is common in broad-leaved woodlands from Zambia to Uganda. This is one of the commonest birds in Akagera NP and adjacent savannah habitats. Its distinctive voice can be heard most of the time when birding in that part of the country.

CHUBB'S CISTICOLA

This interesting species has four disjunct races scattered between Cameroon and Kenya. The nominate race is abundant across much of Rwanda, inhabiting forest openings, scrub, and even cultivated fields above 1500 m.

CARRUTHERS'S CISTICOLA

This monotypic species is endemic to wetlands of East Africa. It is fairly easy to find in many wetlands, including along the Nyabarongo River near Kigali, the Rukuzi Marsh, the papyrus wetlands in the southeast, and in Akagera NP.

STOUT CISTICOLA

Stout Cisticola is fairly common in the drier, taller, and more open grassland of Akagera NP, usually on the hills along the western side of the park.

TABORA (*LONG-TAILED*) CISTICOLA

This is one of the species that reaches the northern tip of its range in Akagera NP. It is fairly common in the southern part of the park and is often found in mixed feeding flocks with other species.

GRAY-CAPPED WARBLER
This weird monogeneric warbler has no clear taxonomic affinities but is probably related to the Oriole Warbler of West Africa. It is restricted to countries around Lake Victoria, where it is fairly common in dense undergrowth, favoring areas close to water. Its loud and distinctive vocalizations mean that it is heard more often than it is seen and it responds well to recordings.

BLACK-FACED RUFOUS-WARBLER
This dapper little bird occurs from southern Cameroon to Kenya. The local race *vulpinus* is restricted to East Africa and eastern Congo. It is shy and skulking but vocal in Nyungwe NP and is best searched for on the lower stretches of the Bururi road, where its distinctive "reversing truck" *deeeep-deeeep-deeep* call often betrays its presence.

BANDED PRINIA
This is another species with four disjunct races scattered between Cameroon and Kenya. The local race *obscura* is restricted to the Albertine Rift and eastern DRC. Some authorities such as HBW suggest that *obscura* and the taxon in western Kenya and eastern Uganda (*melanops*) could be split off as "Black-faced Prinia". They differ from races farther west by having an all-black unbarred throat. However, Clements still regards *obscura* as part of "Banded Prinia", while positioning *melanops* in the "black-faced" grouping. Either way, it is worth checking

well all the dark-throated Banded Prinias in Rwanda.

AFRICAN (RUWENZORI) HILL BABBLER
Although the taxonomy of *Pseudoalcippe* is poorly understood, there are a number of distinct-looking races to which several authors award specific status. The race *atriceps* or "Ruwenzori Hill Babbler" occurs in both the Albertine Rift and in southern Cameroon. This bird is common in Nyungwe and Volcanoes NPs and other montane forests.

GRAUER'S WARBLER
The taxonomic placement of this odd bird is uncertain and potential relationships with the longbills, wren-warblers, and babblers have all been postulated. It might even comprise its own monotypic family. It is fairly common at Nyungwe but is cryptic and usually stays hidden in dense undergrowth. Grauer's is best located by its slow trilling call, similar to that of Scaly-throated Honeyguide. The Karamba and Kamiranzovu trails are excellent localities for this species; other places to listen for this bird include the Uwinka area and the Bigugu trail.

MOUNTAIN ILLADOPSIS
This scarce montane specialist of East and central Africa is uncommon in Nyungwe NP, Gishwati Forest, and Mashoza Parike. As with all illadopsises, it haunts thick undergrowth and is very difficult to see well.

RED-COLLARED MOUNTAIN-BABBLER
This handsome and enigmatic babbler is placed in the genus *Kupeornis* and is uncommon in Nyungwe NP, the most accessible site in the world

for this species. It occurs in mid-story and canopy flocks of up to 12 birds, which are best located by their noisy chatter. They seem to require mossy trees in fairly open, high-altitude forest. The best site is the Bigugu Trail, but they can also found on the trails in the Uwinka area.

GRAY-CHESTED ILLADOPSIS
This enigmatic, illadopsis-like species in the monospecific genus *Kakamega* may actually be a member of the sugarbird family and is treated as such by Clements, whereas IOC considers it a distinct family. Although monotypic, it occurs in two well-separated areas: in East Africa it is distributed widely in the Albertine Rift and Kakamega forest in Kenya but then reappears in the Cameroon-Nigerian mountain chain on the other side of the continent. In Rwanda it is rare in Nyungwe NP.

YELLOW-BELLIED HYLIOTA
Most authorities have recently placed the hyliotas into their own family, which is endemic to Africa and only contains four members. As such, seeing a hyliota has become a high priority for family listers. Although they are widely distributed across Africa, hyliotas are not particularly common anywhere. Yellow-bellied in Rwanda is no exception, although it is occasionally seen in Nyungwe, especially along the Bururi road.

VIOLET-BACKED HYLIOTA
This odd and scarce species has a strange patchy distribution in the rainforests of Central and West Africa. In Nyungwe it is apparently represented by the nominate race, which is also found as far west as southeast Nigeria.

However, this taxonomy is doubtful given the isolation of the population in Nyungwe and eastern DRC. Violet-backed Hyliota is rare in Nyungwe NP and there are scattered records throughout the park.

WHITE-EYED SLATY-FLYCATCHER
Four races are recognized across this species' central and East African range, of which *toruensis* is endemic to the Albertine Rift. Contrary to its name, this subspecies has no white eye-ring and as such can be confused with other species like Ashy Flycatcher. It is common-to-abundant in forest and forest edge habitat.

YELLOW-EYED BLACK-FLYCATCHER
This ARE is fairly common on forest edges and in open areas in Nyungwe at 1300 to 2300 m. It usually perches in the open, making it easy to spot.

CHAPIN'S FLYCATCHER
Although it is an Albertine Rift near-endemic, this species unfortunately does not appear to be regular anywhere in Rwanda. However, given the potential confusion with other members of the *Muscicapa* genus, it may simply be undetected in Rwanda. Chapin's is classified as Vulnerable by the IUCN.

BROWN-BACKED SCRUB-ROBIN
This species is widely distributed but local in Rwanda and Buhanga Forest is a good place to find it. Brown-backed also occurs in moist woodland in Akagera NP and surrounds.

WHITE-BELLIED ROBIN-CHAT
The race *rufescentior* is endemic to the Albertine Rift and may well be split

Gray-winged Robin-Chat, a shy beauty that can be seen at a couple of sites in Rwanda. ©Lee Hunter

from the nominate form that is restricted to the Cameroon-Nigeria mountain range. In *rufescentior*, the belly and undertail coverts are more rufous and the preorbital supercilium more distinctive. White-bellied Robin-Chat is an uncommon bird in undergrowth between 1200 and 2200 m in Nyungwe. The Karamba and Isumo (Waterfall) Trails are especially good for this secretive species, which is most easily detected by its distinctive vocalizations.

ARCHER'S ROBIN-CHAT

This endemic is fairly common in Nyungwe NP in the under- and midstory. It generally prefers higher altitudes and is found between 1600 and 4300 m. It is especially common on the Bigugu trail and around Uwinka. Archer's is also found commonly in Volcanoes NP. Its voice is beautiful and distinctive, with a ventriloquistic quality that makes it tough to track down.

GRAY-WINGED ROBIN-CHAT ●

This species occurs throughout much of Rwanda, albeit patchily. It occurs in Nyungwe NP, including the Kamiranzovu and Karamba Trails, but is rare. It is also found in Mashoza Parike in the southeast.

RED-THROATED ALETHE

The nominate race is fairly common at Nyungwe in the under- and midstory near bamboo, especially around Uwinka and on the Karamba trail. This species often feeds by pouncing on insects disturbed by ant columns or primates and can be remarkably tame. It is also found at Volcanoes NP but it is harder to find.

EQUATORIAL AKALAT

This small robin-like bird is found locally from South Sudan to Kenya and the Albertine Rift. It is quite common but inconspicuous from 800 to 2000 m in Nyungwe NP and is also common in Cyamudongo Forest.

MIOMBO ROCK-THRUSH

There are a few records of this species, suggesting that it is a regular if rare visitor to Rwanda. It has been recorded in exotic *Eucalyptus* plantations in Rwanda.

RUAHA (*WHITE-HEADED BLACK*) CHAT

Although it was once widely considered to be part of the nominate race of Arnot's Chat, a recent appreciation of the subtle differences in this taxon has led to its elevation to species-level: *Myrmechocihla collaris*. The male looks remarkably similar to the nominate Arnot's, being black with a white crown and having white on the shoulder and a completely black tail and rump. The female is mostly black including the crown but has a diagnostic complete or near-complete white collar around her neck. Ruaha (*White-headed Black*) Chat is found mainly in western Tanzania, Rwanda, Burundi, northern Zambia, and extreme eastern DRC. In Rwanda it can be seen mainly around human structures in farmed areas and both degraded and intact savannah. It is frequent throughout much of the county, including near Butare en route to Nyungwe NP and in and around Akagera NP.

WHITE-TAILED ANT-THRUSH ⦿

The race *praepectoralis* is present but uncommon in Nyungwe NP.

KIVU GROUND-THRUSH

Kivu is variously treated as a race of the more widespread Abyssinian Ground-Thrush or as a separate ARE species. It is now very scarce in Nyungwe, although older texts claim

White-tailed Ant-Thrush resides in Nyungwe, but it's far from common. It's mainly found in the park's lower elevations. ©Lee Hunter

it was once common. It is a skulking understory specialist that occurs between 1500 and 3000 m. Kivu Ground-Thrush is best searched for in the very early morning when it may emerge onto paths or be vocal. One of the best areas to try is the moist marsh-side forest along the Kamiranzovu Trail.

ABYSSINIAN (*OLIVE*) THRUSH

This species' taxa are sometimes combined with those in southern Africa and considered to be part of one highly variable species (Olive Thrush). Of late, however, they are more frequently considered to be multiple species within a superspecies complex. The taxon present in Rwanda is *bambusicola*, which is endemic to the Albertine Rift. This species is common in Nyungwe and Volcanoes NPs, including in edge habitats outside the parks.

SPLENDID GLOSSY-STARLING

This big starling is a mainly West African and Congo Basin species that reaches western East Africa. It is most frequently seen in the eastern side of the country, especially in the lush woodland of Akagera NP.

SLENDER-BILLED STARLING

This starling is mainly found in montane forest, as in Nyungwe NP and (less commonly) Volcanoes NP, but seems to wander and can turn up in odd places such as the Rugezi Marsh.

WALLER'S STARLING

This red-winged starling is more common and widespread in Nyungwe than Stuhlmann's and can be found almost anywhere in the park.

STUHLMANN'S STARLING

This scarce starling occurs at low densities in Nyungwe NP. Take care when separating it from the similar but bulkier Waller's Starling.

SHARPE'S STARLING

This beautiful starling is rare in Nyungwe NP. Listen for its beautiful and distinctive "tinkling bell" song and watch for birds perched on bare snags.

BLUE-HEADED SUNBIRD ●

Although endemic to the Albertine Rift, this species is represented by five subspecies, two of which occur in Rwanda. The nominate *alinae* is found in NW Rwanda (Volcanoes NP) and *tanganjicae* in SW Rwanda (Nyungwe NP). Generally, this species is low-density but widespread and ranges widely depending on what species are in flower in different areas. It is partial to *Balthasarea* trees, where it pollinates its long coral-colored flowers. Listen for its distinctive undulating trill call as a clue to its presence. Blue-headed is fairly common in Nyungwe NP and the Kamiranzovu trail is often a good area for this sunbird. It is also present but difficult to find in Volcanoes NP and Mukura Forest.

PURPLE-BREASTED SUNBIRD

In the most visited sections of Nyungwe NP this altitudinal migrant varies between being common (April) and scarce (August) depending on what is in flower. It is highly partial to *Symphonia* trees and when they blossom (Feb-Apr and Oct-Nov) this bird can be surprisingly common between 2000 and 2600 m. Also check giant *Lobelias* and *Albizia gummifera* (generally at lower altitude) if the *Symphonia*

Despite being an Albertine Rift endemic with a restricted range, Blue-headed Sunbird has five different subspecies. ©John Caddick

are not in flower. This species has even been observed in *Eucalyptus*, for example in the buffer zone fringing the park when *Symphonia* is not in bloom. At the time of your visit ask the knowledgeable park rangers where these key tree species are in flower. If they know, this information will greatly enhance your chances of connecting with this sought-after endemic, along with other more common sunbirds. Purple-breasted Sunbird also occurs in Volcanoes NP and Gishwati Forest.

RED-TUFTED (*SCARLET-TUFTED MALACHITE*) SUNBIRD
This scarce species occurs at high elevations in central and East African mountains. The race *dartmouthi* is en-

demic to the Albertine Rift and occurs in the Virungas in northwest Rwanda in Afro-alpine habitat on some of the high mountains of Volcanoes NP, generally above 3000 m. Mount Bisoke is the most accessible place to see this species in Rwanda.

STUHLMANN'S (*RUWENZORI DOUBLE-COLLARED*) SUNBIRD
This highly localized and scarce endemic to the Albertine Rift is taxonomically complex, being represented by four subspecies, two of which occur in Rwanda. The taxon *graueri* occurs in the Virungas (Volcanoes NP), while *schubotzi* is found in Nyungwe NP, which is the best place to search for it. This species is easily confused

with the much commoner Northern Double-collared Sunbird and so take care when identifying it. It is larger, with a much longer tail (almost twice the length of Northern Double-collared) and a longer bill. It can range considerably in altitude but generally prefers higher altitudes – between 2300–3500 m – than Northern Double-collared, especially areas with *Hagenia* and *Erica*. It occasionally comes much lower. Stuhlmann's occurs around Nyungwe's Uwasenkoko wetland and in the forests east of there and less frequently in the central and western parts of the park, as around Uwinka. It has even been recorded on occasions at Gisakura, although Northern Double-collared is much commoner there.

REGAL SUNBIRD

This ARE comprises two subspecies, the widespread nominate that occurs in Rwanda and *andersoni*, endemic to the Mahale Mountains in western Tanzania. It is common in forest throughout Nyungwe above 1600 m and is also found in Gishwati and Mukura Forests and in Volcanoes NP up to 3400 m.

ROCKEFELLER'S SUNBIRD

This species has not yet been confirmed from Rwanda but there have been several reports from Nyungwe NP, mainly from the Uwinka and Kamiranzovu areas. It occurs between 2000 and 3300 m in DRC.

RED-CHESTED SUNBIRD

Red-chested is restricted to waterside and swamp vegetation in the Lake Victoria basin and along the southern Nile River. It is common in papyrus and other wetlands throughout Rwanda. Akagera is a particularly good place to search for it.

MOUNTAIN WAGTAIL

Mountain Wagtail is present in Nyungwe NP but not often encountered, probably because the main roads and trails generally do not run parallel to major streams. The Isumo (Waterfall) Trail is one of the best places to look for it.

JACKSON'S (*GRASSLAND*) PIPIT

Pipits in the "Grassland" or "African" Pipit group have been recorded from Nyungwe NP. Although their identification has yet to be thoroughly established, it is possible that they belong to the taxon *latistriatus*, which is treated as a full species (**Jackson's Pipit**) by Clements.

STRIPED PIPIT

Striped Pipit is rare in Rwanda but has been recorded in wooded savannah in Akagera NP and elsewhere.

SHORT-TAILED PIPIT

This little pipit is scarce throughout its African range and has occasionally been recorded in grassland in eastern Rwanda.

ORIOLE FINCH

Oriole Finch is rare in Nyungwe, particularly in lower forest such as that along the Bururi road and the Karamba Trail.

YELLOW-CROWNED CANARY

This species of the higher mountains is most easily found in the agricultural and edge habitats around Volcanoes NP.

WESTERN (*AFRICAN*) CITRIL

Citril taxonomy is complex and controversial. If Western Citril is split off, as in the current Clements list, this species is restricted to a fairly small area of mountains in western East Africa and eastern DRC. Western Citril is quite common throughout most of Rwanda, even in heavily human-modified habitats such as the Nyarutarama Lake in Kigali.

PAPYRUS CANARY

This canary is rare in and around papyrus swamps, especially in Akagera NP. It was also formerly known from Rwanda's other major wetlands but has become difficult to find in most of those sites.

STREAKY SEEDEATER

Although its range is not huge, this species is generally common wherever it occurs and Rwanda is no exception. It is one of the commonest species, especially in the western two-thirds of the country.

THICK-BILLED SEEDEATER

This inconspicuous seedeater has a disjunct range in Nigeria/Cameroon, Angola, East Africa, and along the Albertine Rift. It is fairly common in Nyungwe NP and is also frequent outside the protected areas. It is usually found in scrubby and open habitat.

BAGLAFECHT WEAVER

This is a variable species with a large but scattered African range. The subspecies in western Rwanda, *stuhlmanni*, is an Albertine Rift endemic. It is common throughout much of the country, thriving even in human-modified habitat.

SLENDER-BILLED WEAVER

This weaver is patchily if widely distributed in Africa, mainly in countries that are rarely visited by birders. This is one of Rwanda's least-common weaver species and is best searched for around wetlands in Akagera NP. It is also often found in agricultural areas in the east, as around Mashoza Parike and Lake Muhazi, where it likes to feed on sorghum.

BLACK-BILLED WEAVER

This striking weaver is uncommon in Nyungwe NP but can be found in many different locations within the park. It can also be found in Volcanoes NP, Mashoza Parike, and Buhanga Forest.

STRANGE WEAVER ◉

This species is fairly common in thick edge habitat in Nyungwe NP. Listen for its Spectacled Weaver-like call. It is also present in Volcanoes NP and Gishwati and Mukura Forests, albeit less commonly.

NORTHERN BROWN-THROATED WEAVER

Northern Brown-throated Weaver is endemic to a small area of East Africa, but widely distributed and fairly common in Rwanda, including the wetlands in and around Kigali. It is also easy to find in papyrus sites in the southeast and in Akagera NP.

BLACK-HEADED (*YELLOW-BACKED*) WEAVER

This beautiful weaver is common throughout most of Rwanda in moist habitats and adjacent scrub.

BROWN-CAPPED WEAVER

This species is uncommon to rare in the lower stretches of Nyungwe NP,

The Strange Weaver creeps through the tangles and thick edge habitats of the Albertine Rift.
©John Wilkinson

including the Karamba Trail, Bururi road, and around Kamiranzovu Marsh.

COMPACT WEAVER
Compact Weaver is scarce in Rwanda, as in most of its range. It has been seen around the Abudada Dam and Mashoza Parike, and also near Kibungo.

CARDINAL QUELEA
Cardinal Quelea occurs sporadically in savannah habitat, mainly in Akagera NP. It seems to be commoner than Red-headed Quelea.

RED-HEADED QUELEA
This quelea occurs sporadically in savannah habitat, mainly in Akagera NP. It seems to be less common than Cardinal Quelea.

WHITE-COLLARED OLIVEBACK
Although no truly reliable sites are currently known, this rare and enigmatic species occurs widely in Rwanda. The marsh near the bridge adjacent to the village of Rwinkwavu on the way to the southern entrance gate of Akagera NP is a good place to search. Sightings are possible in almost any good reedbed or in agricultural areas adjacent reedbeds anywhere in the country. It has been recorded in the Rugezi Marsh, Nyabarongo Wetland, in the papyrus near Bare village, and at Abudada Dam.

YELLOW-BELLIED WAXBILL
This colorful little waxbill can be found in much of the country, especially in the more mountainous western two-thirds. Nyungwe NP is a good place and it can even be found away from good forest habitat.

GREEN-BACKED TWINSPOT
This twinspot is quite scarce in Rwanda but has been recorded in Cyamudongo Forest.

Black-and-white Mannikin is found throughout much of Rwanda, even in agricultural land. ©Lee Hunter

SHELLEY'S CRIMSON-WING

This is one of the most enigmatic of all Albertine Rift endemics and one of the most sought-after of all birds in Africa. It is only recorded very rarely in Nyungwe NP (or anywhere else for that matter). Its occurrence seems seasonal; it may move around the Albertine Rift Mountains, perhaps taking advantage of seeding grasses as they become available. In Nyungwe NP it is most often recorded on the lower portions of the Bururi road.

DUSKY CRIMSON-WING

Dusky is fairly common wherever there is thick edge habitat above 1600 m in Nyungwe NP. It is found most frequently near Uwinka. If you watch carefully as you travel along the road, you can often pick up these tiny red-winged birds as they shoot across the road or flit from the road verge. Morning and evenings, when they sit on the road and eat fallen grass seeds, offer the best possibilities.

ABYSSINIAN CRIMSON-WING

This crimson-wing is rare in Nyungwe NP but has been recorded around Gisakura.

RED-FACED CRIMSON-WING

This is another crimson-wing that is rare in Nyungwe NP and has also been recorded at Gisakura and in Cyamudongo Forest.

FAWN-BREASTED WAXBILL

Fawn-breasted Waxbill is uncommon but can be found throughout the country in scrubby and moist habitat. In particular, watch for it in and around Nyungwe NP, in the Mashoza Parike, around the southeastern papyrus sites, and in Akagera NP.

KANDT'S (*BLACK-HEADED*) WAXBILL

Kandt's was recently split from Black-headed Waxbill and thus became an endemic to the Kenyan and Albertine Rift Mountains. It is uncommon in Nyungwe, preferring moist areas such as around Uwasenkoko Marsh. It is also present although uncommon in the Volcanoes NP area, and Mukura and Gishwati Forests, where human-degraded habitats are actually attractive to this species.

DUSKY TWINSPOT

Dusky Twinspot is very rare in Nyungwe NP. It seems to occur seasonally, preferring the lower-lying areas of Gisakura and the Bururi road.

PETERS'S TWINSPOT

This is another rare twinspot in Rwanda and has been recorded recently in Mashoza Parike.

ORANGE-WINGED PYTILIA

This attractive small bird is rare in Rwanda but has been recorded in Akagera NP.

RED-HEADED BLUEBILL

This beautiful waxbill is always scarce but can show up in small forest patches like Buhanga Forest and the Mashoza Parike. It has also been recorded in Nyungwe, seeming to prefer the park's lower elevations.

RED-BILLED (*BLACK-CHINNED*) QUAILFINCH

This stub-tailed species can be found in Akagera NP both in grasslands and,

especially, in muddy areas along the edges of lakes.

BLACK-AND-WHITE MANNIKIN ○

This mannikin is widespread in Rwanda, often in agricultural areas and preferring overgrown areas along valley bottoms. Nyungwe is one good site; search along forest edges and in open areas. This species has also been seen around some of the southeastern papyrus sites and at Mashoza Parike.

BROAD-TAILED PARADISE-WHYDAH

There are a few records from eastern Rwanda of this generally uncommon species.

PARASITIC WEAVER ○

This odd little bird is generally scarce and sporadic throughout its range and occurs rarely in Akagera NP.

Parasitic Weaver is an odd little bird in a monotypic genus. It is sometimes seen in Akagera NP. ©Ken Behrens

Anderson, J. (2012). First records of Green-backed Eremomela *Eremomela canescens* and Amethyst Sunbird *Chalcomitra amethystina* for Rwanda. *Bulletin of the African Bird Club* **19(1)**: 73-74.

Anderson, J. (2012). Fiery-necked Nightjar *Caprimulgus pectoralis* and Black-shouldered Nightjar *C. nigriscapularis* in Rwanda. *Bulletin of the African Bird Club* **19(2)**: 194-199.

Banamwana, M. (2008). Contribution à l'étude de la dynamique de la végétation de la Résérve Forestière de Gishwati et priorités d'aménagement et de géstion. BSc thesis, Huye, Rwanda

BirdLife International. (2012a). Important Bird Areas factsheet: Akagera National Park. Downloaded from http://www.birdlife.org on 13/07/2012.

BirdLife International. (2012b). Important Bird Areas factsheet: Akanyaru wetlands. Downloaded from http://www.birdlife.org on 13/07/2012.

BirdLife International. (2012c). Important Bird Areas factsheet: Nyabarongo wetlands. Downloaded from http://www.birdlife.org on 13/07/2012.

BirdLife International. (2012d). Important Bird Areas factsheet: Rugezi Marsh. Downloaded from http://www.birdlife.org on 13/07/2012.

BirdLife International. (2012e). Important Bird Areas factsheet: Volcans National Park. Downloaded from http://www.birdlife.org on 13/07/2012.

BirdLife International. (2012f). Important Bird Areas factsheet: Nyungwe National Park. Downloaded from http://www.birdlife.org on 13/07/2012.

Briggs, P. and Booth, J. (2010). Rwanda 4th edition. Bradt Travel Guides, Buckinghamshire, UK

Britton, P.L. (editor). (1980). Birds of East Africa: their habitat, status, and distribution. East Africa Natural History Society, Nairobi, Kenya.

Carswell, M., Pomeroy, D., Reynolds, J., & Tushabe, H. (2005). The Bird Atlas of Uganda. British Ornithologists' Union & British Ornithologists' Club, Oxford.

Claassen, M. Birding Rwanda blog, including contributions by Jason Anderson and others. http://rwandabirdingguide.blogspot.com

Clements, J.F. (2007). The Clements Checklist of Birds of the World. Cornell University Press, Ithaca, New York.

Cohen, C., Ryan, P., Claassen,, M. & Ntoyinkima, C. (2010). Birding Rwanda – in search of Red-collared Babbler *Kupeornis rufocinctus*, Albertine Rift endemics and more. *Bulletin of the African Bird Club* **17(2)**: 229-237.

Cunliffe, S. (2011). Breathing deeply in Rwanda. *Africa Geographic* **19**: 56-62.

Dowsett, R.J. (editor). (1990). Survey of the fauna and flora of Nyungwe Forest, Rwanda.*Tauraco Research Report* **3**.

Dowsett, R. J. (1993) Afrotropical avifaunas: annotated country checklists. Rwanda. *Tauraco Research Report* **5**: 205-211.

Dowsett, R.J., Atkinson, P.W., & Caddick, J.A. (2013). Checklist of the birds of Rwanda. Downloaded from www.africanbirdclub.org on 5 May 2013.

Estes, R.D. (1991). The Behavior Guide to African Mammals: Including Hoofed Mammals, Carnivores, Primates. University of California Press, Berkeley.

Fishpool, L.D.C. & Evans, M.I. (2001). Important Bird Areas in Africa and Associated Islands. Pisces Publications and BirdLife International, Newbury and Cambridge.

Glen, R., Bowie, R.C.K., Stolberger, S., & Voelker, G. (2011). Geographically structured plumage variation among populations of White-headed Black Chat (*Myrmecocichla arnotti*) in Tanzania confirms the race *collaris* to be a valid taxon. *Journal of Ornithology* **152**: 63-70.

Groves, C.P. (2001). Primate taxonomy. Smithsonian Institute Press, Washington, D.C.

Haltenorth, T. & Diller, H. (1984). A Field Guide to the Mammals of Africa. Collins, England.

Kanyamibwa, S. (1998). Impact of war on conservation: Rwandan environment and wildlife in agony. *Biodiversity and Conservation* **7**: 1399-1406.

Kingdon, J. (1974). East African Mammals (3 volumes). University of Chicago Press, Chicago.

Kingdon, J. (1989). Island Africa. Princeton University Press, Princeton, New Jersey.

Kingdon, J. (1997) The Kingdon Field Guide to African Mammals. Princeton University Press, Princeton, New Jersey.

Mittermeier R.A., Rylands A.B., & Wilson, D.E. (2013). Handbook of the Mammals of the World. Volume 3: Primates. Lynx Edicions, Barcelona.

Nielsen, H. & Spenceley, A. (2010). The Success of Tourism in Rwanda – Gorillas and more. World Development Report 2011. Background Paper.

Nsabagasani, C. & Nsengimana, S.J. (2009). Assessment of the current status of endemic bird species to the Albertine Rift in Gishwati Forest Reserve, Rwanda. Albertine Rift Conservation Society and Great Apes Trust of Iowa/Gishwati Area Conservation Program.

Offut, K., Masozera, M. & Gill, E. (undated). Nyungwe National Park Guide. Nyungwe Forest Conservation Project, Kigali and Wildlife Conservation Society, New York.

Plumptre, A.J., Masozera, M., Fashing, P.J., McNeilage, A., *et al.* (2002). Biodiversity Surveys of the Nyungwe Forest Reserve in S.W. Rwanda. Wildlife Conservation Society Working Paper No. 18.

Plumptre, A.J., Masozera, M., & Vedder, A. (2001). The impact of civil war on the conservation of protected areas in Rwanda. Biodiversity Support Program, Washington, DC.

Shorrocks, B. (2007). The biology of African savannahs. Oxford University Press, Oxford.

Sinclair, I. & Ryan, P. (2003). Birds of Africa South of the Sahara. Struik, Cape Town.

Sprawls, S., Howell, K., Drewes, R., & Ashe, J. (2004). A Field Guide to the Reptiles of East Africa. A & C Black, London.

Stattersfield, A. J., Crosby, M. J., Long, A. J. & Wege, D. C. (1998). *Endemic Bird Areas of the World: Priorities for Biodiversity Conservation.* BirdLife International, Cambridge, UK.

Stevenson, T. & Fanshawe, J. (2002). Birds of East Africa. A & C Black, London.

Storz, M. (1983). La Forêt Naturelle de Nyungwe et sa Faune. Projet Pilote Forestier, Rwanda.

Vande Weghe, J.P. (1990). Akagera: Land of Water, Grass and Fire. WWF, Brussels.

Vande Weghe, J.P. & Vande Weghe, G.R. (2011). Birds in Rwanda: an atlas and handbook. Rwanda Development Board, Kigali.

Voelker, G., Outlaw, R., Reddy, S., Tobler, M., Bates, J.M. *et al.* (2010). A new species of Boubou (Malacanotidae: *Laniarius*) from the Albertine Rift. *The Auk* **127**:678-689.

Voelker, G., Outlaw, R.K. & Bowie, R.C.K. (2010). Pliocene forest dynamics as a primary driver of African bird speciation. *Global Ecology and Biogeography* **19**: 111-121.

Wilson, D.E. & Mittermeier, R.A. (2009). Handbook of the Mammals of the World. Volume 1: Carnivores. Lynx Edicions, Barcelona.

Wilson, D.E. & Mittermeier, R.A. (2011). Handbook of the Mammals of the World. Volume 2: Hoofed Mammals. Lynx Edicions, Barcelona.

Numbers in *italics* refer to the page numbers of individual photographs.

Common Name	Scientific Name	Page Number(s)
ACCIPITRIFORMES: Pandionidae		
Osprey	*Pandion haliaetus*	190
ACCIPITRIFORMES: Accipitridae		
African Harrier-Hawk	*Polyboroides typus*	72, 113, 115, 149, 168
Palm-nut Vulture	*Gypohierax angolensis*	48, 110, 156, 184, *187*
European Honey-Buzzard	*Pernis apivorus*	73, 90, 172
African Cuckoo-Hawk	*Aviceda cuculoides*	72
White-headed Vulture	*Trigonoceps occipitalis*	171
Hooded Vulture	*Necrosyrtes monachus*	49, 50, 53, 125, 126, 145
White-backed Vulture	*Gyps africanus*	121
Rueppell's (*Rüppell's*) Griffon (*Vulture*)	*Gyps rueppellii*	171
Bateleur	*Terathopius ecaudatus*	171, 186
Black-breasted Snake-Eagle	*Circaetus pectoralis*	150
Brown Snake-Eagle	*Circaetus cinereus*	181
(*Western*) Banded Snake-Eagle	*Circaetus cinerascens*	156, *168*, 205
Bat Hawk	*Macheiramphus alcinus*	48
Crowned Hawk-Eagle (*African Crowned Eagle*)	*Stephanoaetus coronatus*	*90*
Martial Eagle	*Polemaetus bellicosus*	*163*
Long-crested Eagle	*Lophaetus occipitalis*	48, 148, 195
Lesser Spotted Eagle	*Clanga pomarina*	73
Wahlberg's Eagle	*Hieraaetus wahlbergi*	184
Booted Eagle	*Hieraaetus pennatus*	172
Ayres's Hawk-Eagle	*Hieraaetus ayresii*	59, 156
Cassin's Hawk-Eagle	*Aquila africana*	59, 205
Verreaux's Eagle	*Aquila verreauxii*	156
African Hawk-Eagle	*Aquila spilogaster*	171, 176
Lizard Buzzard	*Kaupifalco monogrammicus*	*163*
Gabar Goshawk	*Micronisus gabar*	53, 149, 165
Eurasian Marsh-Harrier	*Circus aeruginosus*	190
African Marsh-Harrier	*Circus ranivorus*	48, 145, 190
Pallid Harrier	*Circus macrourus*	156
Montagu's Harrier	*Circus pygargus*	156
African Goshawk	*Accipiter tachiro*	48, 110, 184
Shikra	*Accipiter badius*	71, 168
Little Sparrowhawk	*Accipiter minullus*	48
Ovampo (*Ovambo*) Sparrowhawk	*Accipiter ovampensis*	156
Rufous-chested (*Rufous-breasted*) Sparrowhawk	*Accipiter rufiventris*	*66*
Black Goshawk (*Great Sparrowhawk*)	*Accipiter melanoleucus*	110

Common Name	Scientific Name	Page Number(s)
Black Kite	*Milvus migrans*	49, 113, 145, 171
African Fish-Eagle	*Haliaeetus vocifer*	190, *194*
Common (Steppe) Buzzard	*Buteo buteo*	73, 74, 172
Mountain Buzzard	*Buteo oreophilus*	59, 101, 121, 129, 145, 205
Augur Buzzard	*Buteo augur*	*120*
OTIDIFORMES: Otididae		
Denham's Bustard	*Neotis denhami*	156
Black-bellied Bustard	*Lissotis melanogaster*	156, *158*
GRUIFORMES: Rallidae		
White-spotted Flufftail	*Sarothrura pulchra*	107
Buff-spotted Flufftail	*Sarothrura elegans*	85
Red-chested Flufftail	*Sarothrura rufa*	76, 84
African Rail	*Rallus caerulescens*	48, 148
African Crake	*Crecopsis egregia*	48
Black Crake	*Amaurornis flavirostra*	184
Purple Swamphen	*Porphyrio porphyrio*	184
Allen's Gallinule	*Porphyrio alleni*	190
Eurasian (*Common*) Moorhen	*Gallinula chloropus*	50, 149
Lesser Moorhen	*Gallinula angulata*	184
Red-knobbed Coot	*Fulica cristata*	50, 145, 191
GRUIFORMES: Gruidae		
Gray Crowned-Crane	*Balearica regulorum*	110, *110*, 145, 148, 156, 190
CHARADRIIFORMES: Burhinidae		
Water Thick-knee	*Burhinus vermiculatus*	156, *164*, 190
CHARADRIIFORMES: Charadriidae		
Long-toed Lapwing	*Vanellus crassirostris*	48, *48*, 156, 190
Spur-winged Plover (*Lapwing*)	*Vanellus spinosus*	177, 196
Senegal Lapwing	*Vanellus lugubris*	156
Crowned Lapwing	*Vanellus coronatus*	*162*
(*African*) Wattled Lapwing	*Vanellus senegallus*	166
Brown-chested Lapwing	*Vanellus superciliosus*	155, *174*, 206
Black-bellied Plover	*Pluvialis squatarola*	113
Forbes's Plover	*Charadrius forbesi*	155
CHARADRIIFORMES: Jacanidae		
Lesser Jacana	*Microparra capensis*	48, 156
African Jacana	*Actophilornis africanus*	*197*
CHARADRIIFORMES: Scolopacidae		
Common Sandpiper	*Actitis hypoleucos*	112
Green Sandpiper	*Tringa ochropus*	146, 149
Wood Sandpiper	*Tringa glareola*	73, 196

Common Name	Scientific Name	Page Number(s)
Common Snipe	*Gallinago gallinago*	73
African Snipe	*Gallinago nigripennis*	48
CHARADRIIFORMES: Turnicidae		
Small (*Common*) Buttonquail	*Turnix sylvaticus*	165, 206
Hottentot (*Black-rumped*) Buttonquail	*Turnix hottentottus*	156, 206
CHARADRIIFORMES: Glareolidae		
Temminck's Courser	*Cursorius temminckii*	156
Bronze-winged Courser	*Rhinoptilus chalcopterus*	155, 207, *207*
CHARADRIIFORMES: Rostratulidae		
Greater Painted-Snipe	*Rostratula benghalensis*	48, 156
CHARADRIIFORMES: Laridae		
Whiskered Tern	*Chlidonias hybrida*	112
COLUMBIFORMES: Columbidae		
Afep Pigeon	*Columba unicincta*	207
Rameron (*Olive*) Pigeon	*Columba arquatrix*	129
Lemon Dove	*Columba larvata*	70
Dusky Turtle-Dove	*Streptopelia lugens*	59, 129
Red-eyed Dove	*Streptopelia semitorquata*	71, 112, 135, 145, 167
Laughing Dove	*Streptopelia senegalensis*	165
Emerald-spotted Wood-Dove	*Turtur chalcospilos*	51, 111, 165
Blue-spotted Wood-Dove	*Turtur afer*	71, 149, 167
Tambourine Dove	*Turtur tympanistria*	124, 148, 184
African Green-Pigeon	*Treron calvus*	184
CUCULIFORMES: Musophagidae		
Great Blue Turaco	*Corythaeola cristata*	*24*, 59, *70*, 101, 207
Black-billed Turaco	*Tauraco schuettii*	59, *59*, 102, 121, 129, 207
Purple-crested Turaco	*Tauraco porphyreolophus*	155, 184, *188*, 190
Ruwenzori Turaco	*Ruwenzorornis johnstoni*	57, 114, 120, 129, 207
Ross's Turaco	*Musophaga rossae*	*101*, 148, 156, 184, 190, 207
Bare-faced Go-away-bird	*Corythaixoides personatus*	156
Eastern (*Gray*) Plantain-eater	*Crinifer zonurus*	148, 184, 195
CUCULIFORMES: Cuculidae		
Levaillant's Cuckoo	*Clamator levaillantii*	184, 190
Thick-billed Cuckoo	*Pachycoccyx audeberti*	156
Red-chested Cuckoo	*Cuculus solitarius*	121
Black Cuckoo	*Cuculus clamosus*	124
Common Cuckoo	*Cuculus canorus*	172

Common Name	Scientific Name	Page Number(s)
African Cuckoo	*Cuculus gularis*	72, 73
Barred Long-tailed Cuckoo	*Cercococcyx montanus*	59, 114, 208
Klaas's Cuckoo	*Chrysococcyx klaas*	135, 145
African Emerald Cuckoo	*Chrysococcyx cupreus*	94
Dideric Cuckoo	*Chrysococcyx caprius*	190
Yellowbill	*Ceuthmochares aereus*	73, 78, 94, 167
Blue-headed Coucal	*Centropus monachus*	48, 145, 148, 184, 190
White-browed Coucal	*Centropus superciliosus*	124
STRIGIFORMES: Tytonidae		
Barn Owl	*Tyto alba*	35
STRIGIFORMES: Strigidae		
African Scops-Owl	*Otus senegalensis*	*63*
Spotted Eagle-Owl	*Bubo africanus*	156
Fraser's Eagle-Owl	*Bubo poensis*	59, 208
Verreaux's Eagle-Owl	*Bubo lacteus*	71, 156, 175
Pearl-spotted Owlet	*Glaucidium perlatum*	148
Red-chested Owlet	*Glaucidium tephronotum*	59, 208
Albertine Owlet	*Glaucidium albertinum*	57, 208
African Wood-Owl	*Strix woodfordii*	114, 184
African Long-eared Owl	*Asio abyssinicus*	129
Marsh Owl	*Asio capensis*	85
CAPRIMULGIFORMES: Caprimulgidae		
Pennant-winged Nightjar	*Macrodipteryx vexillarius*	156, *175*
Black-shouldered Nightjar	*Caprimulgus nigriscapularis*	156
Montane (*Rwenzori*) Nightjar	*Caprimulgus ruwenzorii*	59, 101, 120, 129, 208, *208*
Swamp Nightjar	*Caprimulgus natalensis*	156
Freckled Nightjar	*Caprimulgus tristigma*	156
Square-tailed Nightjar	*Caprimulgus fossii*	156, 190
APODIFORMES: Apodidae		
Scarce Swift	*Schoutedenapus myoptilus*	59, 101, 129, 209
Mottled Swift	*Apus aequatorialis*	209
Common Swift	*Apus apus*	50
African (*Black*) Swift	*Apus barbatus*	110
Little Swift	*Apus affinis*	112, 145, 171, 174
White-rumped Swift	*Apus caffer*	49, 50, 74
African Palm-Swift	*Cypsiurus parvus*	49, 102, 113, 171
COLIIFORMES: Coliidae		
Speckled Mousebird	*Colius striatus*	71, 111, 112, 135, 168

Common Name	Scientific Name	Page Number(s)
Gray-backed Fiscal	*Lanius excubitoroides*	50, 54, 150, 176
Mackinnon's Shrike (*Fiscal*)	*Lanius mackinnoni*	*106*, 124, 148, 213
Northern (*Common*) Fiscal	*Lanius humeralis*	102, 111, 112, 145, 146, 165
Souza's Shrike	*Lanius souzae*	155, *173*, 213
PASSERIFORMES: Oriolidae		
African Black-headed Oriole	*Oriolus larvatus*	184, 195
Black-tailed (*Montane*) Oriole	*Oriolus percivali*	59, 114, 121, 129, 213, *213*
PASSERIFORMES: Dicruridae		
Fork-tailed Drongo	*Dicrurus adsimilis*	168
PASSERIFORMES: Monarchidae		
African (*Blue-mantled*) Crested-Flycatcher	*Trochocercus cyanomelas*	82, 85
African Paradise-Flycatcher	*Terpsiphone viridis*	121, 124
PASSERIFORMES: Corvidae		
Pied Crow	*Corvus albus*	50, 112, 126, 145, 151
White-necked Raven	*Corvus albicollis*	194
PASSERIFORMES: Alaudidae		
Rufous-naped Lark	*Mirafra africana*	165, 181
Flappet Lark	*Mirafra rufocinnamomea*	165, 176
PASSERIFORMES: Hirundinidae		
Plain Martin	*Riparia paludicola*	50, 76, 146, 171
Banded Martin	*Riparia cincta*	179
Rock Martin	*Ptyonoprogne fuligula*	112, 150, 174
Barn Swallow	*Hirundo rustica*	73
Angola Swallow	*Hirundo angolensis*	50, 74, 78, 112, 113, 146, 150, 174, 176
Wire-tailed Swallow	*Hirundo smithii*	71
Red-rumped Swallow	*Cecropis daurica*	76, 125, 145, 171
Lesser Striped-Swallow	*Cecropis abyssinica*	*42*
Mosque Swallow	*Cecropis senegalensis*	110
Common House-Martin	*Delichon urbicum*	190
White-headed Sawwing	*Psalidoprocne albiceps*	114, 121, 148, 184, 190
Black Sawwing	*Psalidoprocne pristoptera*	213
Gray-rumped Swallow	*Pseudhirundo griseopyga*	156
PASSERIFORMES: Stenostiridae		
White-tailed Blue-Flycatcher	*Elminia albicauda*	59, 102, 121, 124, *125*, 184

Common Name	Scientific Name	Page Number(s)
Icterine Warbler	*Hippolais icterina*	190
Sedge Warbler	*Acrocephalus schoenobaenus*	185, 190
Eurasian Reed-Warbler	*Acrocephalus scirpaceus*	48
African Reed-Warbler	*Acrocephalus baeticatus*	48, 190
Marsh Warbler	*Acrocephalus palustris*	185, 190
Great Reed-Warbler	*Acrocephalus arundinaceus*	48, 190
Greater Swamp-Warbler	*Acrocephalus rufescens*	48, 155, 189, 216
Lesser Swamp-Warbler	*Acrocephalus gracilirostris*	145, 190
PASSERIFORMES: Locustellidae		
Little Rush-Warbler	*Bradypterus baboecala*	145, 185, 190
White-winged Swamp-Warbler	*Bradypterus carpalis*	48, 155, 189, 216
Grauer's Swamp-Warbler	*Bradypterus graueri*	58, *75*, 129, 145, 217
Evergreen-forest Warbler	*Bradypterus lopezi*	59, 217
Cinnamon Bracken-Warbler	*Bradypterus cinnamomeus*	59, 121, 129, *216*, 217
Fan-tailed Grassbird (*Broad-tailed Warbler*)	*Schoenicola brevirostris*	156
PASSERIFORMES: Cisticolidae		
Ruwenzori (*Collared*) Apalis	*Apalis ruwenzorii*	58, *66*, 101, 114, 120, 129, 217,
Black-throated Apalis	*Apalis jacksoni*	59, 102, 121, 217, *217*
Black-faced (*Mountain Masked*) Apalis	*Apalis personata*	*32*, 58, 101, 114, 120, 129, 218
Yellow-breasted Apalis	*Apalis flavida*	124
Buff-throated (*Kungwe*) Apalis	*Apalis rufogularis*	58, 101, 218
Chestnut-throated Apalis	*Apalis porphyrolaema*	59, 102, 115, 121, 129, 218
Gray Apalis	*Apalis cinerea*	102, 185, 195
Green-backed (*Gray-backed*) Camaroptera	*Camaroptera brachyura*	53, 117, 164, 196
Olive-green Camaroptera	*Camaroptera chloronota*	38
Miombo Wren-Warbler	*Calamonastes undosus*	155
White-chinned Prinia	*Schistolais leucopogon*	*79*, 124, 185, 218
Red-faced Cisticola	*Cisticola erythrops*	148, 185, 190

Common Name	Scientific Name	Page Number(s)
Singing Cisticola	*Cisticola cantans*	156
Trilling Cisticola	*Cisticola woosnami*	48, 148, 156, 185, 190, 195, 218
Chubb's Cisticola	*Cisticola chubbi*	48, 59, 102, 115, *115*, 121, 129, 145, 185, 218
Winding Cisticola	*Cisticola galactotes*	145, 190
Carruthers's Cisticola	*Cisticola carruthersi*	*144*, 145, 155, 189, 218
Stout Cisticola	*Cisticola robustus*	156, 218
Croaking Cisticola	*Cisticola natalensis*	156
Tabora Cisticola	*Cisticola angusticauda*	155, *177*, 218
Siffling Cisticola	*Cisticola brachypterus*	80, 102
Zitting Cisticola	*Cisticola juncidis*	179
Wing-snapping Cisticola	*Cisticola ayresii*	156
Gray-capped Warbler	*Eminia lepida*	49, 110, 124, *126*, 148, 156, 185, 190, 219
Black-faced Rufous-Warbler	*Bathmocercus rufus*	*65*, 219
Buff-bellied Warbler	*Phyllolais pulchella*	164
Tawny-flanked Prinia	*Prinia subflava*	50, 112, 150, 180
Banded Prinia	*Prinia bairdii*	121, 219
Green-backed Eremomela	*Eremomela canescens*	176
Yellow-bellied Eremomela	*Eremomela icteropygialis*	164
Greencap *(Green-capped)* Eremomela	*Eremomela scotops*	156
PASSERIFORMES: Sylviidae		
African (Ruwenzori) Hill Babbler	*Pseudoalcippe abyssinica*	59, 115, 121, 129, 219
Garden Warbler	*Sylvia borin*	33, 172
Grauer's Warbler	*Graueria vittata*	58, *91*, 219
PASSERIFORMES: Zosteropidae		
African Yellow White-eye	*Zosterops senegalensis*	52, 70, 105, 112, 117, 125, 140, 196
PASSERIFORMES: Pellorneidae		
Mountain Illadopsis	*Illadopsis pyrrhoptera*	59, 129, 185, 219
PASSERIFORMES: Leiothrichidae		
Black-lored Babbler	*Turdoides sharpei*	49, 148, 156, 185, 190

Common Name	Scientific Name	Page Number(s)
Arrow-marked Babbler	*Turdoides jardineii*	102, 124, 168
Red-collared Mountain-Babbler	*Kupeornis rufocinctus*	57, *97*, 219
PASSERIFORMES: Promeropidae		
Gray-chested Illadopsis	*Kakamega poliothorax*	59, 220
PASSERIFORMES: Hyliotidae		
Yellow-bellied Hyliota	*Hyliota flavigaster*	220
Violet-backed Hyliota	*Hyliota violacea*	59, 220
PASSERIFORMES: Muscicapidae		
Pale Flycatcher	*Bradornis pallidus*	164, 174
White-eyed Slaty-Flycatcher	*Melaenornis fischeri*	59, 102, 115, *117*, 220
Southern Black-Flycatcher	*Melaenornis pammelaina*	156
Yellow-eyed Black-Flycatcher	*Melaenornis ardesiacus*	57, *83*, 220
Spotted Flycatcher	*Muscicapa striata*	54, 172
Swamp Flycatcher	*Muscicapa aquatica*	49, 148, 156, 190, *192*
Dusky-brown (*African Dusky*) Flycatcher	*Muscicapa adusta*	112, 117, 140, 145
Cassin's Flycatcher	*Muscicapa cassini*	38
Ashy Flycatcher	*Muscicapa caerulescens*	156
Brown-backed Scrub-Robin	*Cercotrichas hartlaubi*	124, 148, 156, 220
Red-backed (*White-browed*) Scrub-Robin	*Cercotrichas leucophrys*	164
White-bellied Robin-Chat	*Cossyphicula roberti*	59, *73*, 220
Archer's Robin-Chat	*Cossypha archeri*	57, 114, *128*, 129, 221
Cape Robin-Chat	*Cossypha caffra*	129, *129*
Gray-winged Robin-Chat	*Cossypha polioptera*	59, 156, 185, 221, *221*
White-browed Robin-Chat	*Cossypha heuglini*	*123*, 124, 129
Red-capped Robin-Chat	*Cossypha natalensis*	185
Snowy-crowned Robin-Chat	*Cossypha niveicapilla*	185
White-starred Robin	*Pogonocichla stellata*	59, 115, 129
Red-throated Alethe	*Pseudalethe poliophrys*	57, *89*, 120, 129, 221
Forest Robin	*Stiphrornis erythrothorax*	35, 38, 107
Equatorial Akalat	*Sheppardia aequatorialis*	59, 221
Collared Flycatcher	*Ficedula albicollis*	156
Miombo Rock-Thrush	*Monticola angolensis*	222
Whinchat	*Saxicola rubetra*	146, 165, 172
African (*Common*) Stonechat	*Saxicola torquatus*	53, 71, 102, 112, 165

Common Name	Scientific Name	Page Number(s)
Sooty Chat	*Myrmecocichla nigra*	156
Ruaha (*White-headed Black*) Chat	*Myrmecocichla collaris*	59, 148, 155, 222
Mocking Cliff-Chat	*Thamnolaea cinnamomeiventris*	156
Familiar Chat	*Cercomela familiaris*	150, 166, 174
Northern Wheatear	*Oenanthe oenanthe*	172
PASSERIFORMES: Turdidae		
White-tailed Ant-Thrush	*Neocossyphus poensis*	222, *222*
Kivu Ground-Thrush	*Geokichla tanganjicae*	57, 222
Abyssinian (*Olive*) Thrush	*Turdus abyssinicus*	*66*, 129, 223
African Thrush	*Turdus pelios*	145
PASSERIFORMES: Sturnidae		
Greater Blue-eared Glossy-Starling	*Lamprotornis chalybaeus*	165
Splendid Glossy-Starling	*Lamprotornis splendidus*	156, 190, 223
Rueppell's (*Rüppell's*) Glossy-Starling	*Lamprotornis purpuroptera*	156, 184, 195
Violet-backed Starling	*Cinnyricinclus leucogaster*	156, 184
Slender-billed Starling	*Onychognathus tenuirostris*	59, 129, 145, 223
Waller's Starling	*Onychognathus walleri*	59, 102, 129, 223
Stuhlmann's Starling	*Poeoptera stuhlmanni*	59, 223
Sharpe's Starling	*Pholia sharpii*	59, 129, 223
PASSERIFORMES: Buphagidae		
Red-billed Oxpecker	*Buphagus erythrorhynchus*	156
Yellow-billed Oxpecker	*Buphagus africanus*	*22*, 156, *170*
PASSERIFORMES: Nectariniidae		
Little Green Sunbird	*Anthreptes seimundi*	106
Collared Sunbird	*Hedydipna collaris*	53, 70, 177, 186, 196
Green-headed Sunbird	*Cyanomitra verticalis*	*20*, 49, 110, 121, 124, 156, 185
Blue-throated Brown Sunbird	*Cyanomitra cyanolaema*	107
Blue-headed Sunbird	*Cyanomitra alinae*	57, 114, 120, 129, 223, *224*
Western Olive Sunbird	*Cyanomitra obscura*	102
Green-throated Sunbird	*Chalcomitra rubescens*	156
Scarlet-chested Sunbird	*Chalcomitra senegalensis*	71, 174
Purple-breasted Sunbird	*Nectarinia purpureiventris*	57, *95*, 120, 223
Bronze Sunbird	*Nectarinia kilimensis*	*39*, 59, 121

Common Name	Scientific Name	Page Number(s)
PASSERIFORMES: Passeridae		
Northern Gray-headed Sparrow	*Passer griseus*	112, 126, 145, 171
PASSERIFORMES: Ploceidae		
Red-headed Weaver	*Anaplectes rubriceps*	49, 148, 190
Baglafecht Weaver	*Ploceus baglafecht*	59, *68*, 226
Slender-billed Weaver	*Ploceus pelzelni*	156, 185, 190, 226
Black-necked Weaver	*Ploceus nigricollis*	156, 185
Spectacled Weaver	*Ploceus ocularis*	190
Black-billed Weaver	*Ploceus melanogaster*	59, 185, 226
Strange Weaver	*Ploceus alienus*	58, 101, 114, 120, 129, *140*, *227*, 226
Holub's Golden-Weaver	*Ploceus xanthops*	124, 190, 195
Northern Brown-throated Weaver	*Ploceus castanops*	49, 148, *151*, 185, 190, 226
Lesser Masked-Weaver	*Ploceus intermedius*	156, 190
Vieillot's (*Black*) Weaver	*Ploceus nigerrimus*	*21*, 148, 185
Village Weaver	*Ploceus cucullatus*	102, 145, 150, 168, 179
Black-headed (*Yellow-backed*) Weaver	*Ploceus melanocephalus*	*51*, 102, 129, 145, 195, 226
Forest (*Dark-backed*) Weaver	*Ploceus bicolor*	102
Brown-capped Weaver	*Ploceus insignis*	59, 226
Compact Weaver	*Pachyphantes superciliosus*	185, 227
Cardinal Quelea	*Quelea cardinalis*	156, 227
Red-headed Quelea	*Quelea erythrops*	227
Red-billed Quelea	*Quelea quelea*	151
(*Southern*) Red Bishop	*Euplectes orix*	110, 190, *193*, 195
Black-winged (*Red*) Bishop	*Euplectes hordeaceus*	185
Yellow Bishop	*Euplectes capensis*	145, 185, 190
Red-collared Widowbird	*Euplectes ardens*	190
Fan-tailed Widowbird	*Euplectes axillaris*	145, *147*, 148, 185, 190
Grosbeak Weaver	*Amblyospiza albifrons*	49, 110, *111*, 148, 190
PASSERIFORMES: Estrildidae		
Gray-headed Nigrita (*Negrofinch*)	*Nigrita canicapillus*	*69*
White-breasted Nigrita (*Negrofinch*)	*Nigrita fusconotus*	85, 94
White-collared Oliveback	*Nesocharis ansorgei*	49, 148, 185, 190, 227

Common Name	Scientific Name	Page Number(s)
Yellow-bellied Waxbill	*Coccopygia quartinia*	59, 121, 129, 185, 227
Green-backed Twinspot	*Mandingoa nitidula*	102, 227
Shelley's Crimson-wing	*Cryptospiza shelleyi*	58, 129, 228
Dusky Crimson-wing	*Cryptospiza jacksoni*	*17*, 58, 120, 129, 228
Abyssinian Crimson-wing	*Cryptospiza salvadorii*	59, 228
Red-faced Crimson-wing	*Cryptospiza reichenovii*	59, 228
Fawn-breasted Waxbill	*Estrilda paludicola*	156, 185, 190, 228
Crimson-rumped Waxbill	*Estrilda rhodopyga*	49, 145, 185, 190
Common Waxbill	*Estrilda astrild*	70, 76, 80, 111, 146, 149, 169
Black-crowned Waxbill	*Estrilda nonnula*	59, *81*, 102, 110, 124, 145, 148, 185, 190
Kandt's (*Black-headed*) Waxbill	*Estrilda kandti*	58, 114, 120, 229
Black-cheeked (*Black-faced*) Waxbill	*Estrilda erythronotos*	148
Red-headed Bluebill	*Spermophaga ruficapilla*	185, 229
Red-cheeked Cordonbleu	*Uraeginthus bengalus*	165
Dusky Twinspot	*Euschistospiza cinereovinacea*	58, 229
Peters's Twinspot	*Hypargos niveoguttatus*	185, 229
Green-winged Pytilia	*Pytilia melba*	185
Orange-winged Pytilia	*Pytilia afra*	156, 229
Red-billed Firefinch	*Lagonosticta senegala*	102, 112, 168
African Firefinch	*Lagonosticta rubricata*	49, 110, 124, 185
Red-billed (*Black-chinned*) Quailfinch	*Ortygospiza gabonensis*	229
Bronze Mannikin	*Spermestes cucullatus*	51, 71, 79, 112, 117, 135, 145, 169, 174
Black-and-white Mannikin	*Spermestes bicolor*	185, 190, *228*, 229
PASSERIFORMES: Viduidae		
Pin-tailed Whydah	*Vidua macroura*	102, 112, 135, 150, 168
Broad-tailed Paradise-Whydah	*Vidua obtusa*	229
Village Indigobird	*Vidua chalybeata*	51, 171, 174
Parasitic Weaver	*Anomalospiza imberbis*	156, 299, *229*

General Index

TERM	SECTION (for terms that should not simply be indexed)
Abudada Dam	Site 13
accommodation	This section in intro
Akagera National Park	Site 12
Akanyaru Wetland	Site 2
antelope, roan	152, 155, 160, 203
Bare	193, 227
Bigugu Trail	That section of the Nyungwe site account
biogeography	This section in intro
bird list	That section
Blue Trail	See "Umogote Trail"
buffalo, African	203
buffalo, Cape	*22*, 152, 155, 161, 171, 177, 179, 180, 181, 203
buffalo, Virunga	128, 129, 133, 134, 137, 143, 203
Bugesera	192
Buhanga Forest	Site 8
Buhoro Trail (Gray) Trail	That section of the Nyungwe site account
Bururi	Rangiro / Bururi Valley Road section
Bururi Road	Rangiro / Bururi Valley Road section
Butare	54, 55, 56, 60, 74, 98, 100, 217, 222
Bweyeye Road	Pindura / Bweyeye Road section
cat, African golden	58, 66, 120, 203
chimp	chimpanzee
chimpanzee	15, 16, 26, 57, 61, 88, 90, 94, 98, 100, 101, *104*, 105, 119, 120, 122, 200
civet, African palm	58, 66, 203
climate	This section in intro
colobus, Angolan	16, *34*, 57, 62, 79, 86, 87, 92, 100, 200
colobus, Guereza	Guereza
colobus, pied	colobus, Angolan
Congo-Nile Divide	That section of the Nyungwe site account
conservation	This section in intro
contacts	This section in intro
Cyamudongo Forest	Site 4
Cyangugu	60, 98, 100, 107, 108, 110, 111, 112, 113, 122
driving	This section in intro
duiker, black-fronted	120, 129, 204
duiker, Lestrade's	204